What Matters in Mayhew

What Matters in Mayhew

by Cassie Dandridge Selleck

Obstinate Daughters Press

What Matters In Mayhew is a work of complete fiction.

Names, businesses, places, and events are either products

of the author's imagination or used in a fictitious manner.

All characters appearing in this work are fictitious. Any

resemblance to real persons, living or dead, is purely coincidental.

Published by Obstinate Daughters Press

Lady Lake, Florida 32158

The text of this book is set in Book Antiqua.

Book design by Patricia C. Walker

Cover photography by C. D. Selleck

For my mother, Patricia Veazey Dandridge,

whose voice resonates in my work and in my heart.

I miss you, Mama.

Also by Cassie Dandridge Selleck

The Pecan Man

Contents

Acknowledgements

When I speak of the many wonderful souls who have guided, cajoled, loved, tolerated and supported me through the process of writing this novel, it is usually difficult to decide who to thank first. This time, it's easy. This book would not be a shadow of its current self without the hard work, stellar editing, and incredible insight of Patricia C. Walker, Senior Editor of Obstinate Daughters Press and Senior Instructor in Speech, Communication and Rhetoric at the University of South Carolina. The fact that she is also my firstborn child is just a bonus, and I am profoundly grateful on all counts.

Thanks also to daughters Emily Selleck and Kathryn P. Emily, who are also strong members of our new publishing team, not to mention beautiful, smart and super-talented women in their own right. I have been blessed.

Thanks to my writing group, Gainesville Poets and Writers in Gainesville, Florida, for your inspiring critiques and limitless encouragement. Thanks especially to Jani Sherrard, Kena Schuler, Charlotte Porter, Eldon Turner, Alyssa Karuna, David Maas, U.R. "Bob" Bowie, and Art Crummer – all group regulars who have significantly contributed to my growth as a writer.

To beta-readers Jani Sherrard, James Gantt, Kamilah Marshall, Loretta Armentrout, and Julie Williams Sanon, I am so grateful for your comments and your time.

To advisors and mentors at Goddard College, Annie Abdalla, Michael Leong, Laurie Foos, Arisa White and Jocelyn Cullity, my second reader Michael Vizsolyi, and BFA Program Director Janet Sylvester: you have enriched my life in a multitude of ways, and I bless the day I found my way to Goddard's doorstep. Thank you for your wisdom, encouragement, and high standards.

To my husband, best friend, calm presence, and confidante Perry Selleck, you are the hardest-working man I know, and the kindest. I'll love you forever!

1

Beatrice Bradsher

Will Thaxton followed Beanie down the grassy aisles of polished granite headstones as she silently stopped at first one, then another. The morning was quiet, if you didn't count the occasional logging truck roaring down the highway or the soft swish of Beatrice Bradsher's crinoline petticoat.

"This one's kinda pretty," Beanie said as she pointed to a low rectangular stone with two small, entwined hearts engraved at the top.

"I think that one's meant for two people, Bean," Will said.

"Oh, that's why there's two hearts," Beanie sighed. "But there's only one of me."

"Are you sure you want to do this now?" Will asked.

"I done made up my mind on this one. It ain't every day a body wins twenty-thousand dollars on the lotto. I aim to do something smart with it."

Will wanted to tell her to do something fun with it instead. He wanted to tell her to take a cruise to the Bahamas or buy herself a car or at least a new bicycle, but he didn't waste his breath. She rode her red Schwinn bike everywhere she went. If she needed an occasional trip to Walmart in the neighboring county, she'd tag along with Will on Fridays, like she'd done today - except this time they stopped by the Suwannee Monument Company to pick out a headstone. Otherwise, everything she needed was within a two-mile radius of downtown Mayhew Junction. She did not need to drive a car even if she wanted to, which she did not.

"Why don't you put it in the bank and think about it a while? There's no reason to be in a hurry about this, is there?"

"I should hope not," Beanie snorted. "But you never know about these things. I 'bout got creamed by a chicken truck the other day. Them truckers are plain crazy, barreling through town like they ain't got good sense. I don't know why Sheriff Charlie don't do somethin' about it. Somebody's bound to be

1

killed, though Lord knows I hope it ain't me. Leastways not anytime soon… What was we talkin' about?"

Will laughed. Beanie was a breath of fresh air. Honest to a fault, pure in the truest sense of the word, with very little reason to filter anything that came through her lips. She marched to her own beat, and that's what he liked about her.

Some people — LouWanda Crump, for one — would say Beanie was a spectacle, riding through town on a battered bike, a wire basket on the handlebars filled with groceries, fabric from the quilt shop, or a stack of Avon catalogs to deliver. Will suspected it wasn't that she rode a bike, but how she dressed that gave everyone pause. Beanie Bradsher made her own clothes - skirts with layers of crinoline like the kind made for square dancing, button down shirts decorated with ruffles, hand-beaded trim, or Beanie's personal favorite – rhinestones, and always, without fail, a matching cowboy hat covering the pale reddish hair that fell in curls down her back.

Her face was pale, though her hands and legs sported a healthy tan. She wore enough makeup to compliment her lightly freckled features and army green eyes, but not so much as to outdo her daily attire. And, though no color palette went unexplored in her repertoire of outfits, her lips were always painted the same muted shade of red that Beanie was quick to identify to any potential customer as Avon's Rose Gold #3.

Cowboy boots completed her ensemble. There were two rows of them in her closet, as Will knew because she rented a room from him at The Château. He occasionally went in to make repairs, change the light bulbs, or deal with the temperamental old plumbing.

"We were talking about how you should spend the money you won," Will reminded her.

"Well, I've already decided how to spend it. I'm gettin' my affairs in order. Ain't no one to do it when I'm gone, unless you count my cousin, and quite frankly, I don't. There is no tellin' what she would do if she took care of buryin' me. Prolly just stick me in a pine box with one o' them tacky roadside crosses for a marker and call it done. Or, Lord help me…" Beanie gasped and clutched the mother-of-pearl buttons at the base of

2

her neck. "What do you call that when they put your ashes in one o' them urinal things?"

"Cremation?"

"Yeah, cremation. Lord, the very word makes my butt draw up. I don't wanna be burnt to a crisp and stuck in a urinal for eternity."

"Well, it's not a urinal, Beanie; it's an urn," Will said, stifling the urge to laugh. "But I get your point."

"Whatever," Beanie said. "I don't wanna die without layin' eyes on my gravestone. Better to buy it now and have a few years to enjoy it myself. Besides, I don't think I'm ever going to see this much money at one time again."

"You talk like you're on the cusp of infirmity, Bean. You're forty-two and healthy as a horse. Why don't you do something for yourself for a change?"

"This *is* for me. Ain't no one goin' in there with me, as you just pointed out. So, this is *all* for me. Besides—my mind's made up. Reckon they can do me a pair of boots up there like they done them hearts? I can get this smaller stone for my name, but see where that one heart comes up outta the top there? They could draw me a pair of boots and stick 'em up there in the heart. That'd be nice, wouldn't it?"

"Really nice, Beanie. I think it would be lovely and it would always remind me of you."

"Ha! Now there's some positive thinkin', Will Thaxton! You reckon you're gonna be around when I'm gone? You got ten years on me if'n a day."

Had anyone else said that, Will might have been offended, but he knew Beanie meant no harm. She was only stating the obvious.

"Point taken, Miss Bradsher. Except that it's more like fifteen. And if you're buying it today, I won't have to wait until you're gone, now will I? Let's go talk to Mr. Henshaw and see if they can put a pair of boots in that heart, unless you would like me to put one of mine on your rear end for calling me old."

Beanie's laugh rang out across the field of polished granite.

"I didn't mean it like that, Will, really I didn't..." Beanie protested, choking back giggles.

3

Will feigned offense and led her by the arm toward the office at the back of the yard.

"You're not old, really. I mean, just 'cause you're a widower don't mean your bones is gettin' brittle or anything." Beanie laughed at her own joke, stumbling a bit as Will made a little show of tightening his grip on her elbow and pulling her along.

"Better stop now before you have to find your own way back home," Will said, grinning.

"Wait, I gotta figure out what it's gonna say," Beanie said.

"You can work that out with Mr. Henshaw later. He has to order the stone before he can sandblast the inscription on it, so you have plenty of time."

"Here's hopin'," Beanie chuckled. "Long as I steer clear of chicken trucks anyway."

2
The Talk of the Town

The Mayhew Café sits on the edge of town, across from the Dollarama store and right in front of Mandy's Motel. On a good day, it's a hot spot where you can pick up Mandy's Wi-Fi for free. The café has been open seven days a week for the past thirty-odd years, closing only on Christmas Day and the day Ms. Doshia Cole passed, leaving the restaurant to be run by her capable daughter Edwina.

The café is open early for breakfast and serves buffet style or from the menu until it closes after dinner. By 10:45, the trough is laden with fried chicken, macaroni and cheese, candied yams, fresh cooked greens and cornbread. Depending on the day of the week, there might also be baked chicken, spaghetti, cornbread dressing or pork ribs smothered in barbecue sauce. And, for as long as Edwina remembers, there has always been a Friday night Fish Fry. Certain vegetables make their rounds at the buffet, but green beans are a staple, along with corn and fried okra.

There is one large round table situated directly between the cashier's stand and the buffet, and it is for locals only, though there is no sign of warning anywhere around. The first wave arrives at 5:30 a.m. and a host of good ol' boys stream in and out through the breakfast hours. Anyone sitting within a few feet can learn a lot about Mayhew Junction—impending weather woes, the price of poultry feed, when to plant root crops, the political climate in town, and all the latest news and gossip.

This particular morning, the town is buzzing with excitement about Beanie Bradsher winning the lotto from the Super Kwik market downtown.

"Shoot, I bought two quick picks the same day. I knew I shoulda bought ten a' them things," Randy Kerner shook his head sadly and sipped his tepid coffee.

"I heard it was the Powerball she won," Clyde Owensby said.

"How much she get?" Mac McConnell asked.

"I heard it was over a hun'erd thousand," Eustace Falwell said as he approached the table, swiping his hat from his head as he slid into the nearest empty chair.

"Lord, Useless, where'd you hear that. Wadn't but twenty thousand," Clyde said.

"She got more'n that," Randy said. "LouWanda Crump is hittin' her up for a contribution to the Historical Society."

"Hope she don't get the big head with all that money," Mac said. "We count on Beanie's sewing skills down at the Rotary. She made thirty blankets for our last orphanage project."

"I didn't know she belonged to the Rotary." Eustace said, his eyes lighting up with interest.

"She don't, Useless. She just volunteers for us, so don't get any big ideas." Mac rolled his eyes and looked around for the waitress.

Sissy Reid approached waving a coffee pot in salute. Four hands answered, raising cups to be filled.

"Y'all still talkin' about Miss Beanie?" Sissy asked, deftly filling each mug without spilling a drop. "Useless, you eatin' this mornin'?"

"Yes, Ma'am," Eustace grinned. "I'll have a short stack with sausage."

"Gotcha," she replied. "Anyone else need anything?"

Five hands waved her away in unison.

"Y'all keep it down to a dull roar, ya hear?" Sissy admonished. "I'm sure Miss Beanie doesn't want her business broadcast down the road and back."

Sissy hustled to the kitchen shaking her head as she heard the old boys debating the size of Beanie Bradsher's winnings even as she walked away. They didn't hear a word she said or, if they did, they ignored her as usual.

At 6:30, Suvi Jones parked his Chevy truck in front of the café, grabbed a couple of quarters from the cup holder and made a run for it. The rain started about the time he woke up – 6:00 a.m. sharp, as always. It was only a few steps from his truck to shelter, but he needed to grab a newspaper from the machine by the front door and his size outclassed the roof's slight overhang. By the time he made it inside, his back was drenched.

"Mornin' Suve! I gotcha over there," Sissy pointed at a cup of coffee and small metal pitcher of milk parked at a booth in the corner.

Suvi grinned and raised his newspaper in a kind of wave. Sissy decided where he sat every morning. If it weren't already taken, he'd be at his usual spot, close enough to the coffee pot to refill his own cup if it got too hectic for Sissy to keep up. His table was taken by a trucker this morning.

"Whatcha havin'?" Sissy asked from across the room.

"Scrambled with bacon," Suvi replied, fanning out the sports page as he angled his huge frame onto the red vinyl bench seat. She knew everything else he wanted. No need to tell her he liked his bacon cooked well done, or his toast dry or the side of pancakes he ate every day no matter what style of eggs he chose. He rarely missed a breakfast at the café, even though it was technically his competition. The Big Pig opened each day at 11:00 a.m., though, and the only eggs he cooked were boiled for the chef salad.

Within minutes Sissy reappeared, plates stacked across her arm and a coffee pot in her right hand. He didn't know how she did it, but he wished many a time he could get her to come to work for him. She was fast, pleasant, efficient and reliable, but he did not dare offer her a job. Edwina, a distant cousin and long-time friend, would never forgive him.

"Did you hear the news?" Sissy asked.

Suvi raised the sports page over his head, leaving room for her to situate his food and warm his coffee.

"Which news?"

"About Beanie winnin' the lotto the other night," Sissy said. "Some folks is sayin' she won over a million dollars, but you know how it is around here. You buy a pork roast for Sunday dinner and folks'll have you ownin' a pig farm before the day's done."

"You got that right," Suvi laughed. "And, yeah, I heard."

"Miz LouWanda was sayin' she was gonna see if she could get Beanie to make a donation to the Historical Society. You know they're trying to fix up the old drugstore downtown."

"Mmm-hmm—donated to that one myself. Good cause." Suvi was already back to reading the paper, but he could talk and scan the stats at the same time and Sissy was undaunted.

"If I were Beanie, I know exactly what I'd do with that money," Sissy said wistfully.

"What's that?" Suvi asked, peering over the top of the paper.

"If I won the lotto, I'd buy me a big ol' house in the mountains," Sissy said.

"Really? And leave Mayhew Junction?"

"Well, maybe I'd come back every now and again, just to parade my fancy car down Main Street. Reckon she'll finally get her own car?"

"Wouldja look at that?" Suvi said, squinting at the small print of his newspaper. "Looks like we may be headed for a back-to-back."

There was also no need to tell Sissy who "we" were, or to shoo her away from the table. In Mayhew Junction, there was only one team, and not just because Suvi played there, either.

"I'll check on ya in a minute," Sissy said and headed for the round table, where several of the men, unaccustomed to seeing the bottom of their coffee cups, were staring forlornly in her direction.

"Oh, stop poutin', ya big babies," Sissy fussed. "I'm comin'. God forbid you should have to get up and pour your own."

3

Sweet Lee Atwater

"Tater, get back here this minute!"

Sweet Atwater's youngest son was half-way down the block, still on the sidewalk, but peering hopefully over the curb for any sign of stray candy that might be lingering after the Founder's Day parade on Saturday. His light brown hair, buzzed close to his head once a month whether it needed it or not, glowed yellow gold in the morning sun.

"Tater! Dad-gummit, boy, don't make me come after you!"

Sweet held three-year-old Daisy in one arm as she wrestled with the keys to the front door of Sweet Lee's Dress Emporium in downtown Mayhew Junction. The three-story brick building was a bit on the dilapidated side, but what little work Sweet could get Bubba John to do on it was sufficient for now. She bought the whole building with the idea of having her husband remodel it in his spare time. The only problem she'd found was the gaping chasm between their definitions of *spare*. This morning was a perfect example. Normally he was on hand to help her get their children fed and dressed so she could drive them into town to catch the bus from her shop. There was a school bus stop about three-quarters of a mile from their house, but theirs was the first stop on the morning route. Catching the bus in town allowed everyone forty-five more minutes of sleep. Lately though, Bubba John was up and out of the house before Sweet rolled out of bed. Her day never started out well trying to herd five kids on her own.

"B-Kay! Come gitcher sister. I gotta go get that boy again."

"Aw, Mama! I'm puttin' on my makeup. The bus will be here any second."

B-Kay complained loudly, but slid from the front seat of their old minivan.

"Here!" Sweet said dumping Daisy into her arms. "Thanks, Baby. I'll be right back."

B-Kay sighed and used a make-up smudged baby wipe to scrub the dried snot from Daisy's cheek.

"Tater! I'm tellin' you what, Son, I am gonna tear you up." Sweet's voice carried easily down the two blocks Tater traveled. "B-Kay! Wake your brother up. I hear the bus comin'."

B-Kay plopped Daisy down on the front seat of the car and slid the back door open.

"Mama says time to get up, Tee." B-Kay said, poking her twin brother with her foot when he didn't respond.

"T-Ray! Get up. GET UP! The bus is comin' around the corner! For cryin' out loud, Mama, I only got one eye done and this lump of horse poop won't even wake up!"

B-Kay leaned across Daisy and pushed hard on the center of the steering wheel. The car sounded like a cow in distress as B-Kay pumped the horn over and over. Finally, T-Ray rolled out of the side door, groggily pulling his backpack with him.

"All right, already. Jeez, B! What's up your ass this morning?"

T-Ray wiped at his mouth where drool puddled in one corner. The two eldest Atwater children were twins by birth, but that's where the similarities ended. More than one person pointed out the fairly obvious fact that B-Kay took after her mama, and T-Ray was a bit more laid back like his father.

"T-Ray, watch your mouth, Son." Sweet said, dragging her youngest son to a halt at the car door before stooping to tie his shoe.

"Well, tell B-Kay to lay off then," T-Ray muttered, more to himself than his mother.

"I told her to wake you up. She's already doin' what I told her to do. Tate, zip up your zipper. T-Ray, get Tater's backpack outta the car and tell Bitty to get hers, too. Where is that child? Bitty! Oh, my Lord. Has anyone seen Bitty?"

No one moved or uttered a word, but stood looking at each other with open-mouthed stupor. Everyone except B-Kay, who scooped Daisy up, sat back down in the front seat and proceeded to apply makeup over the head of the docile toddler.

"Where in the world is that child?" Sweet stuck her head into the minivan, lifting a half dozen coats in the rear seat hoping her quiet second grader was asleep beneath them.

"Did anyone see Bitty get into the car this morning? Sweet wounded Jesus, did I leave her again?"

"She was here a few minutes ago. I saw her myself," B-Kay said, dusting her cheeks with powdered blush for the third time that morning.

Just then the bus rounded the corner, its brakes protesting as it squealed to a stop in front of them. T-Ray grabbed Tater by the arm and headed toward the waiting bus.

"I got this one, Mama. You're on your own with the girls." T-Ray said, trudging up the bus steps.

B-Kay thrust the baby back into her mother's arms and grabbed her purse. "Maybe Bitty's inside. I heard her say something about having to pee."

"Tell that driver to wait, then," Sweet said.

"She ain't waitin', Mama. You know she ain't." B-Kay said.

"Then walk slow," Sweet said as she poked her head into the store and hollered for Bitty.

"What are you yellin' about, Mama?"

Elizabeth Atwater climbed slowly from beneath the back seat, brushing crumbs and dirt from her t-shirt and jeans. The generous spray of freckles across her nose and cheeks were the exact same color of her ginger hair which hung in side braids to just below her shoulders.

"What in the world? What were you doing under there? Never mind – don't answer that. Get on that bus right now, young lady! B-Kay! Gitcher sister!" Sweet hollered at her oldest daughter's retreating backside.

"Come on, Bitty," B-Kay called over her shoulder, and Bitty dutifully followed her onto the bus.

"Oh, my Lord, those kids'll be the death of me." Sweet moaned.

Normally her next stop would be the daycare, but Daisy hadn't fully recovered from a stomach virus, so she decided to keep her out another day, which may not have been the best move, considering how the day was shaping up.

"I gotta go potty," Daisy said, looking up at her frazzled mother.

"Hang on, baby," Sweet said and sighed. "I gotta close this car up."

Sweet looked at the van and shook her head in disgust. Clothing and shoes and bags of half-eaten potato chips spilled from the doors as if the car had vomited. She couldn't decide whether to lock up the car, or leave it open and pray someone would walk by and steal something out of it. As she stood mulling it over, she felt a warmth spread across her hip and down her leg.

"Daaaayseeeee!" Sweet screeched.

"I go pee-pee."

"Good thing I own a clothing store, Missy, or you'd be in big trouble right now."

"I gotta go poop," Daisy replied.

"Well, you better hold it 'til we get inside, little girl, 'cause you will not be watching Dora for a week if you poop on me."

Sweet yanked the side door to the right and it ground to a stop just shy of fully closed. Sweet shrugged and turned toward the store giving the door a sideways kick that locked it into place.

Beanie Bradsher

When I was a little girl, my daddy used to take me to the Golden Oldies Matinee over in Taylor County. We never had a movie theatre here, long as I can remember. Anyways, we had a date, every Saturday morning, come hell or high water, and the water rises a lot in this county.

Sometimes we'd see The Lone Ranger, or cartoons or what-not, but my favorite was Roy Rogers. He was so handsome and gallunt, a lot like my daddy. I loved that Palomino horse Trigger, and the dog Bullet, but the best part was his beautiful wife Dale Evans. I always wanted to be just like her, that gleaming white smile and pretty outfits. Best of all, she had Roy.

I don't remember when we stopped going to the movies together. I think it happened kinda gradual-like. Daddy started travelin' some and didn't always come home of a weekend. Mama got snappish and she never wanted to take me no ways. I got into high school and took a sewing class in home economics and I learned that I could be anything I wanted to be, including Dale Evans, if I just dressed right. Now all my dresses look like Dale's and my boots and hat always match. I started sellin' Avon so I could get just the right shade of lipstick to go with my outfits.

Daddy stopped coming home at all and never bought me the pony he promised, so I did the next best thing and bought a bicycle. I ain't never drove a car in my life and don't plan on learnin'. Never once in all them Saturdays did I ever see Roy Rogers drive a car, and what's good for him is good for me. I'm still waitin' on somebody like Roy to come along. Maybe somebody who rides a Palomino, or has a dog. It don't have to be named Bullet. I just want somebody who plans on stayin'.

4
The Château

Beanie was silent almost the entire ride home from Walmart. Will was used to this. Whenever Beanie got tired, she would reserve her energy by not speaking. When his wife was alive, silence meant Marie was unhappy – usually with him, though that was rare. Their marriage was full of conversations and outings and gatherings. It was a good life and they made big plans. The Château was the biggest plan of all; now he was here and she was not.

"Whatcha thinkin' about?"

The question took Will by surprise. He thought Beanie was asleep.

"Oh, nothing much," Will said. "The usual."

"You don't talk about her much," Beanie said. "May help, you know."

"I know, but…" Will sighed then. Beanie thought it felt like a full minute before he took a breath back in.

"I just miss her, that's all."

"Must be hard, livin' here all by yourself. This town ain't easy. You're an outsider for life less'n you're born here. And even still, you know how they say, 'Just 'cause a cat has kittens in the oven, it don't make 'em muffins.'"

Will smiled. "Oh, I don't mind the town at all. People were kind to us when Marie got sick. We'd only been here a few months before she started her chemo."

"How in the world did y'all wind up in Mayhew Junction, for cryin' out loud?"

"Oh, surely I've told you this." Will sounded tired.

"Not that I recollect," Beanie said.

"Well," said Will. "We found Mayhew Junction by accident, really. It was a paddling trip cut short by Hurricane Frances."

"Oooo, I remember that one. Lotta wind and rain."

"Yeah, and not much else, but enough to make us think twice about being on the river."

14

"What were y'all doing on the river if Marie was sick?"

"Well, she wasn't sick then. We'd joined an adventurers' club in Minnesota. It was an annual trip for the club. Supposed to go from White Springs to Fanning Springs in one week."

"Long trip," Beanie said. "I don't know if I could do that."

"I know. I wasn't sure we could either. We'd already traveled a lot. We owned a travel agency, you know."

Beanie nodded. "I 'member that part."

"Natalie was finished with college and starting her own career. Marie wanted some excitement – something different, she said.

"To tell the truth, I was kind of tired. I'd have been happy staying home, but Marie was always our social planner - parties with friends, trips to the theatre, season tickets to all the Vikings games."

"Man," Beanie said, staring wistfully out of the window. "I can't even dream of anything like that. I wouldn't know what to imagine."

"I've seen a lot, that's for sure. But, it was the river. We just fell in love with it. We weren't terribly outdoorsy, other than piddling in our garden. We joined the adventurer's club on a whim. Gosh, if you told me Marie and I would be sleeping in tents, in campsites with no running water or flushing toilets, I'd say no way. But there we were, kayaking down the Suwannee River in October. Amazing. And I remember thinking that I had never seen Marie looking so happy and alive as she did out on that water."

Will cleared his throat twice, then sat silently watching the road.

"I'm sorry I never met her." Beanie said.

"I'm sorry, too. You'd have liked her, I think. Always talking, always planning and admiring things. She adored The Château. That's why we bought it."

"How'd you find it, anyways?"

"The day we left, Frances was forming in the Gulf, but most indications were that it would turn toward Texas. We thought the trip might be cancelled, but I guess true adventurers are seldom daunted. We forged ahead, and the storm grew bigger. It did finally turn, but not quite soon enough and we caught its

15

tail. It was almost impossible to paddle, even going with the current – so much wind! We finally stopped down the road at the bridge and there were several people trying to get their boats out of the water before things got worse.

"That was the first time I ever saw Suvi Jones. Of course, I had no idea who he was, I just knew he was BIG. His boat was already loaded and he was helping an elderly couple get their pontoon boat onto a trailer. Between the wind and the current, the old man couldn't seem to keep the pontoons lined up with the tracks on the trailer. And do you know what Suvi did?"

When Beanie didn't answer, Will glanced to his right. Her hat was pushed back off her head, and her mouth was slightly open, but her eyes were closed. Will smiled and shook his head, then returned his attention to the road.

As the car passed over the blue bridge connecting their neighboring counties, Will remembered how he'd watched, amazed, as Suvi stripped to his t-shirt and waded down the ramp into the frigid water to stand beside the submerged trailer.

"Gun it, Fred!" Suvi hollered, motioning for the old man to try again.

"You sure, Suvi?" the old man hesitated.

"Come on! I gotcha," Suvi shouted above the roar of the wind and the idling motor. "Go back around and aim high. I'll guide her in."

The old man did as Suvi said, taking the boat in a slow sweeping turn to approach from upstream. Aiming for the back of the truck, he pushed the throttle forward to gain speed. The wind whipped the boat's stern toward Suvi at the last second, but he caught the railing with both hands and pushed hard, guiding the pontoons onto the v-shaped tracks of the trailer. The boat slid into place. Suvi made short work of attaching the front hook and winching the boat the rest of the way. Will had never seen anything like it – man against machine *and* the elements. His dark brown skin showed through the wet shirt, outlining abs that were every bit as awe-inspiring as his size. Made Will feel small and insignificant by comparison, though he'd never given his average build much thought before.

Will, Marie, and the paddling group were tired and cold and more than a little worried about finding accommodations in

16

such a rural area. They made inquiries and found that only two establishments nearby could handle such a large group. There was a small motel with ten rooms, and a Bed and Breakfast called The Château, which was once the county courthouse. Will and Marie fell head over heels in love with the place and stayed for a week. Before leaving, they made a casual offer to the owners that was eventually accepted.

Not long after the paperwork was signed on the purchase of The Château, Marie was diagnosed with stage-four breast cancer. There were no signs of the illness before then, just the discovery of a lump on a routine physical exam. When Will looked back on those months of treatment, he wondered how he survived it himself. Marie was a rock, never giving up, never losing hope, even to the day she took her last breath. He missed her every single day, but the funny thing was he didn't miss their friends at all. He was oddly content where he was, living alone the dream they'd dreamed together.

"Will? You okay?" Beanie was leaned back in her chair, but turned her head toward him as she spoke.

"Yeah," he said, with a hint of sadness in his voice, "I'm fine. Why?"

"We been settin' here a good long while. I just wondered, that's all."

Will laughed. "I was seeing how long you would sleep."

"Wadn't sleepin'," Beanie mumbled.

"Then you better go down to the clinic and get your sinuses checked, because you were snoring like a buzz saw."

Beanie smacked Will on the arm and flung open the car door.

"I do not snore, Will Thaxton!"

"Easy there, Killer," Will grinned.

"I didn't hit you that hard."

"I was talking about the door."

"Oh, pooh..." Beanie huffed and rolled out of the car, crinoline crackling wildly as she scooped up her groceries and stomped into the house.

Will chuckled to himself and unloaded the rest of the car.

5
The Big Pig

Smoke rose from the stacks of wood piled teepee style outside the back door of Suvi's Big Pig Barbecue. Hickory logs were started on the outside and brought into the kitchen when they were ready to use in the wide cooking pits where Vesuvius Jones smoked ribs and chicken and pork to perfection.

Sweet Atwater loved the smell, but it sometimes made its way through the back door of the shop, giving her inventory a smoky campfire odor. This might be okay if she was running an outdoor clothing store, but she wasn't. And who wanted to go to a prom smelling like a hunt camp? If she thought about it, though, that might not be a bad thing around Mayhew Junction.

After napping in a portable crib for at least an hour, Daisy woke up hungry, but still in a good mood, and the barbecue smelled so good that Sweet called Bubba John to meet her for lunch. She stuck a "Back at 1:00" sign on the door and closed up shop.

The front doors of the Big Pig sported kissing swine for handles. Sweet swung the doors open and stepped inside. The front room was nearly full, but she could see a few empty booths in the back dining room. She dragged a high chair to a table near the window display featuring a menagerie of ceramic pigs and piglets on a carpet of fake plastic grass. She plopped Daisy into the chair and glanced at the specials board.

AUCE RIBS $7.99 - SWEET TEA EXTRA!

Sold! Sweet thought to herself, as Suvi Jones backed through the kitchen door, filling the entire width with his body and clearing the doorjamb above his head by barely an inch.

Vesuvius Jones was a giant of a man, both in stature and in the community, a hometown hero of sorts, one of the few local boys to make a name for himself outside of Mayhew Junction. Standing six-feet-eight in his bare feet, Suvi played three sports in high school and excelled at them all, though he finally opted for the basketball scholarship offered by the University of

18

Florida over the football scholarship that would have taken him to Miami and too far from home. Sweet graduated high school with Suvi and, from what she could tell, Suvi would probably have never left the county if not for sports. He was drafted into the NBA his senior year in college and ended up in Denver of all places. At the end of four years, he blew out his knee and was back home – financially secure enough to build his mama a big home on the edge of town and buy himself the restaurant he always wanted. Never married, he lived with his mama until she died of a stroke. Though it was over a year since her death, Sweet was sure Suvi was still not over it. His mother was a matriarch, not just of his family, but of his community at large.

"Hey, Suve!" Sweet called out as Suvi made his way through the dining room carrying a large tray of rib baskets. "Where's Cherry today?"

"Sweet Lee!" Suvi hollered over his shoulder, using Sweet's given name as he always did. "Cherry called in again. Dottie'll be here in a few minutes to cover for her. I'll be right with ya."

The front doors swung open and Bubba John lumbered in, kissing Daisy on the top of the head before he plopped down in the chair across from Sweet.

"Hey, Mama, how you holdin' up?" Bubba John grinned across the table at his wife.

That was the smile that always got her into trouble. It was the one that made her fall in love with a man who was just shy of reliable.

"Hangin' in there," Sweet said as she ripped the top off a pack of crackers and handed one to Daisy. "Where the heck were you this morning?"

"Putting out feed," Bubba John said. "Sorry. Meant to be back in time to help. You do okay without me?"

"The kids are still breathin' and they made it to the bus on time. Guess it hasn't been too bad a day, if you don't count the two new outfits me and Daisy are wearin', which came out of perfectly good inventory."

"She gitcha again?"

"Mmm hmmm," Sweet nodded.

"You may ought to think about keepin' some of them pull-up things on hand."

"No, Sir!" Sweet said. "I have bought my last pack of diapers. Period."

"That's what you said after Tater was potty-trained."

"Don't jinx me, Daddy, or you'll be sleepin' on the porch 'til my ovaries are prunes."

Bubba John laughed so loud, several heads turned at once. Sweet glared at him.

"What's the special?" Bubba John said, turning to look at the board.

"Ribs, but if Dottie doesn't get here soon, we may be here all day. Cherry called in drunk again. I don't know why he doesn't fire that girl."

"Cherry Allred," Bubba John said. "Now there's an apple that didn't fall far from the tree."

"Punny," Sweet said, rolling her eyes at the joke she'd heard a thousand times. "Seriously, though. What kind of woman would stick her kid with a name like that?"

Bubba John laughed again, louder this time.

"Do you really want me to answer that?" he asked once he caught his breath.

"What?" Sweet said.

"You know what," Bubba John said. "You know exactly what."

"I don't know what you're talkin' about." Sweet said, barely suppressing a smile.

"Daisy," Bubba John said, handing his toddler another cracker, "your mama is just plain crazy. Best you know that now, baby girl. Save you a world of hurt down the road."

"Kwackers," Daisy said, crumbling it in her fist.

"Kwackers is right," Bubba John grinned and ruffled the blonde curls at the base of her neck.

Sweet stood, throwing her napkin down on the chair.

"Where ya goin'?" Bubba John asked.

"I'm gonna get this show on the road," she replied. "Suvi can't handle this by himself."

"I figured that's what you were gonna say."

"You got her?" Sweet asked, nodding toward Daisy.

"Mmm hmmm," Bubba John said. "Piece of cake."

"Try havin' five of them at once."

"No, I mean: bring us a piece of cake," Bubba John smirked.

Sweet smacked her husband on the arm and headed for the kitchen to wash up and put on an apron. It wasn't the first time she pitched in for the lunch crowd. She didn't mind helping Suvi, and the tips weren't too bad, either. The way Bubba John worked, which was as little as possible, they could use all the help they could get.

She just picked up a pad of lunch tickets when Suvi came from the kitchen with Dottie on his heels.

"I got it, Sweet," Dottie said. "Thanks, though."

"No problem," Sweet said. "I'll go take a few orders while I'm suited up. Front room filled up first, I think."

"Okey dokey," Dottie said. "I'll take the back tables, then."

"Thank God we have plenty of ribs," Suvi said. "I think we can catch up pretty fast if they don't all order burgers and fries."

Sweet managed to sit back down with her husband just as he polished off his second plate of ribs. It didn't take much to convince Bubba John to take the baby home for another nap. She didn't doubt they would both be dozing on the couch until the kids got off the bus from school.

6
Straight to the Source

Dottie Brentwood was through with the toughest shift since the Soweto Gospel Choir stopped their bus on Main Street and piled in unannounced. Untying the back of her Mayhew Hardware nail apron, which doubled as a holder for tips, straws, napkins, order pads and pens, Dottie sat heavily in the nearest booth she could find and started counting her tips. LouWanda Crump, who owned the antiques store across the street from the Big Pig, walked in as Dottie finished stacking her bills with faces pointed in the same direction.

Fresh from a trip to Lynelle's Country Curl, LouWanda patted her bleached blonde beehive, taming any strays jarred loose by the logging truck that blew by before she made it in the door.

"Wooh-wee!" LouWanda said, stomping her size 10 sneakers on the industrial-sized welcome mat. "That boy just needs to slow down, I'm tellin' ya. I'm calling Fred Hewitt the minute I get home. He ort'ta know his drivers is blowin' the hairs outta people's heads."

"LouWanda, if you want a sweet tea, honey, you'll have to get it yourself. My bunion is about to bust. I couldn't pull myself outta this chair if I wanted to, and I don't."

"Bad day?" LouWanda asked, heading straight for the soda station. "Where's Cherry?"

"Fired, I hope," Dottie said and sighed.

"Lord, I hope not," LouWanda said. "Who'll watch the shop for me if you're working here fulltime?"

Dottie was the fill-in for half the stores along Main Street. Suvi used her when Cherry was hungover. LouWanda counted on her to watch her store every time she had a doctor's appointment, which was fairly often since she'd made it to Medicare age. She'd lived an entire lifetime without medical insurance and, now that she was covered, there were a few things she thought needed checking out. Sweet Lee Atwater would call on Dottie if the kids were out sick, or sometimes even if she just needed a break.

"Well, I know, but quite frankly, it'd be good to have a full-time job somewhere, instead of wondering from one day to the next what I'll have coming in."

"Looks like you got a pile of money today. That from the lunch shift?"

"Yeah, I don't know what I'd have done if Sweet didn't show up and help me out. I'll have to split some of this with her, but I'll still make out okay, I suppose."

"Whaddaya mean you have to split with Sweet?"

"She took a pile of orders and got drinks for just about everyone. I can't leave her out, Lou. That'd be wrong."

"Did she bring out the food? Did she bus the tables? I doubt it."

"Well, no, but..."

"Then you don't owe her a dime," LouWanda said. "She was probably just making sure her own food got out on time."

Dottie stopped to consider this. Come to think of it, she overheard Sweet telling Bubba John they'd never get to eat at this rate. But Sweet was always helpful and never expected anything in return.

"I know which ones she helped with. I'll give her some of those. It's not like it's a fortune. Mayhew Junction isn't exactly known for big tippers."

"Speaking of which," LouWanda leaned in to whisper, "Did you hear about Beatrice Bradsher?"

"About the lotto? Oh, yeah, tongues are wagging all over town, no doubt."

"She's about to come into a windfall the way I hear it."

"I'm happy for her. Beanie could use a little good luck."

"Her and me, both," LouWanda said. "I been playin' the lotto for ten years and never got more than a couple of free tickets. I just wonder how she got so lucky."

"Beats me," Dottie said. "Oh, I wish you would look here. Eustace Falwell has put his number on another one-dollar bill. If that don't beat all..."

"Musta been one of Sweet's tables," LouWanda observed.

Dottie's head snapped up.

"Hey, I'm not dead, am I? It's not the first time he's left it, not that I'm interested or anything..." Dottie's voice trailed off. "And besides, Sweet's married!"

"Since when has that been a discouragement to Eustace?"

Dottie held the offending bill up to the light. "Good point, except if he was hoping to score, he could have at least put it on a fiver. No wonder he's never had a girlfriend."

"Well, anyway," LouWanda said, "I think I'm going to give Miss Beatrice a call. I heard it's quite a jackpot she won and I'm bettin' she needs a few tax shelters for her cash."

"Y'all still working on getting that grant for the Historical Society?"

"Yes Lord, and it is not a cakewalk, I'm telling you right now. Paperwork out the wahzoo. We could do with a few contributions to show some matching funds."

"At least it's a worthy cause," Dottie shrugged and scraped her change back into her apron pocket. "You wouldn't believe how many people are trying to figure out how to get some of Beanie's money. Sometimes I feel invisible."

"Honey, I would milk that one for all it's worth, if I was you," LouWanda said, dead serious. "What I would give to be a fly on some of the walls around here."

"There's the difference between you and me, Lou. I have enough problems of my own without borrowing trouble. I'm happy to mind my own business."

"May I remind you that the Bible says we are our brother's keeper? I am doing my Christian duty to watch out for others. And speakin' of Christian, don't call me Lou, for heaven's sake. It's LouWanda or nothing at all. You know I call everyone by their Christian name, even Eustace Falwell, though I have to say I can't argue with his unfortunate nickname."

"Speak of the devil—here he comes now," Dottie said, leaping to her feet and heading for the kitchen door. "Tell him I've gone home for the day."

"But that's a lie..."

"Fine, tell him whatever you want. Make something up."

"Dorothy Brentwood, you get yourself back here. Don't you leave me alone with... Hey, Eustace! How you doin' today?"

Eustace Falwell grinned and swiped his hat off like his head was greased.

"Afternoon, Miss LouWanda. You was just who I was lookin' for," he said and sat down at the table.

"I was?"

"Yeah, I done been over to the Emporium, so I know'd you must be across the way."

"Yeah, business is slow. I closed her up for the day," LouWanda said.

"Where's Dottie?"

"Oh, she's in the back. I think she's hidin' from somebody."

"Really? Well, you tell her if anyone bothers her, she needs to tell me and I will put a stop to it. That is a fine woman right there. I won't stand for nobody harassin' my friends."

"Well, that's nice, Eustace, I'll tell her you said so."

"Who is it, do you know? That just bothers me, somebody messin' with a fine woman like Dottie."

"I do know, but she swore me to secrecy. You know how she is."

"Yea, she is a *fine* woman. Too fine to be tattlin' on anybody, even some ol' banty rooster who comes a callin'. Well, I'll be watchin', I can tell you that," Eustace said, scratching his head with the brim of his hat still clutched tight in his fist.

"So, why are you looking for me today, Eustace?" LouWanda asked, her face a mask of self-control. It wasn't Christian to tease, but sometimes it was too hard to resist.

"Oh," Eustace said, "I am trying to get some information on Beanie Bradsher's lottery winnings, so I came to you."

"Me? Why not go straight to Beatrice yourself?"

"Tried that already. You're the next best thing; you know everybody's business."

"Touché," said LouWanda.

"Huh?"

"Nothin', Eustace."

7
In a Pickle

While the town was busy speculating over Beanie Bradsher's lottery winnings, Will was cleaning up the vestiges of breakfast for The Château's overnight guests. Beanie, being a full-time boarder, generally either helped Will cook and serve, or took care of fixing her own breakfast, which usually consisted of fruit and cereal. This morning Will was surprised when Beanie slept in again. He meant to ask about it, but thought he might be overstepping the boundaries of their friendship, if friendship is what it was.

Beanie arrived on Will's doorstep not long after Marie's death. Several large storms crossed the Okefenokee Swamp in Georgia, causing all of the surrounding rivers to rise to record levels. At first, only the roads to the riverfront homes were inaccessible. Some locals moved to area motels, others took events like this in stride and simply boated in and out; most homeowners near the river kept canoes and small motor boats for just such occasions. Beanie lived in a small ramshackle house in one of the flood zones and, since a bicycle was her only mode of transportation, she moved out immediately. Will offered pro-rated monthly rates to locals needing temporary shelter, and it was one of the few times all the rooms were rented at once. He learned fairly quickly the town was too small and the setting too rural to sustain a bed and breakfast of this size. There were enough visitors to keep the place running, but not enough to see a profit of any kind.

After the flood waters went down, Will took Beanie to check on her home. It was ruined – uninhabitable – and Beanie had no insurance on the place. So Beanie and Will made a deal for her to stay at The Château. He needed full-time help and she needed a place to live, so it worked out for both of them. In fact, she had come to his rescue twice already. It seemed there was nothing Beanie couldn't do. One Sunday morning, Will burned the breakfast frittata beyond repair and, with no stores open in

26

town until noon, he was just praying he would have enough cornflakes to feed his guests. Beanie scrounged through the kitchen, pulled out a bag of frozen tater tots and a can of mushroom soup and, with the sausage she could salvage from the middle of the frittata, whipped up a huge breakfast casserole for the six hungry divers upstairs. On another occasion, a guest dropped a diamond earring into a floor vent. When Will took the cover off, he could see the gemstone glinting down in the bottom of the airshaft, but nothing they had was both long enough to reach it and nimble enough to grab it. With a hair elastic, Beanie secured a nylon stocking over the nozzle of the shop-vac and fed the hose into the air vent, sucking the little earring into the pantyhose net. Will began to think there was no end to what Beanie could do, and he wasn't sure how he ever managed without her.

He was cutting fruit for the next morning's breakfast when Beanie walked into the kitchen carrying a bushel box of cucumbers.

"Hey, Bean." Will looked up and smiled wearily. "Where'd those come from?"

"Found 'em out on the porch with a note. Apparently Useless brought 'em by for me. Says his mama grow'd 'em, but I'm doubtin' that. She ain't worked her garden for years now. Prob'ly stole 'em outta somebody's field."

"Is he still after you to go out on a date?"

"Lord, Will, he's after anything on two legs. You know what they say, eight to eighty... I've done everything I know to discourage him, but he acts like he don't hear a word. Either that or he don't have good sense."

"Do you need me to talk to him?" Will was genuinely concerned.

"And say what?" Beanie asked.

"Oh, I don't know. Something about his intentions being unwelcome?"

"That'd kinda be like tellin' a pit bull not to gnaw on a bone. I'll just keep avoiding him."

"It's a small town, Bean. How long can you keep that up?"

"Long as it takes, I reckon. You want these? I can't even look at 'em without gaggin'."

"I could make refrigerator pickles," Will said. "I got some sweet onions at the market."

Beanie pulled up a chair and sat down with a sigh.

"You wash. I'll slice," she said.

"Tell you what," Will said, "when we finish these and get them in to soak, let's go down to the café for lunch. It's Wednesday..."

Beanie's spine straightened. She slapped the counter with both hands. "Baked chicken day," they said in unison.

Once the cucumbers were washed, sliced, and soaking in brine, Beanie and Will cleaned up and headed to the Mayhew Junction Café, arriving before the local firehouse whistle signaled twelve o'clock noon. It wasn't unusual for a few heads to turn whenever Beanie Bradsher walked into a room. If she noticed the stares or the whispers or even the giggles of children followed by the shushing of embarrassed parents, she never reacted to them.

Today, however, it was as if the Queen of England arrived. The full clamor of the busy diner came to an abrupt and silent halt. Heads didn't just turn - people stopped in their tracks, forks halfway to mouths, spoons full of food teetering in mid-air, jaws gaping and eyes wide. Nobody moved. Nobody spoke. For a full ten seconds or more, they simply stared. Beanie broke the ice.

"Hey, y'all," she said to everyone in general and no one in particular.

Sissy came to her senses first.

"Hey, Beanie! Haven't seen y'all in a month of Sundays."

Sissy handed off two sweet teas and a water to a table of three then hustled over and took Beanie by the elbow.

"Lord, Beanie, you're brave. The whole town is talkin' about your winnin's. Y'all sit over here. Maybe no one'll bother you over here outta the way," Sissy said, leading them both to a booth in the corner which was usually reserved for employees. "Y'all want a menu?"

"Naw, Sissy," Beanie said, still not grasping the seriousness of the situation. "It's baked chicken day. We's both havin' the buffet."

28

"Okay," Sissy said, without conviction, "but don't say I didn't warn ya. What can I getcha to drink?"

"Sweet tea for me," Beanie said.

"Ditto," said Will.

"Comin' up," Sissy said and walked away wiping her hands on the towel tucked into her waistband.

"Let's get this show on the road," Beanie said, scooting across the red vinyl seat. "I'm hungry."

"Beanie," Will said as he scanned the restaurant to see all eyes focused in their direction, "this may not have been a good idea."

"Oh, for pity's sake, Will, how bad can it be?"

Fifteen minutes later they were back in their seats, food cooling on the plates they'd held since loading them. Sissy had long since left huge plastic cups of iced tea on the table, which sweated into puddles on the polyurethaned tabletop.

"Lord, Will, I don't know if I can even eat now."

Beanie stared at the plate piled high with a roasted chicken breast smothered in onions and green peppers, corn bread covered by a healthy spoonful of fresh collard greens, green beans, macaroni and cheese, and rutabagas draped in scraps of bacon used for seasoning.

"Food's cold," Will said. "Why don't you get yourself another plate?"

"No," Beanie said. "It's not that. It's just I'm feelin' depressed is all."

"Who wouldn't feel depressed with all the woe we just heard?"

"I know," Beanie said as if she were surprised Will noticed. "Is it a full moon or something? Seems like they's tragedy all around. Poor Juanita's two kids needin' dental work, Fred's back is out and he ain't been able to work, Mirandy's cousin's friend who's battlin' the cancer. And Amos, bless his heart – his wife with a broken hip and stayin' over at the nursin' home, so he's havin' to eat out every meal. I thought he looked like he gained a little weight. Must be JoEllen's cookin'. I ain't never heard the like of all this misery."

"You've never won the lotto before," Will said, tearing a piece of chicken off the bone.

Beanie stopped shaking hot sauce onto her greens and stared up at Will from beneath her cowboy hat.

"Oooohhhh," she said in wide-eyed innocence.

Will chuckled. "Seriously?"

"I thought they was just bein' friendly," Beanie said, her shoulders sagging.

"Beanie, Beanie, Beanie," Will said, smiling sadly. "When was the last time somebody told you their car was broken down? There are cars being mown around in half the yards in this county and not once has anyone complained to you about needing to fix one of them until today, and I counted Beanie. Three cars and a truck, all desperately needing repairs so someone can get to work, find a job, take their kids to school, or get their elderly parent to the doctor. You do the math."

"I don't have to do the math," Beanie said. "I don't have that much money."

"Well, apparently they all think it's some kind of windfall, because half the people in this restaurant have their hands out in your direction."

"Now I really can't eat," Beanie said, pushing her plate to the side.

"Don't look now," Will said, "but Eustace Falwell just came through the door."

"Oh, Lord, Will – hide me."

Will laughed. "I'm no miracle worker, Beanie. You don't exactly blend in a crowd."

"Yeah, I guess not," said Beanie, tugging at the brim of her turquoise hat with matching sequined band.

"Don't look at him. Maybe he'll take the hint."

Beanie dropped her head and began to eat in earnest.

Eustace Falwell worked every room he entered like a politician up for re-election. He shook hands, remembered names, patted backs, asked after children and parents and spoke just shy of a shout. Certain everyone was just as interested in him as he was in them, Eustace had a story ready for every opening afforded him. Sometimes "hello" was enough. He spotted Beanie as she averted her eyes, but, undeterred, he made a beeline for her table.

"Hey, Will," Eustace said, "How's it going?"

"Afternoon, Eustace."

Beanie's head was still down, her focus on getting as much baked chicken as she could into her mouth. Eustace leaned in playfully and lifted the brim of her hat forcing her to look up with a half-hearted smile. She swallowed the now-dry chicken and washed it down with a gulp of sweet tea.

"Hey, Useless," she said with no enthusiasm at all.

"Hey, Beanie, you get those cucumbers I brought ya?"

"Yeah, I did, thanks." Beanie answered. "We've been putting up pickles all morning."

"Well, ain't that somethin'? Mama'd probably love a jar when you're done. She's got a great recipe for 'em. Ya take a bushel of cucumbers and slice 'em real thin-like..."

"You done give me that recipe last year, remember?"

"Oh, that's right," he said, removing his ball cap and scratching haphazardly at his head. "Hey, you know I heard something about you. Whole town is talking about you winning the lottery and all. That right?"

"Eustace," Will interrupted before Beanie could speak, "I don't mean to be rude, but Beanie's been trying to eat for over half an hour."

"Oh, yeah, I guess everybody's wantin' to know the same thing. Well, I won't keep you. I just thought I'd tell you about this song I been workin' on. Been wantin' to record it, but I got troubles with the I.R.S., and you know how that is. The OSHA guy came out the other day, too. If it ain't one thing it's another. He fined me a thousand dollars, but I won't bore you with all that. It was some little somethin' I forgot to do. You know how they want you to have everything posted where the guys can read it and I got the Mexicans out there can't read English and..."

"Eustace!" Will said.

"Oh, yeah, yeah, I get it." Eustace cackled. "I'm going, I'm going. But let me sing this one little song for you. When you hear it, I know you're gonna want to produce my record. I took this old song and, you know, God just gives me the words to things. Just pops 'em in my head, and I think to myself, now how did I come up with that? It's amazing how all the words rhyme and everything. I think to myself, 'That's good, Eustace.

31

You gotta record them words before they get away from you.' But, you know it cost a pretty penny to get anything recorded. And I can't read a lick of music, so I gotta hire somebody to play for me. But listen up and I'll sing you a little bit..."

***

The phone at The Château started ringing right after lunch and didn't stop until Will Thaxton took it off the hook an hour later.

Beanie took the first four calls. Afterwards, she begged Will to make her apologies and take messages.

"I didn't even know I knew this many people," Beanie moaned. "Leastways not well enough to give 'em money."

"Are they coming right out and asking now?"

"Not in so many words but, hell, the fact they're all of a sudden crawling out of the woodwork is words enough for me. What do they think I am, stupid?"

Will paused.

"No one thinks you're stupid, Bean," said Will, wishing that were true. He knew half the town thought she was a little off, but Will found her idiosyncrasies charming. Boundless energy and positivity, colorful and creative use of grammar, and unpredictable trains of thought made every moment with her both a challenge and a delight.

"What am I gonna do, Will?"

"I don't know, Bean, but we need to do something about the calls. I can't leave the phone off the hook indefinitely. Guests will think I've closed down."

In an age where nearly everyone Will knew carried a cell phone, Beanie Bradsher hated the thought of paying for a phone of any kind. Why should she? She rarely called a soul. If she needed something, she hopped on her bike and rode directly to the source.

"I guess I'm going to have to start getting ugly about it."

"Well, it wouldn't take long for people to get the hint if you just tell them the truth. You don't have any money to spare. Period. The way this town talks, word will spread in a matter of days and they'll leave you alone."

32

"You think?" Beanie asked hopefully.

"I do," Will said. "At least it's worth a try. Just be straight with them. They should be ashamed of themselves, calling you this way when everyone knows you just lost your home."

"I don't think they mean any harm. And I guess some of them really need help, you know?"

"I do know. But I also know this, Beanie. The ones waving their hands in front of your face crying 'woe is me' probably don't need help. If you want to help someone, try looking for somebody who is working too hard to stop and ask for help. These people want to help themselves all right – to your money."

"Well, they's precious little of that to go around, that's for sure. Maybe I ought not get a headstone. I don't want people thinkin' I'm selfish."

"Beatrice Bradsher, there is not a selfish bone in your body. Don't you dare change your plans. This will blow over, I promise."

"Lord, I hope so."

Beanie looked as if she would cry any minute and it broke Will's heart. Without thinking, Will reached out and pulled Beanie toward him for a comforting hug. When she went to lay her head on his shoulder, her red Stetson hit his cheek and slid backwards. They both reached for it at once, his hand closing over hers on the brim as she looked up, half laughing and half crying. He meant only to console her, but somehow found himself leaning in to kiss her.

Will Thaxton was never in his life pushed with such ferocity. Beanie's hands, palms out, caught him squarely in the center of his chest and sent him flying backwards. His feet caught on the first step of the hall stairway, but the rest of him sprawled ungraciously against the banister. There was barely time to gather himself into a sitting position before the front door slammed. He watched through the window as Beanie hopped on her bike and pedaled furiously away from the inn.

Will was still sitting on the stairs when Beanie returned an hour later with a pumpkin pie and a half-gallon of Breyer's Butter Pecan ice cream.

"What are you doin' still settin' there on your behind?" she asked.

"Just waiting, I guess," Will said. "Beanie, I'm…"

"Don't say nothin', Will Thaxton. You'll just make it worser than before."

"I don't know what I was thinking…"

"Well, I don't know either, but you better stop thinkin' it."

"That's just it. I wasn't! I don't know what happened."

"Well, it better not happen again."

"It won't," Will said. "I promise."

"Good," said Beanie. "I got pie for supper."

"For supper?"

"That's what I said."

"All right then," Will said, and followed her to the kitchen.

8
Sound the Alarm

The clock on Bubba John Atwater's bedside table crowed at
7:00 a.m. sharp. Sweet wrapped her pillow around her head like
a burrito and rolled away from the offending noise. The alarm
crowed again. Louder this time.

"Bubba John," Sweet whined, "can ya shut that thing off, for
crying out loud? It's Sunday."

There was no answer, not even the slightest whisper of
movement from Bubba John's side of the bed. Sweet sat straight
up in bed, smacking the empty spot where her husband's ample
frame usually lay.

"Dad-gummit, he did it again."

The rooster crowed exuberantly, lifting its wattled chin up
and down with a mechanical click. Sweet reached across the bed
and slapped the offending clock on its bobbing head, effectively
silencing the beast, if only for a five-minute snooze.

Noticing the bed was empty, Sweet sighed and mumbled to
herself, "Well, at least he put the little ones back where they
belong. Wish to hell he'd remember to shut off the rooster."

Sweet rolled out of bed and stumbled across the cheap
linoleum floor of her mobile home's "master" bedroom and into
the adjoining bathroom. The first wave of nausea hit as she
reached for her toothbrush.

"Whoa, Nellie..." Sweet breathed, catching herself on the
edge of the low-slung vanity.

She ran the water warm and splashed her face until the
nausea passed. She tried to remember what she'd eaten the
night before, but nothing came to mind. The second wave nearly
dropped her to the floor, but she had the sense to fall backward
onto the toilet, grabbing the towel rack on the way down.

What in the world? Sweet thought to herself. And then, *Oh,
good Lord, you've got to be kidding me.*

Steadying herself on the countertop, Sweet flung open the
medicine cabinet and grabbed a thin plastic container. She slid it

open with her thumbs and stared at four rows of plastic bubbles, most of which were smashed flat. Nothing amiss there. No reason to suspect morning sickness over a simple stomach virus. In fact, Daisy threw up yesterday afternoon. *That's all it is,* Sweet reasoned.

She felt the front door open and shut, and the heavy thump of boots coming down the hallway. The boots got quiet before Bubba John reached out to open the bedroom door. She peeked her head out of the bathroom in time to see her husband try to tiptoe into the room.

"What in the heck are you doing?"

Bubba John jumped as if he'd been hit by a cattle prod.

"I thought you'd still be asleep," he said, clearly busted.

"I would have been, if you'da thought to silence the cock's crow."

"Sorry, baby. I was puttin' out feed again. Huntin' season's just around the corner, you know."

"Oh, I know all right. This is the third time this week," Sweet said, brushing her hair back from her face with one hand.

"You're lookin' a little peeked, Mama. You okay?"

"I think I got a touch of Daisy's stomach bug."

"Y'all gonna try to go to church this morning? I came back to help you get the kids ready."

Sweet looked at her handsome, if exasperating, husband and sighed. He did come back for that. Whatever his faults, the man could not tell a lie. He would omit whatever he wanted to avoid, but if asked anything point blank, Bubba John would either answer truthfully or not at all.

"You feel like going?" Sweet asked, knowing the answer.

"Naw, I was thinking about takin' the boys fishing this afternoon. I thought I'd sort the tackle while y'all were at church."

"Well, y'all go on along this morning, why don'tcha? Bitty'll wanna go, you know, but I can keep Tater here if we promise to bake him some cookies. B-Kay'll help."

"Well, I was kind of hopin' to just take the boys, if that's okay. Bitty gets bored awful easy."

Sweet turned and grabbed her toothbrush, slathering it liberally with Ultra Brite.

"That works," she said, catching her husband's eye in the mirror before vigorously brushing her teeth.

Bubba John slipped in behind her and wrapped his arms around her waist.

"You okay, Mama?"

"I'm fine, hon. Just feelin' a little punk."

"Don't be mad at me," he said, bending to kiss the back of her neck.

"I'm not mad, Bubba. I just don't know what's going on with you these days," Sweet said, rinsing her mouth with warm water. "If I was the jealous type, I'd swear you were up to no good."

But you're not," Bubba John grinned. "And I'm not."

"So what is it, then? Why have you been MIA so much?"

"I've got a few irons in the fire, that's all. There's nothing you need to worry about, Sweet, I promise."

Bubba John turned her around to face him and, wrapping his arms around her hips, lifted her until his head rested against her chest.

Sweet wound her fingers through her husband's thick, dark hair and tilted his head back. She bent down and kissed his forehead tenderly. Cupping his face in her hands, she smiled and gazed at the deep blue eyes she loved so much.

"I'm glad, Bubba John. 'Cause I'd really hate to have to kill ya."

A laugh bubbled up from deep in the big man's chest.

"I'd hate that, too, Mama. You hungry?"

"Nope, but the kids'll be up shortly. I'll go make us some pancakes."

***

Bubba John and the two boys made it out the door with an uncharacteristic lack of drama. It was not unusual for the parents to divide and conquer, but the division was rarely without tears. Nobody liked to be left behind. With the twins old enough to help, Sweet was beginning to relax the rules a bit – the rules pertaining to the number of children per adult on recreational trips, that is. More specifically, it was the ratio per

Bubba John that was in question. She didn't think he was deliberately careless; he just didn't have the same regard for safety as she did, which put Sweet in a constant state of emotional stress. Bubba John could only focus on one thing at a time, and if a fish was on his line, a child overboard might go unnoticed. Or so Sweet convinced herself after a few near misses.

Sweet still trusted him with just one small child at a time, and then only with an older child tagging along. It made for a lot of noise when the fact was Bubba John went fishing a lot. And hunting. And four-wheeling. He was a big kid - Peter Pan to her Wendy. The kids adored him, of course. And they always wanted to be where he was, so anytime a child was left out, there would be tears and a lot of them. Sweet went along when she could; not because she was thrilled about fishing or hunting, but for two reasons: 1. She wanted her children safe, AND she wanted them to have fun. 2. She believed in doing things as a family, even if it was a big, chaotic mess of a family.

Normally, Sweet insisted on attending church on Sundays. She would pack up the kids, all five of them, and head off for Sunday School while Bubba John piddled around in his shop out back or snuck down to the river to fish from the bank. She always invited him to go, but he rarely did. After church, they all met back at home for frozen pizza or store-bought subs.

Today, Sweet didn't have the energy for church. Might as well let the boys have a little fun with their daddy. She was happy to stay home and bake. Thank goodness Bitty was too distracted by the rows of cookie dough on the counter to notice Bubba John and the boys sneaking out the front door.

B-Kay almost ruined it ten minutes after they left. Daisy stood on a step stool in front of Sweet, "helping" her roll out sugar cookie dough. Bitty was sorting cookie cutters and lining them up by size: small to large with exactly the same spaces between them. She did this with everything, including the toys in her room and the chairs in the backyard.

B-Kay entered the kitchen in a huff.

"Why didn't you wake me up?"

Sweet looked up, a little surprised and mildly amused.

"I didn't know it was my job, B."

"I wanted to go to church," she said, opening the refrigerator and scanning the shelves.

"Then you should have set your alarm. I didn't feel up to going this morning."

"Where's the OJ?"

"Bottom shelf."

"I don't see it."

"Move the milk."

"Where's Daddy and the boys?"

Two little heads carefully focused on the work at hand popped up in unison.

"B-Kay!" Sweet admonished. "We are making cookies here."

"But I just asked..."

"Brenda Kay Atwater, I'm gonna snatch a knot in you if you don't zip it this instant."

Sweet all but hissed this at her oldest daughter. Then, with only slightly forced enthusiasm, returned her attention to the little ones.

"Bitty, that's great, baby. Do you think you could sort out the sprinkles, too?"

"Where's Daddy?" Bitty asked.

"He'll be right back," Sweet said. "Daisy, that's flat enough, honey. What do you want to make first?"

"Punkin," Daisy said, grabbing the largest cutter she saw.

"That's an apple," B-Kay muttered.

"Punkin!" Daisy said, slamming it into the dough and grinding enthusiastically.

"Nice work," Sweet said. "That's a beautiful pumpkin. Do another one now."

"Great. You're raising a moron." B-Kay said, pouring orange juice into the bottom half of a sippy cup.

"Keep cutting, Daisy-may, Mama'll be right back," Sweet looked pointedly at her oldest daughter and jerked her head toward the utility room door.

Sweet entered first, holding the door open until B-Kay reluctantly slunk in. Sweet shut the door just shy of a slam.

"What is the matter with you this morning?"

B-Kay shrugged and launched herself onto the dryer with one hand.

"Speak, B-Kay. I don't have time to guess."

"He's gone all the time."

"Daddy?"

"No, T-Ray."

"Don't get smart with me, young lady."

"Well, he is. And half the time he's takin' the boys with him. It's not fair."

"Did you want to go fishing?"

"No, Mama, I wanted to go to *church.* But what I want doesn't seem to matter anymore."

"B-Kay, I didn't know you wanted to go this morning."

"I want to go every Sunday, Mom."

"Then set your alarm every Sunday and I'll make sure you get there. But don't you dare wake up with your butt on your shoulders, bound and determined to take your disappointment out on me. Not gonna happen. Is that clear?"

"Whatever," B-Kay said, determined to push it as far as she could.

"Not *whatever.* Not EVER *whatever.* Seriously, what is the matter with you?"

"I don't know, Mama. Something's not right."

"What do you mean, not right? Do you feel bad? Has someone hurt your feelings? What is it, B?"

"Kids at school are talkin', Mama."

"Talking about what? Just spit it out. Is it really that bad?"

"Only if you call Daddy spending time with Beanie Bradsher bad. You tell me."

Sweet felt the air leave her lungs like a vacuum. She wasn't sure how her quivering knees kept her standing, but she managed to open the utility room door with hands she could barely feel.

"Oh, that's silly, B-Kay. Your daddy would never..."

She couldn't finish the sentence. The kitchen table was unrecognizable. Bitty was still focused on arranging the now empty jars of sprinkles, as Daisy patted multi-colored cookie dough into her hair.

"Daisy, noooo!"

If Bubba John Atwater wondered why he didn't smell cookies baking when he returned at 1:30 that afternoon, he

40

didn't say a word to the boys. He followed a trail of sprinkles and smeared dough to the children's bathroom where he found a tub full of purple water and piles of children's clothing on the floor.

"Sweet?" he called softly before opening the bedroom door and peering quietly inside.

His wife snored softly while his two younger daughters lay in a tangled mass of limbs beside her. B-Kay was nowhere to be found.

By the time Sweet woke up, Bubba John had the kitchen returned to almost normal, except for the dough in the creases of the highchair and the underside of the table, which would not likely be discovered for some time.

T-Ray was napping on the couch when Sweet Lee Atwater staggered sleepily into the kitchen. Bubba John was twisting the cap off a Bud Light and didn't hear her come in.

"Put the beer away, Bubba John," Sweet said. "We need to talk."

9
Beanie Spills the Beans

A week or so after the kissing incident, Will and Beanie still tiptoed around each other, awkward and mostly silent. The Château was booked nearly solid on the weekends, with cave divers and hunters trying to get the most out of the time left before the serious cold spells hit. Will paid regular housekeepers to do the turn-arounds, but Beanie always took up the slack, especially if any issues came up after the other staff left. Business was never steady enough to hire anyone full-time, but Will had no problem finding people willing to work on a casual basis.

On Monday, after a relatively busy weekend, Beanie and Will were back in the kitchen finishing up the last of the breakfast dishes. With the plates and glasses all loaded into the industrial dishwasher, there were only the pots and pans to go. Will washed as Beanie dried and put away.

"Reckon you need anything from Tallahassee this week, Will?"

"Actually, yes. I need to restock at Sam's. You need something?"

"Well, they's somethin' I been needin' to tell you, but I gotta ask you not to say nothin' to nobody else."

"Okay," Will said, hesitating. "Is this about the lotto?"

"Yeah, kind'ly, but it's got to do with somebody else, too, and that's why it's important you don't tell nobody what I'm fixin' to tell you."

"You have my word," Will said, handing Beanie a dripping griddle.

"I gotta go to the lotto place to collect my winnings, and it has to be the state headquarters, not regional."

"Oh, well, that's no problem. Tallahassee isn't that much farther away than Gainesville. We can swing by there before we go to Sam's Club for supplies."

42

"They's a little more to it than swingin' by, from what I hear," Beanie said. "Any prize over a million takes a bit of doin'."

"Over a million? I thought you said you were getting twenty-thousand. That's some serious growth there, Bean."

"Well, that's what I been meanin' to tell you; we kept it a secret until we saw a lawyer. It may be a little more than I thought when ever'thing's taken into account, but they'll tell us over there."

"Who's *we?*"

"That's what you gotta keep quiet about," Beanie said, steeling herself to go on.

"It's Bubba John Atwater and me," she said. "But you can-NOT tell his wife, Will. Seriously. It would ruin everything."

Will felt his lungs deflate. He turned off the faucet and rested his soapy arms on the edge of the sink.

"I do take it seriously, Beanie," he said, when he finally caught his breath. "I certainly do."

"Oh, good, cuz we done seen a lawyer and ever'thing's drawed up nice and legal."

"And when are you planning to tell Sweet about all of this?"

"Just as soon as he gets the house all remodeled and ready to move in." Beanie stashed the griddle on top of the refrigerator.

"And you expect me to keep this a secret? That's asking a bit much, don't you think?"

"Why, you gotta keep it a secret. You done promised me you would," she said, wheeling to face Will.

"But, Beanie—dear God—I could not have imagined you taking part in something like this."

"Will, please don't be mad at me..."

"I'm not mad, Bean. I am disappointed. Truly...dreadfully...disappointed."

"Will..."

"Just stop, Bean. Stop. Please." Will pulled the yellow rubber gloves from each hand with a snap and draped them over the dish drainer. "I can't wrap my head around you deceiving Sweet Atwater like this."

"Oh, Sweet is gonna be happy as a lark!"

"Have you lost your mind, Bean?"

43

"But this is a wonderful thing, Will! Sweet has been wanting out of that house for years! You wait. Someday Sweet Lee Atwater will thank her lucky stars we did this for her."

"Who ARE you?"

"Does this mean you aren't going to help me?"

"Of course I'm not going to help you."

"But we won it together, so we gotta go together."

"Then Bubba John can drive you over there himself."

"No, he can't, Will. Somebody will see us."

"Well, you should have thought of that a long time ago. I refuse to be a part of this, and I am amazed you thought I would."

Beanie finished drying the last stock pot and stacked it with the others in the cabinet by the stove.

"Well, don't this beat all?" Beanie said. "We had it all planned out and now it's ruined. I don't know what I'm gonna tell Bubba John."

"I know a few things I'd like to tell him," Will said. "And while I'm at it, there's a few things I'd like to call him, too."

"Well, for cryin' out loud, Will. Bubba John's just tryin' to build a house for his wife. What're you mad at *him* for?"

***

"Beanie, sit down and start at the beginning," Will pulled one of the ladder-back chairs away from the table. "I'll pour you a cup of coffee and you can just start this story over."

"Will, I don't know what in the world you're so fired up about. I was tryin' to help Bubba John surprise Sweet with a new house for Christmas," Beanie said, slouching into the chair he still held.

"Well, there is a God in heaven is all I can say, Bean. I thought you and Bubba John were having an affair."

Even counting the recent kissing fiasco, Will had never heard Beanie Bradsher raise her voice, until now. Beanie snatched the hat from her head and sent it sailing through the kitchen door and down the hallway.

"Well that is the *stupidest* thing I ever heard, Will Thaxton. What in God's green earth made you think such a thing? Here I

44

am, trying my best to keep the biggest secret ever! I knew I shouldn'ta let myself be sucked into espionage. I never thought for a minute he'd go and win the darn thing and now the whole town's talkin' about how much *I* won and I didn't win *anything* but what Bubba John promised me if I'd play those stinkin' numbers at the Indian store every week. Oh, this is just a big, *big* mess."

"Whoa, whoa, whoa…calm down, Bean."

"I am *not* calming down. No, I'm not! And how you could think I would do something so evil and awful and downright ugly, I will never in my life know."

"Here, Bean, drink this," Will said, thrusting a cup of strong black coffee onto the table in front of her.

Bean picked up the mug in both hands and took a huge swig.

"Ow, ow, ow…why that's hot, Will!"

"Of course it's hot. I just made it."

"Well that's adding injury to insult, ain't it? What am I gonna do, Will?"

Beanie folded her arms, laid her head down in the crook of one elbow and wept. Will poured himself a cup of coffee and sat quietly across from her, not daring to touch her for fear of another outburst.

"Beanie, it's going to be fine. Stop crying now. Just sit up and tell me how this all came about."

It took a few more minutes of coaxing before Beanie dried her face on the dishtowel she was still holding and told the rest of the story.

For at least two years, Bubba John Atwater bought gifts for Sweet from the Avon catalogs Beanie carried around town in her bicycle basket. Each time he placed an order, he gave Beanie an extra twenty-dollar bill, which she was to use to play the same set of numbers on the twice-weekly Lotto drawing. Bubba apparently was not adept at lying, and though he didn't mind going behind Sweet's back to spend a few dollars a week, he did not want to be caught doing something she was resolutely against. To Sweet, the lottery was the same as gambling and she was not going to have it.

45

Since Beanie was the most honest person Bubba John knew, he felt like he could trust her to do the right thing if his numbers ever came up. He promised to pay her five percent of his winnings, after taxes of course. The products he bought on a regular basis helped Beanie out financially, and Sweet seemed to look forward to the gifts. Beanie was happy with the arrangement, but she never quite expected he'd win.

And now there was the issue of telling Sweet, but Bubba John made up his mind to pull off the surprise of the century. He hired a contractor in Madison and ordered the survey on his mama and daddy's old property out on the river. He half-expected Beanie to go claim the prize and give him his winnings, until they realized the tax ramifications of such a deal. Arranging meetings with two attorneys and a CPA in a town the size of Mayhew Junction was no easy feat. There were quick stops by the park, or in the grocery store, trying to catch Beanie when he could. He offered to buy her a cell phone, but she thought that was plain silly.

Beanie wasn't sure how Bubba John thought he was going to manage to keep a house a secret, but he was bound and determined to get Sweet Lee out of that double-wide trailer by Christmas.

"I don't know why you didn't tell me this to begin with, Bean," Will said. "I'd have kept your secret. You know that."

"Well, I know, but Bubba John made me promise. He didn't want to take any chances. But then we realized you'd have to take me over there, and he just had to let me tell ya. But, Lord, Will, that did not go as planned, did it?"

"Not at all."

"I'm gonna try to talk Bubba John into tellin' Sweet. I don't think my heart can take all this sneakin' around. Some things get all blown outta hand, don't they?"

Will cocked his head to the side and squinted sideways at Beanie.

"I think you mean blown out of proportion, Bean."

"Whatever. You know what I mean. This thing has snowballed into a whole nother can of worms. I'm just sayin'."

"Do tell," Will said, and went down the hallway to retrieve Beanie's hat.

Hours later, after Will went to bed, Beanie tiptoed downstairs in a terry cloth robe and teal boots, this time no hat. She sat at the hall table and picked up the portable phone.

"Hey," she said, when a man's voice answered. "It's me. Can you come get me?"

The clock on the wall chimed once.

"I know it's late… I know, but… You don't know what I've been through today; it was awful… No, I can't. Okay, yeah, I understand. Okay. I'll see you Wednesday night then. Night."

Bubba John Atwater

From the day I met Sweet Lee Prescott, I have never even looked at another woman, which means — technically — that I've never looked at a woman in the sense that I mean here, since we were both no more than children when we fell in love. What I mean is, I have always loved her. Always. Don't ask me to explain it. I know what most people think about men in general, but I guess I'm like my daddy in that regard. When you are taught by word and by example what it means to be a gentleman, you take that to heart, and to behave any differently is just as insulting to yourself as it is to anyone else.

Jimmy Carter was, and is, my hero. Here is this man, hard-working, humble, Baptist like my daddy — they were cut from the same cloth, I tell ya — the same exact cloth. Leather, actually, though maybe that's not cloth. Tough, nearly indestructible, but soft if it's handled right. Anyway, here is this man who is devoted to his family, teaches Sunday school, loves his wife, works on his peanut farm out in the middle of rural Georgia, and he runs for President of the United States! What in the world ever gave him that kind of courage? I think I know the answer. It was Rosalynn, plain and simple. She made him believe he could do anything — anything at all.

And that's how I feel about my Sweet. I can do anything I set my mind to, including giving her a house for Christmas. I've always wanted to build her a house, but there was never enough money to even think about the kind of house she deserves, and would actually want. I know my wife. She doesn't want some fancy new brick house in a neighborhood. No, she doesn't. She wants a place with a history that means something — like family. And I'm going to give it to her. I am. You watch.

10
The Awakening

Sweet Atwater sat at the kitchen table across from her husband. This table, this very table, was the first piece of furniture they purchased together. Sweet, at eighteen, pregnant with twins and barely able to move—Bubba John, twenty years old, still gangly but growing solid with age and the weight of responsibility. The word itself was foreign to him, but he felt it just the same. Bubba John got his first Christmas bonus and wanted Sweet to have something nice - a necklace, maybe, or a diamond ring. He couldn't afford a real engagement ring. They eloped just after Sweet's eighteenth birthday, picking out wedding bands at a pawnshop in Georgia.

But Sweet wanted a table. A pine farm table, long enough to seat a slew of children. Bubba John would give her the moon on a shining silver platter if she asked for it.

"How am I going to tell my mama I bought you a kitchen table for Christmas?" Bubba John wondered.

"How are you going to tell her you bought me a ring when we're eatin' off a card table?"

"I see your point."

And he did see her point. Sweet was nothing if not practical and responsible – attributes he did not possess. They bought the table together, and they got a nice one, hand-planed and long, with sturdy ladder-back chairs, eight in all. And they filled all but one, slowly but surely.

And now, as many times as Bubba John sat at this table, to eat or to play cards or to clean his guns, this time he couldn't figure out what to do with his hands. Sweet sat directly across from him, her chin resting on her knuckles. She said nothing, just stared at her husband's face.

Bubba John put both hands flat on the table, then reached for the beer he placed at one end, then thought better and entwined his fingers, pressing both thumbs to his chest. After a moment, he began to rub his hands together as if he were washing them.

Finally, Sweet reached across the table and pressed his hands down, effectively silencing the swishing sound. She kept her hand there, firm and strong, but somehow still gentle.

"Talk to me, Bubba," she said.

"What do you want me to say?"

"I want you to tell me the truth."

"I have never lied to you, Sweet. From the day I met you, I have never told you an outright lie and I don't want to start now."

"Then tell me what is going on with Beanie Bradsher."

"I can't," Bubba John said. "You're just going to have to trust me. I'm not doing anything wrong."

"Are you sleeping with her?"

"Um, that would fall in the "wrong" category, so no - absolutely not. I would never cheat on you."

"Bubba John, anything you do with another woman—that you hide from me—is cheating on me."

Bubba John squirmed and pulled his hands away.

"You know what I mean, Sweet. I'm not—you know—I'm not fooling around or anything."

"Then what is it?"

"It's a surprise. That's all I can tell you. It's a surprise and it's for Christmas."

"Oh, for crying out loud, Bubba John, I have a drawer full of Avon supplies I won't use in a million years. What could possibly be such a surprise that I can't know?"

"I can't tell you. It would ruin the surprise."

"The whole town is talking. Do you get that? Your daughter has heard friends talking about seeing you and Beanie meeting at the park. Seriously, Bubba, what the hell?"

Bubba John sighed and scratched the back of his neck.

"Sweet Lee Atwater," he said, looking at her full in the eyes and not blinking once. "I may not be the smartest man on earth, and I may have disappointed you an awful lot these past twenty years, but I love you. I have been meeting with Beanie, but it's not what this town is trying to make it. And come Christmas, you'll see. Could you give me 'til Christmas?"

Sweet looked at his face, searched for any sign of deceit, and found none. He was nervous, but not ashamed — embarrassed, but not guilty.

"Okay," Sweet said. "Until Christmas."

"I love you," Bubba John said. "I really do."

"I love you, too, Bubba John.

"Can I have my beer now?"

Sweet laughed.

"Since when do you need my permission?"

"Since today, I think. I'm not sure."

Sweet picked up the bottle and brought it to her lips.

"Ugh…warm."

"I don't see how. It's cold as ice in here," Bubba John said, the lopsided grin creeping back to his face.

"Don't push your luck, Buster. It'll get a lot colder if I hear another word about you and Beanie Bradsher."

"I can't stop this town from talking, Sweet. You know how it is."

Sweet opened the refrigerator and retrieved a Bud Light from the vegetable bin. Plunking it down on the table, she slid it, unopened, into Bubba John's outstretched hand.

"I'll make beer bread with the hot one," she said.

"Chili, too?" Bubba John asked hopefully.

"I don't see why not," Sweet replied. "And while I do that, you can go see if you can find B-Kay. I think you'd better have a talk with her. She was pretty upset."

"I can do that."

Somewhere in the back of the doublewide, a toilet flushed.

"Kids are up," Sweet said.

"Yep. Need me to get 'em for you?"

"You take care of B-Kay. I got the kids."

Bubba John stood then. To get to the back door, he'd have to either walk around the long end of the table or squeeze past his wife, who stood at the kitchen sink. Somehow, the long way seemed like the wrong way, like he was somehow walking away from her for good. But he wasn't sure she'd want him close to her right now. So he stood for a minute, awkward and silent.

Sweet felt self-conscious, too. What do you do in the moment when trust is the only thing that feels right, but fear and doubt seem the most rational?

Bubba John stepped close to his wife, pressing his wide chest against her shoulders and bending to rest his head close to hers.

"I'm sorry," Bubba John said. "I don't want you to be mad at me."

"I'm not mad," Sweet said. "I'm scared."

"Aw, don't be. Seriously, Sweet…if it helps, I'll tell you the surprise."

"If you told me, would I know the truth?"

"There is no doubt in my mind."

"Then don't tell me."

"Are you sure? I don't want you to feel bad, Sweet."

"I'm okay, I think. But speaking of feeling bad, I can't shake this nausea. I've got a doctor's appointment for Tuesday afternoon. Can you make sure the kids get home from school?"

Bubba John stiffened and froze. "Tuesday?"

"Yeah, my appointment is at 1 o'clock in Tallahassee."

"Tallahassee?"

"That's where my gynecologist is. What's wrong with Tallahassee?"

"Um, nothing. I just wondered, that's all."

"Bubba John…" Sweet trailed off ominously.

"Well, dammit Sweet, I have an appointment over there, too. On Tuesday."

"At the gynecologist?"

"No, in Talla… That was just weird, Sweet."

"Well, I'm confused."

"I know. I'll change my appointment. It's no big deal."

"Let me guess. It's part of the surprise." Sweet said, without an ounce of humor.

"This is not going to be easy, I gotta tell ya," Bubba John sighed.

"I'll see if Dottie can handle the kids. She's watching the store for me. Or, wait, will it spoil the surprise if we ride together? It'd sure be easier if B-Kay can take the car to school and pick up Tater and Daisy from daycare."

"I think I can work it out," Bubba John said. "Hey, let's make a day of it. We can go over early and have lunch. I'll drop you off at the doctor's office before my appointment."

A rumble erupted in the hallway and Bitty's voice rose over the din, "Mama, Mama! C'mere quick! Daisy's done wet the bed and Tater's got pee in his hair."

"Go find B-Kay. I got this," Sweet said and pushed past Bubba John to get to her babies.

***

Bubba John found his daughter in the treehouse. He didn't have to look long, just *up*. B-Kay was asleep, cellphone still in her hand and one leg dangling off the edge of the second level. The three oldest children helped build the treehouse five years before. It started out as one level, but the project was so much fun, they just kept going. Now it was three decks high with a ladder going straight up from the third level to a turret of sorts. It wasn't all that pretty, but it was strong and sturdy and no one had fallen out of it yet.

Bubba John made sure to build the steps to hold his weight. He climbed to the first level and stood up, thus putting him face to face with his gently snoring daughter. She was so pretty it took his breath away, just like her mama. He could never quite figure out how he got so lucky.

"I thought I'd find you here," Bubba John said, catching the phone which slid from B-Kay's hands when his voice startled her awake.

"Daddy! You scared me half to death."

"Need this?" he asked, holding her phone out of reach.

"Not funny, Dad."

Bubba John placed the phone gently into her outstretched hand.

"Mama says you're mad at me."

"Can you blame me?" B-Kay sat up and swiped a hand through her hair.

"Nope. But, I gotta tell you something. It's a secret and you gotta promise not to tell Mama."

"You're kidding me, right?"

53

"Not kidding."

"You've lost your mind," B-Kay said. "Oh, my God...you've lost your mind."

"B. Seriously. It isn't what you think."

"It isn't?"

"Well, duh, of course not. Your mama would kill me if I ever, well, you know... Anyway, I'd be dead and I like being NOT dead too much to do anything stupid."

"Somehow that makes perfect sense. So what gives? Why is everybody talking about you and Miss Beanie?"

"First you have to swear to keep a secret. Biggest secret you ever kept in your life, B. I mean it."

"Is it a good secret or a bad secret?" B-Kay wasn't about to swear to anything bad.

"Good secret. It's a surprise."

"For Mama?"

"For all of us, really, but the surprise part is mostly for Mom, yes."

"Oh, my God, you're buying her a new mini-van aren't you?"

"Nope, bigger."

"A bus?"

Bubba John laughed then, a full out belly laugh.

"What's so funny?" B-Kay felt like laughing, too, but she wasn't exactly sure why.

"Oh, Lord, B...a bus?"

"Well, a bus is the only thing I could think of bigger than a van. I still don't know what's so funny, though."

"No doubt we could use one, but that's another surprise for another day."

"So what is it then?"

"You haven't promised yet," Bubba John said, still laughing.

"For crying out loud, Dad, I promise. I pinky swear promise I will not reveal your stupid secret. What is it?"

"I'm getting your mama a house for Christmas."

"A house?"

"Yep, a house."

"A real house. Not a doll house, right?"

"A real house. With two stories and a porch and a foundation that doesn't roll."

"Wait, what does Beanie Bradsher have to do with building a house?" B-Kay was confused.

"One thing at a time, B…" Bubba John said. "She's helping me and that's really all you need to know for now."

"Okay, that's fine, Dad, but it is almost October already. How the heck are you going to build a house by Christmas?"

"Well, it's not like I have to start from scratch; I'm remodeling Mam-maw and Pap's old house. I wanted to build a brand new house, but something tells me your mama's gonna want the old home place instead."

"Can we afford that?"

"You let me worry about whether or not we can afford it. I have it all figured out, you can trust me on that."

"Hey, wait…does T-Ray know?"

"No, and don't you dare tell him, either. There's no way he could keep a secret this big."

By the time they climbed down from the treehouse and headed in for supper, B-Kay knew about everything but the lottery part. Bubba John was glad he'd gotten her in on the secret. B-Kay would be good at the smaller details, and would help keep Sweet occupied while he worked on the house.

Sweet watched them come in together, both grinning like Cheshire cats. Apparently, he'd smoothed things over with her. B-Kay obviously knew what the surprise was and she was happy about it, from the looks of things.

Good Lord, Sweet thought, *I hope Bubba John isn't doing anything stupid like buying me a ring.* The more she thought about it, the more she was convinced that's what it was. Bubba John was taking out a loan from Beanie Bradsher's lotto winnings to buy her a ring. That had to be it. That's why someone saw them at the lawyer's office together. He was probably getting her to help him pick it out, too.

Lord, help, there is no telling what kind of tacky thing I will end up with if Beanie Bradsher is in on this.

11
Tallahassee or Bust

On Tuesday morning, Beanie was quiet most of the way to Tallahassee.

"What are you thinking about, Bean?" Will asked when the silence became overwhelming.

"I was thinkin' about the money, I guess. I figure I ought to either start paying you some rent or find another place to live."

"Why would you do that?"

"Well, I don't want to overstay my welcome, for one. Plus things is gettin' a little awkward if you know what I mean. I should have enough left over to get me a little trailer or somethin'. Mommer and Diddy's house ain't worth fixin' up, but I still got the land. I can put me a single-wide up on stilts, or better yet, get me a big ol' camper and pull it out ever'time it floods."

"Bean… I want you to do what is right for you, but you don't have to be in any hurry to leave. You've been a big help to me and there is plenty of room at The Château, however long you want to stay. And as for things being awkward, they don't have to be. Really. They don't."

"I know, Will, but it ain't the same anymore."

"Something else is bothering you, I can tell. What is it?"

Beanie took off her lime-green hat and placed it carefully on her lap, but it teetered precariously on the mountain of fabric that was her matching dirndl skirt. The seatbelt across her legs made the crinoline petticoat tilt upwards, so she adjusted by poking the fabric between her knees to make a flatter surface.

"I don't rightly know if I wanna talk about it, to tell the truth. Might make things even more unsettled between us."

"Is it something I've done?"

"No, no…nothing like that. I mean, other than that one thing, but we done hashed that out. Anyways, it's nothing to do with you at all."

"Is it someone else? I heard you talking on the phone the other night. I mean, I didn't hear what you said. I heard your voice and it was late and I just wondered... Oh, shoot, it's none of my business. I'm sorry."

Beanie was more than a little surprised by his admission and cocked her head sideways to look at him.

"I thought you was asleep!"

"I was reading, and I heard the phone dialing. You know it beeps a little on the phone in my room..."

"How would I know that?"

"Oh, right, well it does. Anyway, I heard your voice and just wondered."

"Did you listen on the phone?" Beanie's voice rose incredulously.

"No! Oh, no! Beanie - seriously, I would never do that. I just poked my head out to see who was dialing. I didn't hear what you said."

Will watched as Beanie's hands began to shake and her breathing got shallow.

"Whoa, Bean...what is it? I'm telling you, I didn't hear what you said. Wait, wait...I'm pulling over."

Will pulled his car into the gravel parking lot of a vacant fruit stand and slid to a stop. Placing the car in park, he turned to face Beanie.

"Tell me what is going on. Bean. Look at me. What is it?"

"I been seein' him for a while. I just couldn't tell anyone."

"Who? Bubba John?"

"Dammit, Will! No! I done told you it wadn't Bubba John." Beanie was not yet recovered from Will's wrongful accusation of an affair with a married man. "Why you wanna think the worst of me is beyond my ken. I ain't talkin' to you if you're gonna insult me."

Beanie crossed her arms and huffed. Will leaned forward and bumped his forehead against the steering wheel.

"I give up, Bean. I just give up. I can't do anything right. Can't say anything right. I'm trying to help, really I am, but you are the most confusing person I have ever met, and that's the truth."

They sat in silence for a minute or two, then Will sighed, put the car into drive and started to pull forward. When Beanie spoke, Will could barely hear her.

"It's Suvi Jones."

Will stopped and put the car back into park.

"Oh," said Will. "Suvi?"

"You can't tell nobody, Will. Folks'd run us outta town."

"Why in the world would they do that?"

"Cause he's black, that's why."

"Oh, for pity's sake, Bean, this is the twenty-first century."

"Maybe so, but some things never change in this town."

"How long have you been...I don't even know what to call it...dating? Are you dating him?"

"Not really. Just talkin' is all. We slip away sometimes...go fishin' out on the old rail trestle or something like that. He took me to Valdosta once, but we was nervous the whole time, worried who else'd be there from Mayhew Junction."

"Beanie...there is nothing wrong with you dating a man you like. It's kind of sad, when you think about it."

"I've tried to talk to him about it, but he has a name in this community, a standing, you know? Folks wouldn't like him crossin' a line like that. He's prolly right."

Will raked a hand through his hair, shifted gears again and slowly eased back onto the roadway. Beanie was quiet for several minutes.

"I don't rightly know if it's even worth the effort. Cain't never see him when I want."

"Well, that's a reasonable observation. Are you in love with him?"

"I don't reckon I've spent enough time with him to know the answer. He's good to me."

"When?"

"What do you mean, 'when'?"

"When is he good to you?" Will asked, a little more sharply than he intended. "Seriously, Beanie. *When* is he good to you? You don't see each other in the daylight. You don't go on dates. He obviously isn't giving you rides anywhere, because last time I looked, I was your chauffeur."

Beanie was horrified. She had never seen Will angry, nor heard him use that tone.

"Do you see him at night? Is that it? Do you call and he comes to pick you up? Because that is *not* a relationship, Beanie. That is not *seeing* someone. That is *sleeping* with someone. That's what that is."

"Will?"

"Are you sleeping with him?"

"I really don't think that's none of your business, but if'n I don't say something, you're gonna go off half-cocked and think the worst of me again."

"I guess I'm…I'm just surprised, Beanie. No, not surprised, if I'm honest."

"For cryin' out loud, Will…wouldja stop insulting me?"

"Let me finish. I mean surprised is not the emotion I'm feeling, and the truth is, I'm surprised I'm *feeling* these emotions at all. Does that make sense?"

"Not particularly," Beanie mumbled.

"Well, I'm angry. And hurt. And I know I have no right to be either, but there you have it."

"I don't know what to say," Beanie said.

"You don't have to say anything. It is what it is. I'm sorry I put you in an awkward position. Maybe it is too awkward. Maybe you *should* think about moving."

"If that's what you want…"

"No, I don't want that. But I can't make myself happy about you sleeping with a man who won't be seen in public with you. Gosh, Beanie, I don't want *you* to be hurt."

"First of all, I am not *sleeping* with Suvi Jones. Truth of the matter is, I ain't never slept in a bed with another human being in my life. Not that I know of, anyways."

"You know what I mean," Will said, petulant now.

"Well, I'm not doin' *that* either. I'm not the fool you think I am, Will Thaxton. Hard as it is to believe, you're lookin' at a forty-two year old virgin."

Will said the first thing that came to mind.

"How is that *possible*?"

Beanie, embarrassed now, pulled her hat down over her face and spoke from behind the rim.

"Do you really want me to answer?"

"No...I don't know, do you want to?"

Uncovering her face, Beanie turned to face Will, her crinolines crackling under the strain of the seatbelt.

"Listen, Will, I don't want you thinkin' they's anything wrong or peculiar about me; it just ain't never happened and I'm not even sure I care. If Suvi wadn't so goll-darned upright, I probably wouldn't be where I am now. But Lord knows I ain't never wanted children, so I guess it's all for the best."

Will stopped to think for a moment. He hadn't spoken to his daughter for a couple of weeks, but that wasn't unusual. Natalie used to call Marie almost every day and they would talk for hours, but somehow, when Will got on the phone the conversation dwindled quickly. On the other hand, he couldn't imagine not having the relationship at all. What would it be like *not* to have children? He found the idea rather sad.

"You didn't want children?" Will asked.

"Well, first off, I never had a husband, so it was kind'ly out of the question from the get-go. But no, I never pictured hitchin' my horse to that wagon."

"It can be a heavy load, that's for sure," Will said, "but I wouldn't trade it."

Will flipped on his turn signal and guided his car onto Capital Circle.

"I think we're almost there," Will said, "Can you hand me those directions I printed out?"

Beanie didn't respond; she was squinting at the traffic down the road.

"Oh, look, there's Bubba John's truck up ahead. He knows where he's goin'. You can just follow him the rest of the way to the Lotto Headquarters."

Two hours later, the paperwork was done, and the requisite photos were taken with the assurance their names would not be published for at least six months. Afterwards, Will took Beanie to the Cracker Barrel out on the interstate for a late lunch. All the awkwardness seemed to dissipate over fried chicken livers and meatloaf and they chatted non-stop all the way home.

As they came back through town, Will suggested they stop by the bank and deposit Beanie's check.

"Oh, Lord, Will... I never even thought of that. Now everybody's gonna know how much I won."

"We can do this discreetly, Bean. It's a bank...they have to keep it confidential."

Beanie looked at Will like he had two heads.

"It don't work that way here. Oh, they mean well...but if I hand them a check this big, somebody in bookkeeping is bound to tell her husband, and then he'll tell his best friend and within a week or two, it'll be on prayer chains across the county."

"Prayer chains?"

"Why, yeah...

"Well, that's ridiculous -" Will began.

"Of course, it's ridiculous, but that don't make no difference to them church ladies. First they'll calc-a-late how much is ten percent of a hun'erd and ninety-seven thousand dollars, and then they'll pray for my discernment about tithes."

"Are you serious?"

"As a heart attack. It'll be printed in church bulletins across the county under *Prayers and Praises.* Cross my heart and hope to die!" Beanie drew an emphatic X across her chest and ended with one hand raised in a four-fingered salute.

"So what do you want to do?"

"Reckon I'll hang onto this check 'til I figure that out."

12
All is Not Well

Sweet and Bubba John woke early on Tuesday for the trip to Tallahassee. After calming a minor row between B-Kay and T-Ray over who would be driving the van, the kids were packed off to school in good order. Sweet was hesitant to let either of them drive with the other children in the car, but B-Kay was by far the cooler head of the two. T-Ray would sulk for days, but he would "live and not die," as Sweet's mama used to say.

It wasn't often Sweet and Bubba John took time away together. Even the looming doctor's appointment didn't spoil the hour-long ride. Sweet was staring quietly out the window when Bubba John spoke.

"Whatcha thinkin' about?"

"Nothing really. Just realizing I'd forgotten how beautiful it is here. Hard to enjoy the scenery when you're hauling five kids around."

"I've always loved this land. Been thinking about Mama and Daddy's place settin' there decaying. You think you might want to live out on the river someday?"

Sweet sighed. "Always been my dream, you know that."

"I been thinkin' about cleaning it up a little, you know, just in case."

"Just in case what…we win the lottery or something?" Sweet laughed.

Bubba John choked, but recovered quickly.

"Yeah, right. Kinda hard to win the lotto when you're not allowed to play."

"I never said you weren't allowed to play, Bubba. If you want to gamble what little money we have, I can't stop you. But I think it's silly. What are the odds of us winning anything?"

"Pretty slim," Bubba John said. "Kinda fun to dream, though. You ever thought about what you'd do if we struck it rich?"

"Not really," Sweet said. "Well, maybe every once in a while, I do. When the mini-van farts in the school pick-up line, or the pipes bust at the shop. But, on the whole, I wouldn't change much."

"Really?"

"Yeah, really. Would you?"

"Well, yeah," Bubba John said. "I'd change lots of things."

"Like what?" Sweet asked, a knot forming in the pit of her stomach.

"Like the farting car, for starters," Bubba John laughed and reached for the radio dial. Sweet caught his hand and squeezed gently.

"I'm kind of enjoying the quiet, if you don't mind." Sweet smiled at him before turning her attention back to the landscape.

Bubba John glanced over at his wife, her head resting against the side window as she gazed at the endless rows of piney woods whizzing past. Sometimes she took his breath away. Her hair, long and naturally wavy, was always pulled back. He'd watched her do it a million times. As soon as breakfast was in front of the kids, she dashed to the bathroom, washed her face, brushed her teeth, threw on lipstick, blush and mascara and tied her hair back with one rubber band. Brush, brush, pull, twist, wrap twice and he swore it looked like she just came from a salon. But she hadn't seen the inside of a hair salon since the day they were married. He wondered if that would change now. God, she was beautiful.

"I love you, Sweet Lee Atwater."

Sweet turned her head without removing it from the window.

"I love you, too, honey," she grinned.

"Hey, we have about an hour before your appointment. Wanna go look at new cars? You know, just for fun..."

"Oh, that's a great idea – show me something I can't have and then I'll walk away wanting it."

"I knew you'd say that, but listen - I picked up a side job and I think we might be able to handle a new car payment. The van is falling apart, Sweet. I want you to have something nice."

"Is this the surprise, Bubba? A side job?"

"Well, kind of... Boy, I am not good at this at all."

Bubba John swallowed hard and reminded himself he wasn't actually lying. He did pick up a side job of sorts. He'd be working closely with the contractor to get the house done by Christmas, which was a job in itself. He didn't have to tell Sweet *whose* house he was working on. He didn't plan on buying a car yet, but now that Sweet brought it up, and now that he was actually collecting the money – well, it seemed dumb to wait for the house to be built to make his wife's life easier.

"Honey," Sweet said, "I appreciate the thought, but honestly, if we have a little extra income, I have an entire list of things that need to happen before a new car. I have to say, I'm a little relieved. I thought you were in cahoots with Beanie Bradsher to buy me a ring or something. And, speaking of which, what *does* Beanie have to do with the surprise, if it's not a ring?"

"Oh, well," Bubba John stammered, "Beanie helped me get the job, that's all."

"You're right. You are not good at this."

"Crap."

"Bubba John…"

"Sweet, you said you'd give me until Christmas. Stop trying to trip me up."

"Good Lord…"

"Humor me, Sweet. If you were going to get a new car, what would it be?"

"Well, I always wanted a Corvette," Sweet grinned.

"Right," Bubba John said. "And how would you fit five kids into a Corvette?"

"Good point," Sweet said. "And the way it's looking now, it could be six. Could you pull over? I think I'm going to throw up."

Ten minutes later, Sweet was fine and Bubba John was nauseous. He knew Sweet had not been feeling well, but he thought she was just tired. They were back on the road before Bubba John found his voice.

"How could this happen?"

"Same way it happened all five times before," Sweet said.

Bubba John was silent.

"Look, let's wait and see what the doctor says. It could be a stomach bug, but I want to make sure."

"I love our kids, Sweet..."

"But you don't want any more. I get it."

"Do you?"

"I'm not trying to get pregnant," Sweet said carefully, "but, I would never change what God brings to us."

"I'm worried..."

"Yeah, me, too. But let's not spoil this day worrying. Let's go look at cars."

Sweet patted her husband's thigh and smiled. Bubba John relaxed and breathed deeply for a moment. He was a lucky man and he knew it. If another child was coming into their lives, so be it. He reminded himself in a few hours they would be millionaires. That in itself was a load off anyone's mind. He almost broke down and told her right then, but he was too excited about his plan. He wanted to see his wife's face when he pulled down the long dirt driveway and revealed the best Christmas gift ever.

After checking out a host of minivans and two SUV's, then grabbing breakfast at Hardee's, Bubba John dropped Sweet off at the doctor's office, promising to pick her up in two hours.

Sweet signed in at the front desk and sat amongst the throng of people in the waiting room. It was a busy place, but she felt at home there, and no wonder. She spent many an hour in this room over the years. She loved watching the other women. Some were obviously pregnant – tired, but excited, too. The larger they were, the sooner the reward for all that suffering. She knew it was wrong, but Sweet made the time go faster by playing her favorite mental guessing game: *Why is She Here?*

The ones who were trying to get pregnant were all business. Their partners were with them, and there was usually a notebook or reference materials in one of their hands. The ones who hoped they weren't pregnant were alone and nervous, or brought a mother or a friend along. They spoke in whispers and rarely laughed. Those who were hoping for a positive test spoke the loudest and laughed the most often. They already had an inkling and were happy to tell everyone. The women who were there for a checkup were either bored or relaxed. And then there were the women like her, unsure and a little nervous. Something just isn't right.

"Sweet Lee Atwater?"

The nurse's voice cut through Sweet's reverie and she stood.

"Hey! Gloria! You're back!"

Sweet smiled at the tall, gorgeous woman whose skin contrasted so starkly with her white uniform.

"Long time, no see," Gloria replied and hugged Sweet warmly before ushering her through the office door.

"Gosh, I know, I haven't seen you since before *you* joined the ranks. How's that baby doing?

"She's almost three now. It has been awhile. You know the drill, weight first."

"You took some time off, didn't you?" Sweet asked, stepping onto the scale and setting the caliber weight automatically on 100.

"A little bit. I think I was out when your last baby was born. Wait, that's not right..." Gloria said, peering at the scales.

Sweet looked, too. The lower counterweight was pushed all the way to the left and the top bar still had not moved. Gloria adjusted the scale and looked again.

"Ninety-eight pounds."

"Well, I thought my jeans were a little loose, but that's just crazy."

"Let's finish up your vitals and I'll get your history in the room. You'll be in Exam 2 today. Any chance you might be pregnant?"

"I'm still on birth control, but knowing me, I'd say I need to pee in a cup to be sure."

An hour later, Sweet was buttoning up her top and waiting for the doctor to return. She was concerned, but not overly worried. The exam was uneventful as those things go, but the pregnancy test was positive, so he ordered an ultrasound. If this was one of the physicians she knew - Dr. Palomino, who delivered three of Sweet's babies and had children of her own, or Dr. Desmond, the incredibly handsome older man who put everyone at ease with his calm, friendly demeanor – Sweet might already know what to expect. But this was a new guy, young and serious, and a little on the nervous side, Sweet thought to herself. He said little during the test, but pointed occasionally at the screen and directed the technician to print certain views.

Dr. Anderson came in as Sweet put her shoes back on.

"Hey, Doc," Sweet grinned, determined to make him smile. "What's the good word?"

"Is your husband here?" Dr. Anderson asked.

"Not at the moment," Sweet said. "He's picking me up, though. What's wrong?"

"I just think you may want him here to discuss this – your situation."

Nervous was one thing. Patronizing was a whole different matter.

"Where's Gloria?" Sweet asked.

"The nurse?" Dr. Anderson looked bewildered.

"Yes, Gloria. Your nurse. Where is she?"

"She's with another patient, why?"

"Because I think you may want *her* here to discuss *your* situation."

"I'm confused."

"I can see that," Sweet said. "And I don't mean to be rude, Doc, but you're definitely confused if you think I can't discuss my body without my husband at my side. I have given birth to five - count 'em, Doctor, they are all right there in the chart you're holding - five children without having my husband at a single appointment. Just tell me, for heaven's sake. What is wrong with me?"

"You're pregnant."

"Well, for crying out loud, why didn't you say so? You scared me half to death."

"That's not all," he said. "I'm sorry, Mrs. Atwater, it's not viable. We need to do surgery immediately."

13
The Risk You Take

Bubba John Atwater was on top of the world. On his way from the Lotto Headquarters to the doctor's office, he could barely contain himself. At every red light in Tallahassee, he popped open the glove compartment of his truck and patted the check atop the owner's manual therein. Just before he reached the office, he noticed a SunTrust bank on his right and, flipping on his blinker, turned quickly into the parking lot. He was certain Sweet would be in no hurry for him to get to the office. She'd told him it would take at least two hours. It didn't occur to him a check like the one he was carrying would cause such a stir, but it did. By the time he spoke with the new accounts representative and made an appointment to meet with a trust officer later in the week, Bubba John was well over thirty minutes late to pick up his wife. He was relieved she wasn't in the waiting room when he arrived.

Gloria caught his eye through the glass window and motioned for him to come on back. Bubba John noticed the frown on Gloria's face.

"Hey, Gloria! Long time no see," Bubba John said as he came through the patient door.

"Hi, Mr. Atwater," Gloria said, still not smiling. "Sweet is talking with the doctor right now. She's been waiting for you."

"Is everything okay?"

"Well, not exactly, but it's best if you go on in. Last door on the left."

Aw, hell, Bubba John thought to himself. *I shoulda known better than to stop at the bank. Sweet's probably mad as a hornet.*

Bubba John peeked his head in the door, expecting to see an examination room, but it was not. The office was large and a little on the dark side, despite the light coming through two windows on the west wall. Sweet sat in one of two chairs facing an imposing desk, with a wiry, bespectacled man in a lab coat at the other side. The man rose immediately, offering his hand as he spoke.

"I'm Dr. Anderson," the man said. "And you are?"

"Bub..., uh, John Lewis Atwater. Sorry I'm late."

Bubba John sat in the chair beside Sweet. Something was not right, he could feel it. Sweet sat too stiffly, too tall. It wasn't like her.

"Sweet?"

"We were discussing some options for your wife's condition," Dr. Anderson said. "I hope you can help us make a decision here."

"Condition?"

"I'm pregnant, hon." Sweet twisted a tissue around her index finger before dabbing it to her nose.

"Okay," Bubba John said slowly. "So what kind of decision do you need to make? I don't understand."

"I'm not sure I do, either. Maybe the doctor can shed some light on it for you."

Bubba John turned back to the doctor and waited for a response.

"Your wife has what we call an ectopic pregnancy. This means the egg has been fertilized, but is now lodged in the fallopian tube. There are only two options for dealing with this type of pregnancy which, quite frankly, I personally don't consider a pregnancy at all."

"What are the options?"

"Well, we can try a round of Methotrexate first, but I'm not sure I recommend it in this case."

"Why? Does it hurt the baby?"

"Mr. Atwater, I would encourage you to use the term embryo, here. I'm not trying to be cruel, but there is not going to be a baby. This is a fertilized egg with no womb to grow in and is, thus, not viable. The only safe thing for your wife is to expel the embryo. We can do this one of two ways. Methotrexate is an injectable drug that prevents cells from dividing further. I don't recommend it at this point, though I'm willing to try."

"So what's the other option?"

"I believe surgery is the best choice here. I think we've caught it in time, so the surgery can be done laparoscopically, which is a much less invasive procedure."

"Sweet? What are you thinking?" Bubba John reached over and took his wife's trembling hand.

"I can't abort this baby," Sweet said. "I just can't."

"Mrs. Atwater," Dr. Anderson said, more sharply than he intended, "this is not an abortion. Not by any stretch of the imagination."

"If you cut me open and remove a fetus from my body, you are aborting it."

"It isn't a fetus yet. I explained that to you already. We don't consider an embryo a fetus when it has not even attached to the uterine wall. Mr. Atwater, please understand, if your wife refuses to have...refuses this treatment...she will be risking her life. Plain and simple. An ectopic pregnancy cannot go full term. If the embryo continues to grow and ruptures her fallopian tube, the surgery will be an emergency procedure aimed at saving the mother's life. Either way, the pregnancy will not continue."

"Sweet, honey..." Bubba John pleaded.

"Look, I'll try the Metho-whatever, but I'm not having surgery unless it is absolutely necessary."

"In my professional opinion, Mrs. Atwater, it *is* necessary."

"But you gave me an option..."

Dr. Anderson sighed and placed his hands, palms down, on the desk. He knew his bedside manner was not the best. He always felt awkward and inept speaking with patients, and he knew he blew it with this one, though his intentions were honorable. The damage was done. Might as well tell her straight, in the same abrupt manner she used with him.

"This is probably going to be the wrong thing to say, given my earlier faux pas with Mrs. Atwater, but I can't let you walk out of here without giving you my best advice and it is this..." Dr. Anderson paused and took a deep breath, long enough to make Sweet and Bubba John simultaneously look up.

"Your wife is stubborn and contrary and way too sensitive, if you ask me, but she is also - obviously - strong and self-sufficient, and that is to be admired regardless of how many

70

feathers she ruffles. However, what she is *not* is invincible. And, as she was so quick to point out..."

"Could you please stop talking about me like I'm not here?"

"Absolutely. As *you* were so quick to point out, *you* have five..." Dr. Anderson held up a thick manila file folder and tapped it with his index finger. "...count them, five reasons not to take risks with your life. Now what I want to know is, what is the real reason you don't want this procedure? Is it really philosophical, or is there something else going on, because I cannot understand your resistance."

"Hold up," Bubba John leaned forward in his chair, as if to stand. "I don't know exactly what happened here, but I know I can't let you speak to my wife that way."

Sweet put her hand on her husband's wrist.

"It's okay, Honey," Sweet said and Bubba John immediately relaxed. "He's right."

"So what is the problem?" Dr. Anderson said with gentle, genuine concern.

"We can't afford surgery right now."

Bubba John slumped and covered his head with both hands.

"You have insurance," Dr. Anderson said.

"Yes, but the deductible is high and I still have a 20% copay. I want to try the cheaper route and see. If it doesn't work, we'll do the surgery."

"I wish you would reconsider..."

"Sweet," Bubba John said, "schedule the surgery. Money is not a problem."

"Well, of course it's a problem..."

"No. It's not. Doc, do you mind stepping out for a minute. There is something I need to tell my wife."

***

After a brief discussion alone in the doctor's office, Sweet and Bubba John spoke with Dr. Anderson a second time. Sweet remained adamant she wanted to try the shot of Methotrexate first, reasoning it would take at least a few days to get the kids squared away. If surgery were necessary, she would at least have things in order. At Dr. Anderson's insistence, they made an appointment for blood work on Friday. They would monitor her hCG levels closely, he said. If they rose at all, he would insist on performing the surgery right away.

Sweet was quiet on the ride home. She didn't know what to make of Bubba John's news. There was a tiny kernel of joy rolling around her chest, but each time she thought about letting it loose, she remembered there was also a baby forming in her gut and, one way or another, it would not be allowed to live. She could tell herself it was cells – but she kept thinking of the pictures she saw throughout her pregnancies. She loved to gauge the baby's size from week to week. The tip of a pen, an eraser on a pencil, a blueberry, a grape, a peanut. She estimated seven weeks since her last period. This was the eraser week, with the baby's head starting to form, but no eyes quite yet. She knew it was irrational, but she kept imagining that tiny thing struggling to find its way to her womb, becoming trapped, bewildered, frightened. She knew the feeling all too well.

"Whatcha thinkin' about, Hon?"

Bubba John's question was perfectly timed.

"Just…you know…" Sweet said, unable to put her sorrow into words.

"I'm sorry, honey. Truly sorry. For everything."

"I'm not mad at you, if that's what you're thinking. I'm just sad, that's all."

Sweet leaned her head against the window and the tear poised to come down her cheek detoured across her upper lip.

"It's the craziest thing," she said, swiping her arm across her face. "I mean, I'm relieved that you've decided to sell your grandparents' old house. It's the answer to a prayer, really. We can do a lot with that money, but I don't know… I guess I always thought we'd fix it up for us, or build a new one on the property. It's been in your family so long, it's like selling part of your history, you know?"

And he did know. It was why he'd never actually considered selling his family home, despite the ruse now. This property was more than sentimental, it was part of his heritage, his legacy. His paternal grandfather was Timucuan, a tribe indigenous to the area between the Suwannee and Aucilla rivers. He had learned the ancestral ways from his father before

72

him and taught Bubba John to farm using crop rotation, and to harvest local timber for building. The home and sixty acres around it had been in his family longer than there was documentation to prove it.

Every year they paid the taxes, he and Sweet had talked about selling, but neither of them wanted to part with it if they could help it. His wife always dreamed of having a house on the river and he was, by God, going to give it to her. She would forgive him for lying when she saw what he would do with that beautiful old farmhouse she loved.

"Sweet, it's going to be all right. *You're* going to be all right. Just let me worry about the money and you focus on getting well."

"I want to, I do, but I can't make sense of it. How did this happen? How did I even *get* pregnant? I didn't miss any pills at all. I don't understand."

"Neither do I, hon. But, I don't guess it matters, does it? It isn't really a pregnancy, the way the doctor explained it."

"Oh, it's a pregnancy, Bubba John. Trust me...I'm pregnant. I know my body."

"But it won't produce a baby. Why don't you have the surgery and get it over with?"

"I don't think you understand - I already feel a connection to this life, to this baby's spirit. I don't *want* to just get it over with."

"So make me understand, Sweet. What is the point? Are you hoping for a miracle or something?"

"Maybe."

"You heard what the doctor said. If this thing ruptures, you could die. Do you get that?"

"I do."

"And you're willing to risk your life for this pregnancy?"

"What mother *wouldn't* risk her life for her child?"

"One who has five children and a husband who would be lost without her, Sweet. Dear God, it's one thing if you were having to choose your own life *or* a child's, but this baby doesn't have a chance and you do."

"I have to do what I think is right," Sweet said. "I'm sorry if you disagree."

73

Bubba John sighed, a signal Sweet knew meant he was giving in. He would not change her mind and he knew it.

"I'll take you back on Friday."

"I'm going to call and see if Dr. Desmond will be there. I'd feel better if I talked to him about this."

"That's a great idea. If he recommends the surgery, will you consider it?"

"I've been considering it."

"You know what I mean."

"I'll talk to him Friday."

"There's another thing we are going to do Friday, and I'm not taking "no" for an answer, dammit."

Sweet looked long and hard at her husband. He rarely swore, nor did he ever raise his voice.

"We are buying a new car," Bubba said, without a trace of a smile. "When Mam and Pap's place sells, we'll be able to pay it off. I want you to have a decent car, especially if you are going to have to traipse back and forth to Tallahassee for the next three weeks."

Sweet reached for Bubba John's hand and held it the rest of the way home. Bubba John clung to her hand like his life depended on it. What would he ever do without Sweet Lee? And what would she do when she found out he just told a whopper of a lie?

14
It's Getting Thick All Right

LouWanda Crump was always welcome at the round table inside the Mayhew Café, though under normal circumstances she was more of a spectator than a participant in its often-lively political discussions. It wasn't that she had no opinion; she was just tired of being constantly talked over and thus often kept her opinions mostly to herself. This morning, however, LouWanda held court with a status given only to those holding the most fascinating fodder to consume.

"I'm tellin' ya, fellas, this just thickens the pot."

LouWanda swept a stray piece of hair up the back of her head and, producing a black bobby pin from thin air, tucked it firmly into place.

"Dottie is over there now watchin' that store and, low and behold, Beanie Bradsher and Bubba John's nowhere to be found. Word's gettin' around Beanie and Bubba done run off together to get that lottery money, and I'm bettin' Sweet Lee Atwater ain't gonna stand for that. She's probably tracking 'em down now."

"She ain't gonna get very far without a vee-hickle," said Eustace Falwell. "I noticed her mini-van down at the high school this mornin'. I was pulling through the Senior Parking lot this morning and stopped when I saw her car door open. I remember exactly, 'cause I thought to myself, *that Sweet Lee is sure lookin' good this morning. I need to see what she is doin' to keep that young, healthy look.* Course then I realized it was her daughter, and not Sweet at all. B-Kay sure is pretty, just like her mama. She's got to be sixteen now if she's drivin' and all. I waved at her, but I didn't stop. They don't like it when anybody stops. That school resource officer will come right over and invite you to leave. I know, because it's done happened to me twice't so far. Anyways, Sweet ain't drivin' her car today, so that ain't it."

"Well, she wouldn't be following in her car, anyway. How would she keep from being seen if she did that?" LouWanda asked.

"Y'all got all this wrong," said Clyde Owensby. "I saw Sweet and Bubba John myself this morning. They were headed toward Tallahassee, all right, but Beanie wasn't in the truck. Did Dottie say where Sweet was off to?"

"Well, of course she didn't say," LouWanda huffed. "She don't never tell me nothin'. I got to drag it out of that hateful old thing. I saw her opening up the shop this morning and I waved at her like I always do, and do you know what she said to me?"

"We need some more coffee." Clyde held up an empty cup and shook it at Sissy as she passed the table.

"Hold on, Clyde," said Sissy. "I'll be right back."

"She said, 'Don't even ask, LouWanda.' Now, is that any way to talk to your best friend?"

"Well, what I wanna know," said Randy Kerner, "is what is going on with this lotto thing? Did Beanie win it or not?"

"Oh, she won it all right. And I bet that's why Bubba John is leaving his wife," LouWanda said, pouring milk from the stainless pitcher into her own cup. "Who can resist all those millions?"

"Well that would account for what happened the other day over at the courthouse. I wondered why Bubba John was applying for a building permit out at his mama and daddy's old place. I thought maybe he and Sweet were finally gonna get a real house, but when I mentioned it to Bubba, he acted all nervous and asked me how I knew. I said the county commission always has to approve applications for building permits on the river and he said, oh, he hadn't thought about that."

"You see what I mean? The pot thickens," said LouWanda.

"I think you mean, 'plot', not pot, LouWanda," Randy said, shaking his head.

"Whatever," said LouWanda. "It's getting sticky is all I can say."

Sissy reappeared with coffee, refilling cups around the table. For a moment there was silence, save for the clinking of spoons in cups.

Two tables over, Suvi Jones peered over the edge of his morning paper and cleared his throat. He folded the paper neatly, plopped a ten-dollar bill on the table and stood to leave. His great bulk cast a shadow over the round table as the morning sun shone through the front windows. All heads turned and looked up. Way up.

"Mornin', Randy," Suvi said.

"Hey, Suvi, I didn't see you come in."

"That's because I've been here awhile. Matter of fact, I was just leaving."

Suvi tucked his shirt in neatly and brushed off his pant leg, then turned and headed for the door. He was almost past the table when he stopped short and shook his head. Turning to face the now silent cluster, Suvi placed both hands on the back of Eustace Falwell's chair.

"I heard what y'all said about Beatrice Bradsher and Mr. Atwater and I'd like to put your minds at rest. I can assure you, nothing could be further from the truth."

"Oh, we were just speculating, Suvi," said Randy with a dismissive laugh.

"I understand, I understand," said Suvi. "But if I were Mr. Atwater, I'm not sure how I'd feel about my county commissioner discussing my private business."

"What?" Randy asked. "I didn't say anything that wasn't in the public record."

"Oh, I see, I see. Well," said Suvi, "y'all have a nice day."

"You too, Suve," Randy smiled.

With his hands still resting on the chair back, Suvi nodded twice. Then he brought himself upright, smiled at the group, and left the café.

15
Driving and Dancing

Beanie and Will sat in the kitchen drinking coffee and staring at the check in the middle of the table.

"What in the world am I gonna do with all this money?" Will scratched his head.

"I don't know what you're going to do, but I know what this means for me. I'll be finding someone else to help me around here."

"Why? Are ya kickin' me out?"

"Of course not, but why would you stay? You could get your own place and have plenty left over."

"Well, I've thought about puttin' a double wide up on stilts on my river property, but I've also thought about sellin' that land and movin' closer to town. Truth is, I've kind'ly gotten used to it here."

"I've said it before, you are welcome to stay."

"Reckon we can stop by the National Bank over in Live Oak on Friday? Oh, wait, they have a branch here, better make it that other bank, the one that sets out by the interstate."

"If it was me, I'd want to have that branch close by or you're going to need a car to get anything done."

"Oh, right, and Lord knows I am not ready for a car."

"I don't know why you don't let me teach you to drive, Beanie. There's nothing to it."

"I don't want to drive. Never have, and prolly never will."

"We could go down into Mallory Swamp – plenty of roads down there and almost no traffic."

"Less'n you count the turtles crossin' the road," Beanie said with a snort, "which, by the way, is one o' the reasons I don't never want to drive. I couldn't bear the thought of smashing my car into an animal. It's bad enough when I'm the passenger."

"I know what you mean," Will said, lifting his coffee cup with both hands. "I never saw so much carnage in my life until I moved here. You need a strong stomach just to go to the store."

"I'll never understand why so many turtles get hit though. It ain't like they can dash out in front of you like a deer."

"And if a deer crosses in front of you, you better brake, because there's at least one more inside the tree line. Why do they wait until you are right up on them to make a move?"

"They's just dumb animals, that's all. But I do know how they feel, I think."

Will looked at Beanie, trying to think of something encouraging to say and failing.

"They's too many things comin' atcha to figure out what to do. And by the time you think of something, it's too late. It's too much pressure, that's all."

"Beanie, you are not some dumb animal, if that's what you're saying," Will said, after a brief, awkward silence.

"Well, I know that, Will, but every time I see a turtle smashed to smithereens out on the highway, I just think, Lord, if people cain't make their way around a thing as slow as a turtle, how they gonna avoid me if I make the wrong move?"

She had a point and Will knew it, but he pressed on.

"Look, once you have control of your own vehicle, you learn to process things quickly and *you* can do the avoiding. It's not as hard as you're making it out to be."

"I ain't never wanted to be in control of anything barrelin' down the highway. That's all they is to it."

"And yet, you ride your bicycle out there all the time. It doesn't make sense to leave your safety in the hands of the fools out there now. You add texting to the mix and you're a sitting duck on the side of the road. Seriously, Beanie...you need a car."

"How 'bout a scooter? I can take it one step at a time, don'tcha know?"

Will put down his cup and, laying his hands flat on the table, leaned forward and spoke firmly.

"Beanie...if you were to ride a motorcycle of any kind, you'd have to get a whole new wardrobe, or at least make sure your underwear matched the rest of you, because that's what you'd be showing to the world."

"Oh," said Beanie. "Ooohhh! You got a point there, don'tcha? Ha! Wouldn't that be a sight?"

"It would," said Will, in all seriousness.

"Well, here's the thing," Beanie said, covering her mouth with her hand. "They *do* match, but I ain't settin' out to show them to nobody, that's for sure."

Will let out a whoop and both of them collapsed into fits of giggles and snorts. Every time Beanie would try to breathe, Will would let out another whoop. And if Will calmed down, Beanie would try to follow suit, which resulted in a series of *whoooo-weeee's* from Beanie. Every who-wee made Will relive the mental image of Beanie Bradsher racing down the highway with one hand on her cowboy hat and a face full of crinolines. It was too much.

"We got to stop, Will," Beanie gasped. "I'm 'bout to pee my pants!"

"You're not wearing any pants!" Will shouted.

And there they went again, laughing and spitting and slapping the table. They didn't see Suvi standing in the doorway of the kitchen until he'd been there a while.

Suvi Jones was not a jealous man, nor prone to anger, but it occurred to him this was the first time he'd ever seen Beanie laugh like that and it cut him to the bone. She'd invited him over to talk. Said there was something important to tell him. Said it was okay because Will knew all about their… What was it exactly? Friendship? It wasn't a love affair – that word was never spoken, nor had anything physical happened. They just talked. Mostly about why they couldn't be seen in public together.

Will and Beanie were seen in public all the time, and yet no one thought a thing about it. Or at least no one *said* anything. Oh, no, they preferred the salacious twist of Beanie and Bubba John. But Suvi knew better than that. Beanie wouldn't hurt a fly, much less another human being. That's what he loved about her.

This is not good, Suvi thought as he stood there watching Will and Beanie laughing like an old married couple.

"What's so funny?" Suvi asked, trying desperately to keep his voice light.

"Suvi! Hey!" Beanie said, beaming over her shoulder. "Oh, Will, I forgot to tell you Suvi was comin' over. We're goin' fishin' this morning."

80

And just like that, the party was over. Will excused himself as soon as he could, saying he had a headache.

***

Suvi leaned back against the rusted metal truss of the long-abandoned railroad trestle. Bracing one foot against the opposing truss, which formed a "V" in the opposite direction, he stared off into the distance. His fingertips worried a handful of broken twigs, snapping tiny pieces and dropping them into the river below. Beanie sat nearby, her legs dangling high above the water's surface, hat perched beside her to avoid disaster. One strong breeze and the hat would be in the river, a fact she learned the first time she and Suvi came "fishing" out here.

Now, however, Suvi seemed to be fishing at something else entirely, though Beanie couldn't quite put her finger on what it was. Neither of them was all that skilled at communicating, and both were perfectly happy with long periods of silence. But this had gone too long, Beanie thought, and felt uncomfortable in Suvi's presence for the first time ever.

"What is it, Suve?"

Beanie squinted against the morning sun, shielding her eyes to bring his dark features into focus.

"I don't know," Suvi said, flicking another twig fragment into the river. "I guess I'm just worried, is all."

"What about?" Beanie asked, fully knowing the answer.

"Everything, actually."

"That narrows it down."

"I'm sorry, Bean," Suvi sighed. "I wish it weren't so complicated."

"You use that word a lot."

"I do?"

"Yeah, you do. And I ain't so sure it's as complicated as we're making it."

Suvi rested his head against the truss and closed his eyes.

"Suvi?" Beanie leaned back on her elbows to look up at him from around the metal plate blocking her view.

"Yeah?" Suvi did not open his eyes.

"I'm kind'ly gettin' tired of settin' on the fence."

81

Suvi sighed and crossed his arms over his face.

"Can't say I blame you. It's not very comfortable up here."

"No, it ain't. And no amount of settin' is going to solve the problem, neither. What I want to know is, what are you scared of? And don't say 'it's complicated,' less'n you want to pick yourself up outta this river."

Suvi grinned and sat up. *God, she is pretty*, Suvi thought as he looked down at Beanie, still resting on one elbow and peering solemnly up at him. Her hair, glowing golden in the sunlight, spilled curls down her arm and over her shoulder.

"Not a day in my life have I ever felt jealous of another man – until today. I didn't like it. Not one bit."

Beanie rose up on one hand and shook with pure indignation.

"What do you mean you didn't like it? We wasn't doin' a thing in the world but talking."

"I mean I didn't like the feeling, Bean. I didn't say you did anything wrong."

"I'll say I didn't do nothin' wrong. And what's *wrong* mean, anyway? For your information, Will tried to kiss me the other day. I didn't let him, but it ain't 'cause they'd be anything *wrong* with it. Lord knows *you* ain't never tried to kiss me. I don't think I owe you a blessed thing, Suvi Jones. Seems to me you ain't got nothin' to be jealous about."

Pushing himself off the truss, Suvi stood up straight. Taut with anger and frustration, Suvi towered over Beanie, his massive arms bowed and his hands folding in and out of tight fists. The moment Suvi recognized fear in Beanie's eyes, he relaxed his shoulders and the rest of him followed suit. He dropped to one knee and held out his hand to her.

"Beanie, I'm sorry."

She sat up and turned away, ignoring his outstretched hand.

"I didn't mean to scare you."

"I ain't scared of nobody."

"I know you're not. You're one of the strongest women I've ever met. And the prettiest, and I know I've never told you before, but I'm telling you now. I think you're beautiful and smart and funny and there's nothing I'd like more than to kiss you, but..."

82

Beanie turned back to face him, eyes wide until the "but," and then they narrowed into a glare.

"But, what?"

"But there are other people to think of besides ourselves."

"Such as?"

"Friends, family, hell…the whole town."

"I ain't got no family left to speak of, and the only friends I have think the world of you. So, here's the thing, Suvi – this ain't about *my* family and friends; it's about *yours*. And I'm thinkin' *you're* the one with the real problem here. And I'm tired of waiting for you to figure it out."

"So what are you saying?"

"I'm sayin' it's time to poop or get off the pot. I ain't waitin' forever, and I just realized something I ain't never even thought of before."

"What's that?"

"I have options."

"And Will Thaxton is one of them. I get it."

"Well, I reckon he is, but the fact is I don't want Will Thaxton. I want you."

Suvi smiled and dropped his head for a moment. Then, rising to his feet, he took both of Beanie's hands and pulled her up with him.

"What are you doing?" Beanie asked when he gently placed her hands on his shoulders.

"I just realized we've never danced together before," Suvi said as he pulled her close.

"Prolly not," Beanie said, "but now's a funny time for dancing, don'tcha think?"

"It's as fine a time as any, Beatrice Bradsher. Fine a time as any."

And so they danced on the bridge that no longer led to anywhere or anything. And Suvi hummed a soft tune Beanie didn't recognize. He would tell her later it was *My Funny Valentine*, a song his daddy used to sing to his mama. And it was his mama who always told him you should never kiss a lady until after your first dance.

Vesuvius Jones

I had an edge over most everyone I grew up with down in the Quarters. I knew I was destined for bigger things and no one ever told me any different. I never had to throw my weight around, even though I easily could have. I stood at least a head taller than everyone in my class, including the biggest white boy in school. I think some of the teachers thought I was held back, but they learned soon enough that there was nothing slow about me, except my temper. Takes a lot to rile me up. Hasn't happened often. May have been why I was favored by coaches in both basketball and football. Those boys never could get to me. Not the white ones who called me nigger, or the black ones who called me Uncle Tom. It wasn't that I didn't care, I have to admit that. The problem was I cared too much. I kept a tight rein on my temper, because I was dead positive if anything would take me down, it would be that. I got a cousin in jail for life. That could easily be me. I focused on the ball and my target and everyone else might as well not even be there.

Always thought I would coach college ball, but the knee injury killed my career too soon. I'd thrown half the money I made playing pro-ball into a house for my mother, thinking the money would be there for years. I'd do it all over again, too. In a heartbeat. My mom took care of me when I blew out my knee, so when she got sick, I happily returned the favor.

Some people think I sacrificed a family life for my mother, but that's not really true. I dated in high school and college, but I never had time for anything serious, playing two sports like I did. Then there was the NBA. It was a lifestyle I didn't even know existed and, quite frankly, don't miss. Don't get me wrong, I had a good time, but the circles we ran in scarcely contained anyone I'd want to take home to meet my mother.

So now Mom is gone and there's this thing with Beatrice Bradsher. I spent a lot of time steeling myself against what other people might think. And the truth is, I don't want to hurt anyone, least of all Beanie. I don't know where this will go, but I have to give it a shot. Lord help me, I don't think it's going to end well. Somebody in the godforsaken town is going to say the wrong thing at the wrong time and there's going to be a lifetime of back-pull on my fist when I let it fly.

16
The End Justifies the Means

If there was one thing Bubba John Atwater hated, it was lying and sneaking around. Never mind the fact that he wasn't good at it, the truth was, it did a number on his heart, not to mention his emotional health. But, he had committed to this thing and he was going to see it through. September was nearing a close and he needed to get the design part of the house going. With any luck, he would have the house remodeled by Christmas to surprise the love of his life.

Speaking of which, luck sometimes went in his favor, like the chance discussion with the manager of the flooring department at the DIY box-store in neighboring Suwannee County. Bubba had the idea book Sweet had been keeping since the twins were in elementary school, and was using it to choose tile for the bathrooms. A black ring-bound folder that had seen better days and more than its share of coffee spills and heat damage from being forgotten in her car, the book was filled with pictures of rooms clipped from outdated magazines Sweet picked up from the recycle box at the public library. Sweet often took the book to the shop and worked on keeping it up to date.

The manager was accustomed to *women* bringing in photos and clippings, but watching Bubba John thumb through Sweet's well-worn idea book made him do something he swore he would never do.

"You need some help, Sir?" Jack Crawford asked Bubba John.

"That's a loaded question," Bubba replied.

"And that's a loaded design book," he said, bending to pick up two pages of magazine photos that had slid to the floor unnoticed.

"It's my wife's," Bubba said.

"I could have guessed," Jack said and handed the pages back to Bubba. "My wife has several of those at home. She drives a school bus for the benefits, but she's always dabbled in interior design. She's got an eye for it."

"Really," Bubba said, the wheels already turning. "Well, believe it or not I'm trying to surprise my house with a wife—dammit all—my *wife* with a *house* for Christmas. She doesn't know."

Jack smiled. "That's the nature of surprises, isn't it?"

"Obviously, I am out of my element here. The answer is yes. Yes, I do need some help. Big time."

Jack Crawford would later tell his wife that it was the first time in his career he'd almost been moved to tears. Here was this tall, sturdy man, wanting desperately to give his wife something spectacular and, for once in his life, perfectly capable of making it happen.

"Money is no object," Bubba said. "Time is my problem. I only have until Christmas. Can you help me with that?"

The earnestness of this plea made Jack Crawford refer a DIY customer to his wife. Not entirely ethical since Jack worked on a commission, but desperate times called for desperate measures. And if this wasn't desperate, Jack didn't know what was. He called his wife at home and explained the situation.

After brief consideration, a meeting was arranged between Bubba John and Jack's wife, Nonie. It took a couple of phone calls to decide the location and time. Nights didn't work for Bubba, and Nonie only had a four-hour window on weekdays. She had an office at home, but neither man was comfortable with that, since Jack worked every day at the store. They couldn't meet at the store, nor could Nonie go to the Atwater house. They finally settled on 10:00 a.m. the following morning at the Waffle House out by the interstate. It was the safest place, and least likely to cause a stir. The two men shook hands and silently congratulated themselves on their foolproof plan.

***

"You don't look like a school bus driver," Bubba John said the next morning when Nonie Crawford shook his hand and introduced herself.

"Thanks, I think." Nonie's smile put Bubba immediately at ease. She was petite and a little on the plump side, what Bubba John's daddy always called "soft," which was a fitting

86

description for Nonie Crawford in many ways. And yet, she was striking and not at all what he expected of a bus driver who did interior decorating on the side.

"I don't mean to rush you, but I only have about an hour before I have to leave."

"Not a problem – shouldn't take us long at all. I was up for hours looking at your wife's idea book last night. She has an interesting aesthetic."

"Is that a good thing?" Bubba John asked.

"Oh, gosh, yes," Nonie said. "I think this may turn out to be my favorite job yet. I was trying to put a name to her style, and *eclectic* is about the best I can do. It has elements of contemporary design – some shabby chic, but with cleaner lines, and without the kitschiness of Junk Gypsies. Does she watch that show?"

"She does, but it's not her favorite. What she loves is Fixer Upper, and what's that other one? Oh, shoot…the one where the girl buys up old houses…Rehab something."

"Rehab Addict," Nonie said.

"Yeah, that's the one. She likes when you don't change the character of the house too much."

"You can kind of tell that from looking through her book. It helps that she makes notes all over the pages. You know, I was a little worried when Jack came home and told me about you. I've never done a 'surprise' house before."

Bubba John grinned. "Me, either."

"I almost feel like I know your wife already. I'm excited to meet her. December, right?"

"Yeah, if you think we can do it."

"It's a short timeframe, no doubt."

"I know," Bubba John said. "I worry about it a lot, but I got the idea in my head now, which Sweet says is the Atwater curse. Come hell or high water, I want this to be the best Christmas present ever."

"Well, I have a lot of ideas, but I want to see the house before I make any big decisions. Do you have a copy of the floorplan?"

"Not yet. I'm not going to change the structure itself, except for interior walls. I want to make the kitchen bigger and create an open floorplan, but I'm still going to have it engineered with new blueprints. Everything will be properly permitted. I hired a contractor out of Madison to do the bulk of the work."

"Good idea. Any surprises could set us back. I'd like to drive out there one day this week and see exactly what I'm dealing with."

"I hope you have an imagination, 'cause it's pretty rough right now. The main section was built in 1934 and a wing was added in the forties when the children kept coming. My dad was the last of eleven children. Unfortunately, the house has been empty since my parents were killed in a car accident..." Bubba John coughed and cleared his throat. He was surprised and a little embarrassed that talking about it still choked him up.

Nonie reached out and covered Bubba's hand with her own for a moment.

"I'm so sorry," she said, meaning it. "I can't even imagine..."

Bubba John cleared his throat again.

"It was rough," he acknowledged. "I've mostly avoided going out there, and the house has been neglected the worst. I don't want to completely change it, but it's probably best if we make it our own home and not a replica of the old one."

"I think we can do that. How much help will you need with the layout?

"I'll need some help with the kitchen design, for sure. The only thing I know for certain is Sweet likes things convenient. She complains all the time about the refrigerator door opening the wrong way and about not having space to move around."

"Perfect. Jack and I both love to cook, so I know what does and doesn't work in a gourmet kitchen. If money is no object, we'll give her the kitchen of her dreams."

"That's what I'm aiming for," Bubba said.

Nonie and Bubba John spent the next half hour making notes about design plans and wrapped up their meeting with a time selected for Nonie to visit the house the next day.

17
Stubborn as a Mule

Friday morning, having told the children they were going to buy a new car and omitting the part about the doctor's visit, Sweet Lee and Bubba John headed for Tallahassee.

"Did you hear what T-Ray said before they left?" Sweet asked.

"About the car wash?"

"Mmm-hmm."

"Yeah, what was up with that? Since when do they offer to clean the car?"

"Uh, that would be since they think the van will be theirs now. Ha!"

"It's not a bad idea, though. They can go straight to school instead of stopping in town to catch the bus. And even better, you won't have to get Dottie to come in every afternoon so you can pick them up."

"Don't think I hadn't thought of that," Sweet said. "But I figured we'd sell it to help with payments. I'm not sure I'm ready for my crew to have that much freedom every day. I made straight A's in school until I got a car."

"I remember that car," Bubba grinned and squeezed Sweet's thigh.

"I'll bet you do," Sweet said, remembering, too. The car in question was much more comfortable to snuggle in than the beat-up old Chevy Stepside Bubba drove in high school.

"Did you ever stop to think that every single car you and I have owned, including the one I bought when I was thirteen, we've both driven at one time or another?"

Sweet poked out her bottom lip and nodded. "I'll be darned...we have, haven't we? Crazy."

Other than her first kiss, which was a disaster from the start, and Bubba John's semi-sordid fling with a rail-thin cheerleader who now sported breast implants that looked like balloons tied to a signpost long after the party is over, Bubba John and

89

Sweet's adult lives were a series of firsts. Now it was a new car. A brand new one with a warranty and a new-car smell and whatever color she wanted as opposed to whatever they could afford. Sweet protested at first, but Bubba John convinced her they'd be better off making payments on a car with a warranty.

An hour later they were at the Chrysler dealership scanning row upon row of Town and Country minivans. As hard as Bubba tried, Sweet was adamant. With five kids, not even the Chevy Suburban Bubba fancied seemed wise to his practical wife. Sweet did her homework. She wanted the basic model in metallic grey and was thrilled to learn it came with stow-and-go seats and a DVD player in the back. It was like that pine table she always wanted. Sleek and pretty and built for a family.

Later, Sweet would remember the fresh-faced Puerto Rican man who greeted them when they arrived. A hint of an accent and his bright, ready smile allowed Sweet to let down her guard enough to practice her rudimentary Spanish skills. He was tickled by her attempts and his laugh was contagious. They were all three laughing like old friends before they were even properly introduced. Angel was his name.

"Angel? Like....Angel?" Sweet blurted.

"Want to see my wings?" He laughed and winked at Bubba John.

"I've been praying for an Angel," Sweet said. "Looks like God has a sense of humor."

"Dios es bueno," said Angel.

"Todo el tiempo," Sweet replied and leaned into Bubba John's embrace.

He always seemed to know what she was thinking and when there would be tears. He pulled her close and kissed the top of her head, giving her enough time to compose herself before she pulled away.

"Darned allergies," she sniffed and swiped at her face with a napkin hastily pulled from her purse.

They were sitting in Angel's office, waiting for him to finalize the paperwork that would seal the deal when Sweet suddenly grasped both arms of her chair and sucked air in through her nose. She would also remember how it felt, like a guitar string pulled tight and released with a twang. Except it

90

never stopped ringing - just increased in sound and vibration until the noise of the pain spread through her gut, rose through her chest and exited through her ears. Like everything was in reverse. Bubba John leapt from his chair, but his arms and mouth moved in slow motion and she could see, but not hear, the words on his lips.

"Sweet? Sweet! What is it? Sweet! Oh my God, somebody call 9-1-1. Call 9-1...."

***

Sweet Lee Atwater awoke to a sea of blue-green hovering over her in a room with walls of ice. At least that was what it felt like as she opened her eyes and struggled to make sense of the surroundings. Something that sounded like waves crashing one after another, but the tempo was too consistent and closely spaced to be waves. Unless she was on an ice floc somewhere, which could account for the floating sensation.

I'm in an igloo, Sweet thought and shook her head, trying to bring the blue blobs into focus.

"Hold still, honey," a disembodied voice somewhere behind her spoke kindly, but with authority.

Sweet tried to open her mouth to speak and found it was already open, taped so her jaw could not move in either direction. Nor could she make a sound. She tried to swallow and felt something blocking her throat.

"Who's scrubbing in on this?" Another voice, this time to her left side.

Hurts, hurts... Sweet reached for the offending tube in her mouth, but her hand was gently pushed back down.

"Anderson, I think. Hold still now, hon. The E.R. doc sent her up. Desmond consulted, but he's got a C-section in progress. Multiples."

"Great. How soon before she's out again?"

"Working on that now. We may need restraints, Leo. What's the patient's name?"

"Um...wait, I'll tell you. Atwater, I think."

Sweet. My name is Sweet.

"Yeah, Atwater. Sweet Lee Atwater."

"Sweetly?"

"Maybe, but it's two words. Sweet Lee."

Call me Sweet. Sweet turned her head and tried to focus on the voice to her left.

"That's unusual. Hold still, Sweetie, you're doing fine."

"History?"

"Let's see…"

"I know her history," said another voice, breaking through to her right.

"Dr. Anderson, just in time. BP is dropping."

"Gravida 6, para 5, and stubborn as a damned mule," he said.

"Okay, then…" said the voice behind Sweet's head. "Looks like there's more than *one* history here."

His was the only face Sweet would recall later - the young Dr. Anderson, scowling at a clipboard and barking orders that made the blobs move faster. She squinted at him, willing him into focus, just before the darkness closed in once again.

What she would not remember, but would be told later by a nurse who came by to check on her in ICU, was how, as Sweet's blood pressure and respirations dropped to dangerously low rates, Dr. Anderson slammed the clipboard closed and jabbed it into the air above him.

"This woman has five – count 'em people – five reasons why we are not going to lose her today."

And then, even as the surgical nurse reminded him to finish scrubbing in, the normally staid and ultra-calm surgeon ranted all the way out of the operating room.

"I told that woman. I told her, but would she listen to me? Oh, no, she would not. Dammit to hell, she better not die on me."

They all laughed about it later, but once Dr. Anderson came back into the room prepped and ready for surgery, it was back to the business of saving lives.

18
Lost in Translation

After a week in Intensive Care, and three days back in a private room, Sweet was finally recovering from her ordeal. As sick as she was, to hear it told at the Mayhew Junction Café was another story entirely. At first she wasn't expected to live at all, then she suffered amputations of both legs and would be in a nursing home for months, none of which was true.

LouWanda Crump and Randy Kerner nearly came to blows at the round table.

"LouWanda, for crying out loud, I talked to Bubba John myself. Stop blowing this out of proportion," Randy said, reaching for a piece of bacon on the side of LouWanda's plate.

LouWanda, feeling slighted from every direction, slapped the offending hand a little harder than she intended.

"I'm saving that for Duke," LouWanda snapped. "And I don't know how it could be out of proportion. She liked to have died right there on the operatin' table. I know, 'cause we got her on the prayer chain and I stood in for her at church. They laid hands on me and everything, and I know somebody was prayin' over my *legs*, whether she lost 'em or not."

"Well, she hasn't lost her legs. Bubba said she was out of the coma and the infection was getting better by the day."

"And, praise the Lord for that, I'm tellin' ya. Just praise – the – Lord," LouWanda said, raising one hand in the air.

"Bubba said his Aunt Dilly was only going to be around another couple of days and then she's going back to Alabama. I don't know how he's going to deal with all those kids without Sweet there. He said she'd be in there another week for sure."

"Dottie's got a signup sheet started for meals, I think. I know the ladies at our church are taking turns now, sending casseroles and what-not out there. Well, speak of the devil..."

Dottie Brentwood, looking utterly exhausted, pulled out a chair at the round table and sank into it with a sigh.

"Lord, I have never worked this hard in my life," Dottie said, waving a hand at Sissy and then tipping an imaginary cup to her lips to order coffee.

"Be right with ya, Dottie!" Sissy hollered on her way to the kitchen with a pile of dirty dishes.

"I am awful glad Sweet doesn't open on Mondays or I think I would be tearing my hair out right now," Dottie said, to no one in particular.

"How's Sweet doing?" LouWanda asked. "I heard she lost both her legs."

"Lord, LouWanda, where'd you hear such a thing? No, she did not lose her legs. She lost her u....well, you know, her female parts," Dottie said, not wanting to offend the menfolk at the table.

"What female parts?" Randy asked, horrified.

Dottie dropped her forehead onto the table.

"I give up," she muttered into her napkin. "I just give up."

"What'd I say wrong?"

"Nothing, Randy. Nothing. She had a hysterectomy, okay? That's all. She can't have kids anymore."

"Well, praise the Lord for *that*," LouWanda said, and meant it.

"That's an awful thing to say, LouWanda!" Dottie raised her head abruptly.

"Why's it awful? She's got five kids already. She don't need to be worried about havin' no more."

"It's still awful. Sweet loves those kids."

Randy stood, swiping his hat off the table beside him.

"On that note, I'm going to go see what's shaking at the courthouse."

"You don't want to know what's *shaking*, Randy. Trust me on that one." Dottie smirked at LouWanda.

"Have a great day, ladies." Randy shoved a dollar bill beneath the rim of his breakfast plate and joined the line at the cash register.

"Lord help Sissy if that's all the tip he's leaving," Dottie said under her breath.

"Oh, that's all we ever leave," LouWanda said in full voice. "They's eight of us here most mornings, why that's eight dollars an hour for one table."

"Shhhh…" Dottie whispered as heads turned across the restaurant. "First off, most of you are here at least two hours in the morning, and longer on the afternoon shift."

"So?"

"Never mind. Y'all are awful, I'm just saying. You try busting your butt waiting on people who tip a dollar no matter what, and see how you like it."

"Sissy don't seem to mind, Dottie. What is wrong with you today?"

"Oh…I'm just tired is all. I've been having to keep Sweet's dress shop open all by myself. I thought about asking B-Kay to come in, but she's got her hands full with the little ones. And I hate to complain because there isn't much Sweet or anyone else can do about it, but I don't make as much money at the shop as I do waiting tables for Suvi."

"I thought you said…"

"Not everyone in this town is a cheapskate, LouWanda."

"Well, fine then," LouWanda plucked a dollar and a quarter out of her ample bra and slapped it down on the table.

"Jesus help me," Dottie said, and laid her head down again.

19
Family Meeting

At the Atwater home, things were not going well. A week without their mother took its toll on everyone. Bubba John's Aunt Dilly was a blessing at first, but she did not have the constitution for chaos, and everyone was happy to see her go. Unfortunately, Bubba John got a big dose of reality Sunday morning not long after Dilly was out the door.

Bubba John called a meeting with the twins while their younger siblings napped.

"When's Mom coming home?" B-Kay asked.

Bubba John absent-mindedly rubbed his hand back and forth over the top of his head.

"That's what I need to talk to you about," he said. "I talked to the doctor this morning and he thinks it could be another week, maybe two."

"Two weeks?" T-Ray snorted. "Aw, man, that's not good."

"We can't see her for two more weeks?" B-Kay asked.

"Well, maybe not that long, but it'll be a while, B."

"But why, Dad? I don't understand." B-Kay looked stricken.

"I'm trying to tell you now. Just listen, okay?" Bubba John struggled to find the right words. "So, you guys know Mom had two surgeries, right? She had the one when her tube ruptured that first day, then she got an infection and they had to do a hysterectomy."

"I know that's what you said before, but what does that mean, actually?" T-Ray asked.

"It means she can't have any more children, for one thing," Bubba John said.

"Okay...but that's not a terrible thing. I mean...we have enough, don't we?" He asked quickly when his sister glared at him.

"Well, yes and no," Bubba John said. "But that's not even the worst of the problem now, though your mama might beg to differ. The problem now is, the infection is not cleared up.

96

They're trying some new antibiotics today, but they had to put some kind of drain in yesterday, and it just needs extra care. And right now they don't want any kids coming in. So, I know I promised we'd all go over today, but we just can't."

"I talked to her yesterday, Dad. She needs underwear and stuff," B-Kay said.

"Right, I know. I'm gonna take her what she needs this afternoon. Right now, I just wanted to make sure you guys knew what was going on. I think we're on our own for a while, so I just need to know I can count on both of you to help."

Bubba John paused a moment to let that sink in. He was fairly certain neither of them realized what all that would entail. He wasn't completely sure himself. Fortunately, he underestimated his wife's mini-me. B-Kay morphed into her mother right before his eyes.

"Aunt Dilly did the laundry before she left. Said to tell you there's a bag of Mom's clothes sitting on top of the dryer." B-Kay said. "And don't forget those library books on the kitchen table."

"Got it," Bubba John said, as if he'd remembered the books, which he did not.

B-Kay grabbed a pencil and notepad from the side of the refrigerator.

"What's that for?" Bubba John asked.

"We have to make a list."

"A list of what?"

B-Kay looked at her brother and rolled her eyes.

"Everything, Dad. Pick up times, schedules, school projects. These things don't happen by osmosis."

T-Ray snorted again.

"What's so funny?" Bubba John asked.

"Dad," T-Ray shook his head.

"Never mind," B-Kay held up one hand to silence her brother. "I gotta think. Let's see, I think Bitty has early dismissal on Wednesday and goes to dance right after. I'll call Samantha's mom and see if she can take Bitty, too. Then I'll pick her up when we get out."

"*We'll* pick her up," T-Ray interjected.

"Whatever, T. That leaves Daisy and Tater, and that's where it gets a little hairy."

"Right," T-Ray said. "Tate gets out early, too."

"And Daisy only goes to daycare half days," Bubba John said. "I know all this, so y'all don't need to act like I'm totally clueless."

"Sorry, Dad." T-Ray tried to smooth it over. "We don't think you're clueless, just…"

"Clueless, I get it. Well, I'm not," Bubba John said. "I can pick them up sometimes…"

"Shhh…I'm trying to think," B-Kay said. "The problem is not just pick-up, Dad. Who's going to take care of them while we're in school? We don't get home until almost four. Mom usually keeps them at the store with her, but Dottie can't watch the kids and the store by herself."

"Well, I can watch them, I guess, but I'm supposed to be working on the…um…project."

"What project?" T-Ray sat straight up in his chair, suddenly interested.

"Nothin', Tee." B-Kay said, with a bit too much pride for her brother to let it slide. "It's a secret."

"That's not fair, Dad! How come B-Kay knows and I don't?"

"Because I can keep a secret and you can't, that's how come."

"Are you kidding me?" T-Ray protested. "Dad!"

"No, it's okay. It's not really a secret anymore," Bubba John said.

B-Kay sighed.

"We're fixing up Mam and Pap's old house," Bubba John said, then added "so we can sell it."

"I don't get it. What's the big deal?" asked T-Ray.

"What?" B-Kay interjected. "You said it was a Christmas present!"

"Aw, man," Bubba John said, rubbing the back of his neck. "I'm never gonna keep this straight."

"I'm confused, Dad, which is it?" B-Kay asked.

"Okay, listen, y'all have to help me and not breathe a word of this to a soul. I told your Mom I was fixing the house up to

98

sell, but it's really for us, and I only have until Christmas to get it done."

"Damn, Dad, that's some Christmas present." T-Ray leaned his chair back on two legs.

"Watch your mouth, Son," Bubba John said. "And seriously, please don't tell your mother. It'll ruin everything."

"So," B-Kay said, getting back on track. "Who's keeping the little ones until Mom comes home?"

"I'll ask around in town. Surely somebody can give us a hand," Bubba John said. "Make sure you both remember. Don't mention a word about the house to your mother."

"We won't." The twins answered in tandem and rolled their eyes at each other in uncharacteristic solidarity.

20
Decisions to Make

A few hours later, Bubba stood at Sweet's bedside with a large bag of books, but no laundry.

"What in the world is that?" Sweet asked.

"The ladies at the library all send their love," Bubba John said. "Apparently they know what you like."

"How thoughtful of them; I have been just about to crawl out of my skin from boredom. Let me see..." Sweet stretched her hands out to receive the plastic library bag. "Oh, wait, better put them here beside me. I'm not supposed to lift anything more than a dinner tray."

Bubba John placed the bag on the bed beside her, and leaned down to kiss her.

"Hey," he said.

"Hey, yourself," Sweet said and smiled.

"How you feeling?"

"Better today," she said. "Yesterday was rough. They cleaned the wound before they put in the drain tube. That was not pleasant."

"I bet."

"Did you remember to bring clean underwear?"

"Aw, crap!" Bubba John said.

"Bubba..." Sweet said.

"Oh, no, I brought the bag. I just left it in the truck. I'll run back down in a minute."

"I almost called B-Kay to make sure you brought it with you."

"Oh, ye of little faith."

"Oh, I have faith alright," Sweet grinned.

"What'd Ms. Janice send you?" Bubba asked to change the subject.

Sweet opened the bag and peered inside.

"Oh, yay, my favorites. I guess they've met me before."
Sweet laughed. "I can't believe they sent this one over. There's usually a waiting list for new releases."

"Oh, that's right," Bubba said. "Ms. Janice said to make sure you send the Jan Karon book back as soon as you get through. They bumped you up on the list."

"I'll give her a call tomorrow. You'll probably be able to take it back by Tuesday. Lord knows I don't have anything else to do."

Sweet reached for the cup of water on her tray table, but winced in pain just as her hand connected. The Styrofoam cup tilted, spilling half its contents on the bed and half on the floor.

"For cryin' out loud, look what I've done," Sweet said. "Can you get me some of those paper towels, please?"

Bubba John spun around, looking for the dispenser.

"By the door, by the door," Sweet said, the cold water spreading beneath her.

Bubba grabbed a few towels and handed them to Sweet, then went back for more.

"I'm so sorry..." Sweet said, mopping at the bed while Bubba John wiped at the puddle on the floor.

And this was how Dr. Anderson found them when he and the charge nurse stopped by for afternoon rounds.

"What in the world?" The nurse was the first to speak.

"Oh, I knocked my cup over," Sweet said. "My bed is soaked."

Bubba stood and carried a dripping wad of towels to the garbage can, squeezing awkwardly by the doctor to grab another handful of towels. The nurse stopped him on his way back with one hand on his arm.

"That's what the call button is for," she said. "Sit. I'll get housekeeping in here when we leave."

Bubba did as he was told.

The relationship between Sweet Atwater and Dr. Anderson did not improve much during her time in recovery, so Sweet was glad her OB-GYN physicians alternated rounds.

Leave it to perfect timing, though, thought Sweet. *I am so busted.*

Dr. Anderson's grim-lipped look of disapproval spoke volumes.

"I wanted to talk to you about when we might send you home, but I think I just got my answer. I hoped you'd be ready within the next week, but I need to be absolutely certain you won't overdo it when you get there. I have a feeling it won't matter a bit what I say; you'll overexert yourself the first day home."

Sweet didn't bother to argue. She relaxed back into her pillow and covered her eyes with one arm, the wet paper towels still clutched in her fist. He was right, and she knew it.

"It's a little dicey with your insurance company. I can get approval to move you to the rehab center for a couple of weeks, but you'd still have a pretty hefty bill, which I know is a concern for you."

"Which rehab center," Sweet asked.

"There is one in particular I'd prefer for you; their wound care is excellent, which we really must consider in your case."

"It's in Tallahassee?"

"Yes, a couple of blocks from here, actually."

"I haven't seen my kids in forever..." Sweet trailed off, close to tears.

Dr. Anderson sighed and thought for a moment.

"I could set you up with a home care nurse, but that only covers coming in to check the wound and repack the dressing. You'd have to travel back to Tallahassee at least twice a week for a while. But I cannot, in good conscience, let you go home unless I know for certain there will be someone there to help."

"The older kids do help," Sweet offered weakly.

"Remind me how old your children are?"

"Daisy's three, Tate is almost six, Elizabeth is eight, and the twins are sixteen."

"Do all of them attend school?"

"All but Daisy, the youngest. She goes to daycare half days, though."

"And who watches her the rest of the time?"

"Well, normally me, but Bubba John has been filling in since his aunt left.

Dr. Anderson wrinkled his brow and glanced sideways at Bubba John, who sat mute since he'd been chastised by the nurse.

102

"How is that working for you? Are you taking sick leave or something, or do you just have an understanding boss?"

Bubba John and Sweet answered the question simultaneously.

"I set my own hours."

"He's self-employed."

Dr. Anderson glanced from one to the other, sizing up the too-quick answer and deciding two euphemisms at once was a clear indicator Bubba John Atwater was unemployed.

"What kind of work do you do?"

"I'm in construction mostly," Bubba John said. "I work shut-downs at the paper mill when they need me, and I fill in for a couple of construction companies in Suwannee County, but mostly I work odd jobs - deck building, land clearing, tree trimming, stuff like that."

"So you're flexible, then," Dr. Anderson said.

Bubba John heard the disapproval in his voice and, forgetting the goal was to get Sweet home, added, "But it has gotten pretty busy lately. I just picked up a job remodeling a house."

"Okay then, we'll get approval for the rehab center and see if we can't get you moved over there in a couple of days," Dr. Anderson said and made a note on the chart.

"Wait, wait," Sweet said, glaring at Bubba John before turning her attention to Dr. Anderson again. "What if we got someone to come in and help, *and* I promise not to overdo it? Could I go home instead?"

"What kind of help?" Dr. Anderson asked.

"Well, I'm sure there are some CNA's in the area who are looking for work. And I can ask at church, too. Surely someone will be willing to come in until I'm better."

"I can't make a decision based on possibilities. I need to be sure you won't be picking up children, or laundry, or casseroles, for that matter, and you absolutely *must not* drive a car until I specifically clear you to do so."

"I promise I won't. Lord knows I do not want to deal with *you* if I break my promise, either."

For the first time since Sweet laid eyes on her stern young physician, Dr. Anderson broke into a grin and emitted a guttural blast that passed for laughter. His nurse struggled to maintain her all-business composure, and tilted her head toward the floor so as not to give away her smile.

"Ha!" Sweet said and pointed gleefully at her doctor. "I made you laugh! Does that mean I get to go home?"

"*I'm* not promising *anything*," Dr. Anderson said, shaking his head in mock defeat, "but here's what we'll do: I have a couple of days to clear everything with the insurance company and see if they have a bed over at Southland. If, in that time, you arrange for reliable, *around-the-clock* help, I'll discharge you to go home. If not, you'll go on over to Southland to finish your rehab. Deal?"

"Deal," said Sweet.

"I'll come back tomorrow and see what you've come up with and we'll go from there, okay?"

"Sounds like a plan," Sweet said.

Dr. Anderson slapped the chart closed, hung it back on the end of Sweet's bed and nudged his nurse toward the door.

"Let's get out of here before she talks me into something else."

He brushed past her, nodded at Bubba John, still sitting mute in the chair by Sweet's bed. The nurse followed, but spoke on her way out, "I'll let the front desk know you need a bed change."

The room was quiet for a minute. Bubba John broke the silence.

"Sorry, hon."

Sweet sighed. "I just want to go home."

"I know."

"Then why did you say that about your so-called new job? How in the heck am I supposed to find 'around-the-clock' help?"

"Sweet, please don't fuss at me. I'm sorry, all right? I just didn't want him thinking I was…you know…lazy or something. I work hard."

"I know you do," Sweet said. And she did know, though it probably didn't show.

Bubba John sat staring at his hands, which he worked almost incessantly whenever he was uncomfortably idle. Sweet loved his hands, despite their sandpaper texture. They were the hands of a working man, and one would only have to glance at them to know. And Sweet knew.

She was forever after him to fix one thing or another inside the house, or pick up the kids, or stay home when one of them was sick. The truth was he did work hard. Their yard was always mowed, and one acre of the property was routinely planted with crops that fed her family throughout the year. Bubba John was better at canning and freezing than she would ever be and, though Sweet was inclined to complain about the time her husband spent at the hunting camp, she wasn't sure what she'd do without the supply of venison he provided each season. Sometimes the work he did on the side wasn't exactly income-producing, but Sweet couldn't ignore the fact that Bubba John bartered land-clearing often enough for them to have a full side of beef or a butchered hog, and even once lamb meat from the Wiley's farm. Even so, it was impossible to pay the mortgage and insurance and gas without cash, so to keep from hiring a full-time clerk at the store, she relied on Bubba John to help when she needed him. And she knew it embarrassed him for people to think he was lazy, when exactly the opposite was true.

"Honey, it doesn't matter what Dr. Anderson thinks. You don't have to explain a thing to him or anyone else, for that matter."

Bubba John sighed and worked his hands harder.

"What's wrong?" Sweet asked.

"I'm trying to think of someone we can get to help. I think I've probably exhausted every willing person at church. I can't think of a soul who could work full-time."

"There has to be someone."

"Well..." Bubba trailed off.

"Spit it out," Sweet said.

"I hate to even mention it, but Beanie's the only one I can think of who doesn't have a full-time job, but has the experience you need. She took care of both of her parents and never put them in a nursing home."

"I thought she was working at The Château," Sweet said.

"She is, but I think they're pretty slow now. Will's started renting out by the month, which doesn't include breakfast, and she could still help him on weekends if he needed her."

"Sounds like you've got it all figured out," Sweet said.

"Have you got a better plan?" Bubba asked.

"No, but I bet we can think of one if we try hard enough," Sweet replied.

"What's wrong with Beanie helping us?"

"Oh, for crying out loud, Bubba, the whole town thinks you're sleeping with her."

"Do *you* think I am?" Bubba asked.

"No, but I'll be darned if I'm going to add fuel to *that* blaze. No way. No. Freaking. Way."

For someone who truly hated lies, he was sure tangled in a slew of them. What was that old saying about desperate times? Because he sure felt desperate right now. He was either going to confess the entire thing, lottery, house and all, or he was going to have to break a few of his own rules.

"Sweet," he said, "I need you to trust me. You and the kids are all I've got."

"You got a funny way of showing that," Sweet said, her head cast sideways toward the wall.

"I'm going to tell you something, but you have to swear you won't repeat it. Beanie'll kill me."

Sweet snapped her head up and glared at her husband. *You have got to be kidding me!*

"Just listen," Bubba John said, throwing both hands up in mock surrender. "Seriously, Sweet, listen. Beanie is seeing someone, has been for a while."

"Who?"

"I'm not sure exactly, but it isn't me. That's all you need to know."

Sweet stared hard at her husband.

"Wow," Sweet said. "That's all I need to know? Really?"

"What do you want me to do, Sweet? I'm doing the very best I can. You know...?" Bubba stood and picked his car keys off of Sweet's tray table. "You aren't the only one this happened to, honey. We're *all* doing the best we can. Maybe Dr. Anderson

106

is right. Maybe rehab is the best option right now, because quite frankly, I'm all out of ideas."

He made it to the door before Sweet spoke.

"Fine," Sweet sighed. "Do you want to call Beanie or should I?"

Will Thaxton

I have never loved anyone remotely like Beanie Bradsher. It is an incomprehensible thing, and I'm hard-pressed to make sense of it myself, let alone explain it to anyone who knows me. There aren't many who know me, though. Especially not here.

I am a foreigner, an outsider, a Yankee for heaven's sake, though the term itself seems incongruous, old-fashioned, absurd. My wife brought me here and convinced me to stay. We fell in love with the river and this old rambling building that is in no way what she dreamed we would make it. She did all this not knowing if she would survive to see it through. And she was gone before I grasped that I might lose her.

I loved Marie. I miss her like you might miss an index finger. You can get by without it, but it is always going to feel strange. Well, that sounds clinical, doesn't it? What I mean to say is my wife was like a part of me. We did everything together, including raising our daughter. I had my own career, of course, but I managed it on her schedule. I may have it wrong, though. Perhaps I was her index finger. Lord knows she was the driving force behind everything we did. Wow, I just keep sinking lower and lower into this abysmal recollection of a marriage that was far more than a schedule.

I miss the easy friendship, and knowing that I was part of a relentlessly loyal team. I miss the laughter that was always close to the surface. I miss the noise of living with Marie. She was exceedingly upbeat, thoroughly outgoing, never met a stranger, and never pulled punches. I liked myself around her. The thing is, I find that I still like myself, even though I've settled into the quiet that is life without her.

And now there is Beanie, but there isn't Beanie at all. The girl makes a statement without saying a word. For someone with little to say, she speaks volumes. Her education is woefully inadequate, yet I have never known anyone who could make me feel more like a fool without even trying. She is an enigma, a paradox, a puzzle with no solution. She loves someone, but it is not me.

I could pack up and leave; I know this. I could sell The Château, though I can't imagine what kind of fool would buy it. A fool like me, I suppose. Anyway, what I'm getting at is, I don't want to leave. I promised Marie I would see it through and I intend to do just that. As for Beanie, I don't know. A man can hope, can't he?

21
Beanie Says Goodbye

Will Thaxton did not take Beanie's news well. Despite the fact that business had been slow for over a month, Will was accustomed to Beanie's help with cleaning, cooking and general upkeep of The Château. More importantly, he was happy.

She broke the news just as the breakfast hour was ending on Monday morning. Will brought in the last of the dishes from the table while Beanie rinsed and loaded them into the dishwasher.

"What's on your agenda today?" Will asked, scraping all but the meat scraps into the compost bin.

"Suvi and I thought we'd ride over to Carrabelle for some seafood. I'm not too crazy about shellfish, but Suvi likes raw oysters and crab and you cain't get those anywhere in this county. I'm mostly goin' along for the ride."

"It's a pretty day for a drive," Will said. "When are you heading over?"

"Soon as Suvi gets back from the farmers market, I reckon."

"I take it you guys got everything worked out now," Will said, clearly fishing.

"Well, I wouldn't say *everything* just yet. We ain't exactly advertisin' it yet, but things is goin' along okay."

"That's good," Will said, stacking the last of the plates beside the sink.

An awkward silence followed. For nearly five minutes, neither of them spoke a word, just washed and dried and restored the kitchen to order.

Beanie was the first to speak.

"They's somethin' else I got to tell ya," Beanie said.

"Okay..." Will braced himself for the worst.

"Sweet Atwater called me last night..." Beanie hesitated, searching for the right words to soften the blow.

"Oh, yeah? How's she doing?" Will allowed himself to relax a bit.

109

"A little better, I reckon, but she's kind'ly got a long row to hoe. Doc ain't gonna let her come home less'n she has somebody to take care of her and the kids."

"I guess I didn't realize she was that sick," Will said. "I hope they find someone."

"Well, that's what I'm tryin' to tell ya. They did. It's me."

Will looked confused.

"I hate to just drop it on ya like this, Will, but I'm gonna stay at their house for a while. I don't wantcha to think I'm ungrateful or nothin' but things's gotten kindly touchy here, and I think it's prolly for the best, don't you?"

Will wiped down the counter for the third time in several minutes. Then he turned to face Beanie.

"You want my honest answer? Not really. I mean, I thought we were doing fine."

"We are, and I'd like to keep it thataway."

"I guess I just don't understand, Bean. Isn't there somebody at their church or something?"

"Shoot, Will, them church ladies is good to bring casseroles and such, but ain't nobody can possibly manage two families at once't."

"But why *you?*"

Beanie shrugged. "It's kind'ly what I do. Mommer was the same way, 'cept she used to birth babies, too. I ain't never been too keen on that, though I helped with a few when I was little."

"Your mother was a midwife?"

"Shoot, no…my mama couldn't be bothered to take care of *me* half the time, much less somebody else. Mommer and Diddy was my granny and grandpa. They took me and Mama in when my daddy left."

"Ah, I see," Will said, though he wasn't sure he did.

"So anyways, I'll be leavin' this weekend."

Will's shoulders dropped. "I hate it, Beanie. I really do. I…I got used to having you around, you know?"

"Well, I was thinkin' of leavin' anyway. I gotta figure out what to do with my winnin's." Beanie said. "Speakin' of which, I think it's time I done somethin' with that check, too. Suvi said he'd take me by the SunTrust in Tallahassee tomorrow morning

110

so I can open an account. Says that's the onliest way to keep the locals from knowin' my business."

"I think that's a good idea, Bean." Will dropped the kitchen towel into the garbage can.

Beanie frowned and cocked her head slightly.

"You okay, Will?"

"Fine, why?"

"Oh, nothin'."

Beanie waited for Will to turn his back and scooped the towel out of the trash.

Will peered into the refrigerator as if he lost something.

"Whatcha lookin' for?"

"Coffee," Will said. "Would you drink another cup if I made half a pot?"

"Um...sure, but...um...Will? The coffee's right here."

Beanie pointed to the canister, which sat right by the coffee pot and always had.

"Are you sure you're all right?"

"Absolutely." Will took the milk from the refrigerator, leaving the door wide open. "Never better."

"Okay, if you say so."

"Matter of fact, I'm thinking of getting a dog."

"Oh, really? What kind of a dog?"

"I'd have to say the friendly and loyal kind. The kind that will stick around awhile."

"Oh," Beanie said, and closed the refrigerator door.

***

Over the course of the next week, Will helped Beanie pack and occasionally hinted that she might want to stay.

When the day came for her to leave, he offered to take her out to the Atwater home, but Beanie said Suvi would be by later to help her move. This, Will thought, was a bit like rubbing salt in his wounds, but he said nothing. He poured a cup of old coffee, heated it in the microwave and went upstairs to his room without so much as a fare-thee-well.

Beanie puttered around the kitchen, which seemed like a cave without Will sharing the space. She felt a pang of something she couldn't quite identify. The Château had become her home and, quite frankly, a sanctuary. Beanie's world was never exactly normal, a fact which was not lost on her, but moving into The Château provided her with more than stability and a routine – it gave her a purpose, made her feel useful, wanted, happy.

Well, she would be useful and wanted at the Atwaters' house, too. And maybe the next move she made would be a permanent one. It could happen.

A short blow of a car horn shook Beanie from her thoughts. She patted the worn kitchen tabletop on the way out of the kitchen and went to greet Suvi at the door. In short order, Beanie's bags and boxes were neatly tucked into the back of Suvi's truck, and they were ready to go. Will did not come down to help, even though Beanie was sure he heard Suvi arrive.

"Ready?" Suvi asked, sliding into the driver's seat beside her.

"As I'll ever be."

Beanie meant to sound enthusiastic and bright, but her words fell flat and both of them noticed.

"You okay?" Suvi asked.

"Yeah, I'm fine."

"You sure? 'Cause you don't really sound--"

"I'll be right back," Beanie said, and bolted from the truck without waiting for Suvi to respond.

She found Will sitting, not in his own room upstairs, but hers. Her old room, that is.

"Will..." Beanie sat on the bed beside him, tucking her arm through his.

"I'm sorry, Bean."

"You ain't got to apologize, Will. I'm the one should apologize, leaving you out of the clear blue. I just..." Beanie struggled to find the right words. "I just think it's for the best, ya know?"

"It isn't my call. It's yours. I hope you're doing the right thing, I think I understand, but if I'm honest, I don't think it is – for the best, I mean. And I'm rambling. Why am I rambling?"

Will stood and faced Beanie.

112

"Maybe I'm being selfish. I got used to you being here and, quite frankly, I don't like being alone. But it's more than that, Bean. I like your company. You make me laugh. You light up a room the second you walk in. And, dammit, I'm going to miss you."

Will raked his forearm across his eyes, then held his hand out to Beanie and helped her rise.

"Suvi's prolly wonderin' what's takin' so long." Beanie could not bring herself to look at Will's face, so she stared at the floor instead.

"I wish you the best. I mean that."

"I don't wanna leave it this way. I don't want it to be all awkward and dumb..."

"It'll be fine next time I see you, and I hope that's soon. Take care of yourself, and don't be a stranger."

Will brushed past Beanie and left the room, throwing a quick, "See ya, Bean," over his shoulder.

"See ya, Will," Beanie said to the empty room.

Suvi stepped out of the truck when he saw Beanie exit the front door. In a few strides, he was at the passenger door, holding it open for her to climb in.

"Everything okay?" Suvi asked again.

"Yeah, I just forgot to tell him goodbye, that's all."

Bean folded her crinolines under her legs, adjusted her neckerchief, and busied herself fastening the seat belt. For some reason, she couldn't look at Suvi either. Her face felt hot and her hat heavy. She placed the blue Stetson on the seat between her and Suvi, who was already turning the key in the ignition.

"I'm worried about you, Beatrice Bradsher," Suvi said, and backed the car down the driveway.

22
Moving In

Sweet Lee and Bubba John's doublewide mobile home was not nearly big enough for another adult, so figuring out where to put Beanie Bradsher was a real dilemma. Sweet's plan was to let B-Kay sleep on the couch, so Beanie could have one of the bunk beds in the girls' room. Daisy still slept in the well-worn crib, which was a hand-me-down when the twins were born. With only three bedrooms, and none of them terribly large, it was a tight fit in the Atwater household. Of course, B-Kay was not all that thrilled with the idea, but she brightened up when Bubba John reminded her she'd be able to watch TV long after the boys were in bed. Unfortunately, no one stopped to consider how much room Beanie's attire required.

When Suvi pulled into the Atwater's front yard, Beanie took a deep breath and exhaled with a whistle.

"Kind'ly small, ain't it?"

Suvi nodded, but said nothing.

"They's seven people livin' in that thing."

"Eight now," Suvi said. "You sure you want to do this?"

"Sweet needs me, and I told her I would. Cain't hardly go back on my word."

"I wondered how it was going to work, but I guess I figured the house would be bigger. I take it you've never been here, either."

"Naw," Beanie said. "Ain't never been invited before and I don't exactly get out this far on my bicycle. Good thing Bubba's plannin' on fixin' up his grandparents old place with his lottery winnings. Oh, shoot, I kind'ly promised I wouldn't say nothin' about the house. Sweet don't know. It's a surprise."

"How's he going to pull that one off?"

"Beats me, but he thinks he can do it by Christmas."

"Have you thought about where you're going to live once Sweet's recuperated?"

"Well, not exactly...why?" she turned to face him, surprise and delight in her eyes.

"I wonder if they might want to sell you this place. It's just the right size for one person and you'd have plenty of room for a garden."

Beanie's face fell and she slumped back in her seat. "That'd never work."

"I don't see why not."

"How would I get to town?"

"Well, I could take you sometimes," Suvi said, missing the point entirely. "Anyway, it's something to think about."

"I'll say it's something to think about," Beanie said glumly.

"Welp," Suvi said, as Bubba John opened the front door of the doublewide and took five deck stairs in two strides. "Looks like there's no turning back now."

"Suvi!" Bubba John extended his hand as Suvi exited the truck. "I'm surprised to see you! Beanie told me somebody'd offered to bring her out, but I assumed it was Will."

Suvi tried to smile, but it came out more like a grimace. "Nope, just me."

"Ahhh, so...is this..." Bubba John said, waving a finger between Suvi and Beanie, "a thing now?"

"Oh, Lord," Beanie said under her breath, then smoothed her skirt as if her life depended on it.

"Did I say something wrong?" Bubba John asked.

"No, no...it's fine," Suvi said. "It's not really public yet, but yes, we are...whatever you call it these days."

Beanie excused herself and went inside to greet the kids.

Bubba John and Suvi stood for a moment, the awkward silence deafening.

"I guess we should just take all this stuff inside, then." Bubba John pointed at the back of the truck.

"I'll follow you," Suvi said.

In the grand scheme of things, Beanie traveled fairly light. What little furniture and housewares she owned were left in the flood-damaged home she vacated in March. Her clothing, however, was another story entirely. The boots and hats and matching cowgirl outfits took up more than one closet's worth of space. Beanie had only to enter the front door to know with utmost certainty extra space was not to be found in a household now numbering eight.

As Bubba John and Suvi piled box after box in the living room, T-Ray pointed out the obvious, and none too gently.

"Um, Dad? Where the heck are we going to put all *that* stuff?"

Suvi shifted uncomfortably from one foot to the other.

B-Kay entered the room in time to hear Bubba John say, "I guess it'll have to go in the closet in the girls' room. That's where she's sleeping."

B-Kay squinted and cocked her head sideways. "I don't think so, Dad. We're pretty packed in there, even without Daisy's diapers. I know Mom needs help, but I'm not sure we thought this one all the way through. Sorry, Ms. Beanie, no offense."

"None taken," Beanie said, though it came out more like a question.

"I think I'll just be goin' now, unless there's something else you need." Suvi, normally poised and confident, looked like he didn't quite know where to put himself.

Beanie threw her hands up and shook her head. *Whatever,* is what she thought but dared not say out loud.

T-Ray offered the only solution that would work, which was to bring Bubba John's old Airstream home from his hunting camp for a month or so. With hunting season just getting started, Bubba John was not thrilled with the idea. On the other hand, he was pretty sure this season was a wash if there was any hope of getting the house ready by Christmas. They left Beanie's boxes by the door and made plans to retrieve the camper in the morning.

Beanie felt immense relief. It was true; she did not think this through very well. In her rush to leave an awkward situation at The Château, she forgot about the fact that she never shared a room with anyone in her life. And, from the looks of things, that may well be what she ought to have engraved on the headstone she ordered.

***

116

The next afternoon, Bubba John and T-Ray drove out to the hunt camp to retrieve the travel trailer. It took some serious effort to dislodge the aging behemoth from the spot where it sat anchored for the past five years. First on the agenda was to check the tires for dry rot. With at least ten miles to go getting it back to the house, they could not afford a blowout. The tires still had tread and no flat spots, so Bubba John reckoned he'd chance it.

While T-Ray raised the trailer jacks, Bubba John checked the interior for loose items that might break during transport. Tucking everything he could into the cabinets in the kitchen, he stuck the coffee pot in the sink and the tower fan in the non-functioning shower stall and called it done. It smelled a bit like campfire and dirty tennis shoes, but they could clean it when they got home. By the time they got the camper attached to the back of the truck, both father and son were out of sorts.

"I don't know why she's even coming here, Dad." T-Ray said.

"Who, Beanie?"

"No, Dad…the Queen of England."

"Hey, what was that for? I just asked a question, T. Jesus," Bubba John shifted in his seat and eyed his son.

"Why do we even need her? We can handle things 'til Mom gets well. It's not like it's gonna be forever."

"I already explained that," Bubba John said. "The doctor won't let her come home unless there's someone to take care of her. And you know your mama, she does *not* like being away from you guys."

"Well, why's it gotta be Beanie Bradsher, for crying out loud. She's just embarrassing, if you ask me." T-Ray leaned toward the passenger door and dropped his head into the corner of the seat. "I hate this whole thing."

"Thomas Raymond Atwater," Bubba John slipped into Sweet's role like he'd done it all his life. "That doesn't even sound like you. What do you have against Beanie? She's one of the nicest people I know, even if she is a little odd."

"I'm not talkin' about *how* she is, Dad. I'm talkin' about *who* she is. And the whole town is talkin', too. You'd be embarrassed, too, if you went to my school."

"Son, you have got to ignore stupid people. Seriously."

"I wish it was that easy, Dad, but it's not. I'm sick of it. So's B-Kay. And now you have her moving in, for crying out loud."

As they approached the turn-off for their road, Bubba John slowed the truck to a crawl.

"I need you to work with me here, son. You can't make Beanie feel unwelcome. If she leaves, I'll never be able to get this house done by Christmas. How are you gonna feel if you spoil your mom's surprise?"

"Oh, surprise my ass, Dad. That house is a wreck."

"I've made a lot of progress, T. I'll take you out to see it if it'll make you feel better, but I am working on it and it *is* going to be done by Christmas."

"Right…"

"Look, Son, whether you believe me or not, I need Beanie's help. If we don't have someone taking care of your mom, she'll have to go back to the hospital and stay until she's well. Do you want that?"

T-Ray snorted and squirmed in his seat. "I want her well," he said. "I want things back to normal."

"Then, Beanie Bradsher is your only option and I'm not kidding, son, you'd better be nice."

Beanie was waiting outside when they pulled down the long driveway and made a wide circle around the back of the double-wide. She had already swept the concrete pad where the camper would be set.

"Lord, Bubba John," Beanie said, leaning on her broom, "that's the biggest trailer I ever saw. Looks like I'll have plenty of room in that thing."

"Hope so," Bubba John said. "T-Ray, unhook those running lights for me and run down that tongue jack while I set these blocks."

T-Ray said nothing, just did as his father asked, then went inside as soon as his chores were done.

"Go on in, Beanie, and, uh, welcome home," Bubba John grinned and braced himself for a reaction.

Beanie fumbled with the door handle and stepped up in to the camper. The smell hit her first. "Whooo, Lord," Beanie gasped. "I think we might need to air this thing out."

118

"What, you don't like Eau de Wet Dog?"

"It's a bit noisome, that's for sure. I'll just open up some windows."

"Yeah, well, good luck with that," Bubba John said. "Some of 'em work. And if you open up those vents on top, there's some fans that'll pull some of the rank outta there."

By the end of the day, the camper was livable, but just barely. Beanie was fairly certain she just bit off more than she could chew.

23
Something to Talk About

News of Beanie's departure from The Château spread, as Beanie would say, like bedbugs in a roach motel. It was the main topic of conversation at the café Wednesday morning. Clyde and Randy didn't want to appear like they approved of the sordid affair, but secretly they were a little in awe of Bubba John's prowess. They'd never heard of anyone moving his mistress into his own house with his wife and children. Well, there was the one incident where Leo Hornbuckle brought his cyber-girlfriend to stay in the rental cottage next door, but Leo's wife caught on pretty quick and called the woman's husband to come pick her up. He was confused, of course, since his wife drove her own car to the cottage, saying she needed some time away to start writing a romance novel. Romance, indeed.

Agnes Hornbuckle did not have the foresight to realize taking a hatchet to the vehicle's windows and tires would not exactly speed up the hussy's exit. The car was towed to the only repair shop in the county, and the husband was just angry enough to explain to the incredulous mechanic how and why his wife's car was butchered.

Leo ate sandwiches for an entire month over that affair, until he figured out if he ate lunch at the café, he could pop over to the library to go online. Agnes hacked his computer, in the same manner she'd hacked the car, and he didn't have the nerve to buy another one.

At least that was how the story was told at the café.

And now, here was Bubba John Atwater moving Beanie Bradsher into his home, with his wife still recuperating in the hospital. LouWanda was just about to head to the shop when Eustace Falwell stopped by the round table to catch up on the gossip du jour.

"Hey, y'all." Eustace tugged the greasy cap from his head and plopped it onto the table, right on top of Randy's silverware.

Randy picked up the offending hat with two fingers and hooked it gingerly over the back of Eustace's chair.

"Oh, sorry 'bout that," Eustace chortled. "Hey, what's goin' on down at The Château? I heard Beanie Bradsher done run out on ol' Will."

"That ain't the half of it," Randy said, elbowing Clyde.

"Oh, yeah?"

LouWanda sat back down. "You ain't gonna believe this, Useless. Bubba John has gone and moved Beanie in right under Sweet Atwater's nose."

"Noooo!" Eustace slumped in his chair, and shook his head in disbelief as if to say *another one bites the dust*.

"Yes!" said LouWanda "And Sweet not even out of the hospital yet."

Eustace perked up. "Does Sweet know? Is she gonna leave him?"

Randy rolled his eyes. "I swear, Useless, you're like a damn buzzard waitin' to pick the first bones you see."

Eustace grinned and slapped Randy on the back.

"Yep, that's me. I'm the clean-up crew," Eustace snickered.

"It wasn't a compliment," Randy said.

"That's all right, ol' son. Even a buzzard gotta eat."

"That's enough of that," LouWanda sniffed. "I swear, you boys are getting' downright vulgar these days."

"Well, anyway, word is Beanie Bradsher packed up and left The Château Monday evening. Reckon' ol' Suvi is running a taxi service these days. Somebody said he picked her up and carried her out to the Atwater place himself." Randy was determined to get the conversation back on track.

"I don't know why he'd need to do that, unless the Big Pig is goin' under. Now that I think about it, business does seem to be slowin' down," LouWanda said.

Suvi Jones, four tables away, shook his head in amazement. He wasn't in the habit of listening to other people's conversations, but these people weren't even trying to lower their voices. Even the newspaper, which he read from cover to cover every single day at this very table, couldn't distract him from the blaring horns of speculation going on right now. He rose, tucked his folded paper under his arm and approached the crew at the table.

"Suvi!" Eustace spoke first. "Good to see ya! We was just talkin' about you."

"So I heard."

"Oh, well, it wadn't nothin' bad. We was just wonderin' if you were startin' a taxi service, what with the restaurant slowin' down and all. Town could use a taxi, 'specially in the Quarters. I think that's great."

Suvi took a deep breath and tried not to grind his teeth too hard.

"I am not starting a taxi service, and barbecue is selling as well as ever. Matter of fact, I'm looking for some help so I can start taking a little time off to spend with my girlfriend."

"Well, I'll be…" Eustace scratched his head, puzzled. "I ain't never hear'd of you havin' a girlfriend before. Anyone we know?"

"Matter of fact, you do know her. You have been sitting here talking about her for the past half hour, and I'd appreciate it very much if you would stop."

For a moment, the table got quiet enough to hear the two flies that had been dive-bombing their plates all morning.

Randy was the first to recover, though not very well.

"You're dating Sweet Lee?"

"Of course not, Randy!"

"Well, who is it then?" LouWanda demanded.

"I'll give you a hint," Suvi said, swiping one massive hand down his face. "I moved her out of The Château on Monday."

"Oooooh," was the collective response, followed by stunned silence.

"So, now while you're *speculatin'*, at least it'll be about something that's true for a change."

Suvi did not wait for a response, but slipped his customary ten-dollar bill to Sissy on his way out the door.

This time it was Eustace who broke the silence.

"Bubba John is not going to be happy about this turn of events."

24
What He Didn't See

On Beanie's first night in the camper, Bubba John took the kids to Live Oak to pick up pizzas for supper. They polished most of it off in the car and were full and ready for baths and bed by the time they made it home.

Bubba John spent the rest of the evening thinking about the project he was determined to have complete by Christmas. Sweet didn't watch much TV, but the shows she DVR'd and they watched together after the kids were in bed were the ones about remodeling houses. They made it look easy, of course, but Bubba John practically grew up in his grandparents' house. He knew exactly what needed to be done. It would be a tight deadline, but for the first time in his life, he didn't have to worry what anything would cost.

The large sprawling farmhouse was structurally sound, but required new footers to bring it up to code and to build the addition they would need. The heart pine floors were covered with linoleum and carpet, the plaster walls were bare in places, and the last time he'd gone out there, he noticed a family of squirrels had taken up residence in the attic. The roof needed replacing and they would have to install an HVAC unit and ductwork because the house was never air-conditioned, unless you counted the two window units his parents installed when they moved in to care for Mam and Pap.

Bubba John remembered those years with a mix of joy and pain. As he and Sweet added to their family, there were plenty of "grands" to spend time with his kids. They spent countless hours in that house helping his parents deal with the aging and subsequent death of his grandparents. He'd expected to do the same with his own parents. He couldn't think of it without his stomach knotting up. It was why he rarely went to church anymore, and why Sweet understood and didn't press the issue.

They'd all been to the early service the day his parents were killed and were planning their usual Sunday dinner out at the river. As always, they would swing by their house first to change clothes and pick up the casserole Sweet left in the oven. Bitty cried to ride with his parents and he was happy to switch the car seat over for her but Sweet, pregnant with Daisy at the time, was desperate to get to a bathroom and couldn't wait. If anything ever made Bubba John consider the fragility of life, it was that his wife's bladder saved his daughter.

A teenage boy driving home after a night of partying in the woods passed a line of vehicles on a sweeping curve. Racing to beat an approaching car, he whipped back into the lane in front of the Atwater's sedan, but misjudged the length of his long-bed pickup. His bumper caught the driver's side of his mother's car and sent it spinning into the path of an oncoming tractor-trailer rig. His parents were killed instantly, their bodies trapped in the vehicle long after the life-flight helicopter carried the trucker to Shand's Hospital in Gainesville. The teen in the truck walked away without a scratch, and was still at the scene when Bubba John and his family arrived. He was glad he didn't know at the time who caused the accident. He was not a violent man, never laid a hand on any of his children, but he didn't even want to imagine what he would have done if he knew. To this day, he could not get past his anger. It settled in his gut and rose up whenever he thought of it. He told Sweet later he no longer believed in God, but she knew better and so did he. You can't be mad at something you don't believe in. Still, the void left in his life was palpable.

He missed Sunday dinners and Friday night fish fries, tending the garden he and his daddy planted twice a year. There was always enough to freeze or can, and plenty to share with neighbors. He missed the hours he spent in the woods with his father, who had patiently taught his grandchildren to respect the land and to handle guns safely, just as Bubba John learned as a boy. He missed his mother's laugh, and the hymns she played on Mam's old upright piano. And he missed the house. He'd avoided it over the past few years, neglected it even, but it was time to move on, he thought. Time to start some new memories out there while they still could.

By community standards, it wasn't unusual for an old family home place to sit vacant until it was in ruins. Bubba John hated the thought and so did Sweet, but they didn't have the resources to restore it. Now they could do whatever they wanted, maybe even build a new house someday, but for now, Bubba John wanted to reclaim some of the old life he loved, make something new from it, surprise Sweet with the home of her dreams. He knew the idea was crazy and not likely to work, but he couldn't get the image of her face out of his mind, and by God he was going to try.

He figured he'd get T-Ray out there to help remove the old carpet and linoleum, and clean up the yard. If he played it right, Sweet would never know they were doing anything other than making it suitable to sell.

He roused himself out of his reverie, got the coffee pot ready for the next day, checked on the kids and went to bed feeling a little nervous, but excited. Hopefully, now that Beanie was here, he could devote a little more time to getting the project rolling.

***

The next morning, Beanie, unsure of what was expected in the way of household duties, arose early and traipsed through the maze of plastic toys and wheeled objects littering the path to the back door of the house. After a moment's hesitation and a glance around the stoop looking for anything that might serve as a place to hide a key, Beanie reached out and tried the doorknob. It turned with only a faint squeak. She was not surprised. It wasn't unusual for country folk not to lock their doors. Bubba John, standing at the coffee pot in boxer shorts and a t-shirt, nearly jumped out of his skin when Beanie stuck her head in and crooned, "Anybody home?"

"Crap!" Bubba dropped his coffee cup onto the counter and took off down the hallway.

Beanie startled so hard she knocked her hat off sending it sailing end over end and landing it squarely on its brim in the cat's litter box which, apparently, had not been emptied in at least a week. As Beanie, red-faced for more than one reason, tried first to assess the damage and then to decide whether she was better off with the hat on her head or in her hands, Bubba John returned to the kitchen. Now dressed in a pair of jeans, he struggled to button a long-sleeved flannel shirt over the dark stain still spreading on his t-shirt.

"I'm so sorry," Bubba John stuttered. "I didn't expect…I didn't know…I didn't think you'd be up so early."

"It's no problem," said Beanie. "I just…"

"Dammit," Bubba John said, now unbuttoning the shirt.

"I'm sorry," Beanie said, feeling chastened and indignant at the same time.

"No, no, it's not your fault. I just burned the crap outta my stomach, that's all. I gotta get this shirt off." Bubba ripped the flannel shirt off, stripping the sleeves wrong side out, and pulled the stained cotton undershirt over his head. The skin on his scalded abdomen glowed red.

"Oh, my," said Beanie. "That looks bad."

"Yeah, I was just taking the first sip when the door opened. Dumped the whole cup out. Yee-ouch, that hurts." Bubba grabbed a sale paper from a stack of unopened mail on the counter and fanned it futilely over his torso.

"Where do you keep the ice?" Beanie asked, reaching for the upper door on the refrigerator.

"Not there," Bubba John said.

Beanie took one look at the packed freezer and closed it immediately.

"I was afraid of that."

"Try the cooler on the back porch. If not, there's always some in the deep freeze out back."

Beanie found the red Coleman cooler on the back porch beside the washing machine and opened it to reveal six bottles of Bud Light swimming in an icy mix of mostly water. She grabbed a dishtowel from the pile of dirty clothes spilling out of three laundry hampers and thrust it into the cooler.

"Well, at least it's cold," Beanie said as she came back into the kitchen with the dripping towel and twisted the worst of the water out over the dirty dishes in the sink. She was just spreading the towel out over Bubba John's chest and abdomen when T-Ray appeared in the doorway.

T-Ray squinted at the scene, tilting his head to the side as he tried to make sense of it. His father, naked from the waist up and arms outstretched, his shirt on the floor at his feet, stood facing the opposite direction. Beanie…it had to be Beanie, though all T-Ray could see was the flounce of her bright red skirt peeking out on either side of his father's legs, stood close to him, too close. And what the hell was that patting noise and why was his dad *breathing* like that?

"What the…WHAT?" T-Ray bellowed.

Bubba John wheeled to face him, catching the towel just below the beltline as it dropped from his belly.

"Oh, my God, Dad, what are you doing?"

Beanie recoiled in horror.

"Get out!" T-Ray flung his arm wide and pointed in the direction she was already moving.

Beanie clapped both hands over her ears and sank to the floor in a puddle of petticoats.

Bubba John froze for a moment, unsure what just happened. He felt the wet towel seeping cold water into the front of his jeans and looked down.

"Wait, no. No, Tee, no. It's not at all what you think," Bubba John said, followed immediately by the thought, *Jesus, what* does *he think?*

B-Kay, hearing the cacophony in the kitchen, burst from her room down the hall and met her twin head on at the kitchen door just as he wheeled to exit. The impact sent T-Ray sprawling backward. He landed with a thud beside the long pine table and stayed there, too stunned to move.

"What in the world is going on in here?" B-Kay asked.

"Just give me a minute, and I'll explain. It's just a big misunderstanding, that's all."

Bubba John helped Beanie to her feet and guided her to the table. Once she was seated, he reached for T-Ray's hand.

"Don't touch me," he hissed and pulled himself up into the closest chair.

"T-Ray, stop. I burned myself, that's all."

"Right," he said and wiped his nose on his sleeve.

"Well look for yourself," Bubba John said, pointing at the red skin above his navel. "I was drinking my coffee and I heard Beanie come in the back door."

"I didn't mean to scare ya," Beanie said.

"Well, it didn't actually scare me."

"Then why'd ya spill your coffee?"

"Because I was in my underwear, for Pete's sake."

"Wait, I don't get it." B-Kay said.

"You're in jeans!" said T-Ray, glaring at his father.

"Oh, my God…just stop it, Tee." Bubba John said. "I spilled a whole cup of hot coffee down the front of my shirt. Once I got *dressed*, I realized my stomach was burned pretty bad, so Beanie soaked this towel in ice water and put it on the burn to cool it down. And that's when T-Ray walked in."

"So what?" B-Kay said.

"So that's not what I saw," T-Ray said.

"No, that's what you *didn't see*," Bubba John said. "There's a difference."

"Now I *really* don't get it." B-Kay twisted her hair into a long strand on one side.

"What he *thinks* he saw, and what he *didn't see* are two different things. What he didn't see, was Beanie was putting a cold rag on a burn. That's it."

"So what does he think he saw?"

"You'll have to ask your brother, honey,'cause quite frankly, I do *not* want to know."

"I got some burn cream in the camper," Beanie said. "I'll bring it back in a little while, but if it's all the same to you guys, I think I'll skip breakfast this morning."

***

Bubba John was mopping the kitchen floor when B-Kay came back in with Bitty and Tater, both dressed and ready for school. She sat them both at the table and poured cereal and milk into their bowls.

"Why are you mopping over there?" B-Kay asked.

Bubba John stopped and looked up at his daughter. She was the spitting image of her mother, just a hair or two taller, which wasn't saying much. As far as both of them were concerned, they were ten feet tall and bulletproof, a fact that both impressed and perplexed him on a daily basis. He flipped the mop up into the wringer and pressed the handle down hard.

"One thing leads to another, I guess. The more I mopped, the more I *had* to mop to make it all look even. Looks like it's been awhile."

"Ya think?" B-Kay said.

Bubba John wheeled to face his daughter again. "What is that all about?"

"Is what T-Ray said true?"

"Look, B., I don't know what T-Ray thinks he saw, but I'm telling you the truth. I burned myself with coffee and Beanie was trying to help."

"Well, he's convinced it wasn't as innocent as all that. Just so ya know."

"Dammit," Bubba John said, wringing the mop with his bare hands this time.

"Whatsa matter with Daddy?" Tater piped up from the table.

"Nothing, Tate," B-Kay answered for him. "Finish your cereal and run get your backpack. You, too, Bitty. We gotta leave soon."

T-Ray appeared with Daisy in his arms. Her face and hands were covered with liquid makeup.

"What in the world?" B-Kay asked.

"Apparently, you left your makeup AND the baby unattended." T-Ray said, thrusting Daisy toward his sister.

"Since when is it *my* job to watch *all* the kids. I had Bitty and Tate." B-Kay complained. "Dad!"

Bubba John threw his hands up and shook his head. "I don't know what to tell you, B. We all have to be careful about leaving things out. Get her cleaned up for me, would you? I need to talk to Tee."

B-Kay reluctantly took Daisy from T-Ray's outstretched arms and headed toward the back of the house.

"Look, son, you're gonna have to pitch in around here, too. B-Kay's right, it's not fair to put it all on her."

"I do help. Besides, I thought that's why Beanie was here. Or did I get that wrong, too?"

"That's enough, Tee. You know better than that."

"She should not be here, Dad. Seriously, it's disgusting what people are saying."

"You know what…I can assure you of one thing: people's imaginations are far more disgusting than anything I have done, or would do for that matter. We can talk about this later. You guys are going to be late to school." Bubba John said, resting both hands on top of the mop handle, "Right now, we need Beanie's help."

"Maybe you need her, but I sure don't. I need my mom…"

T-Ray's face crumpled and all Bubba John could do was stand and stare as an array of grief, fear, and embarrassment to boot swept across his features.

"Aw, son, it's okay," Bubba John recovered and reached for T-Ray, tossing the mop handle to the floor. "Mama's coming home soon. Is that what this is all about?"

T-Ray pressed his face into his father's chest and wept openly for the first time since Sweet's surgery.

Bubba John tucked T-Ray's head under his chin and rocked him side to side.

Bitty got down from her chair and padded across the kitchen floor. She said nothing, but rested her head on T-Ray's hip and patted him on the arm. After a minute or two, T-Ray squeezed his sister's shoulder and pulled away from Bubba John's embrace.

T-Ray shrugged, took a deep, snuffling breath, and smiled down at Bitty's worried face.

"I'm fine, Bitty, really. Go get your dance stuff and take Tater to the potty, K?"

Bitty hesitated, but turned to do her brother's bidding. As they left the room, Bubba John reached once again for his oldest son.

T-Ray spun away and left the room, leaving his father there with arms outstretched.

25

Unsettled

Sweet Lee Atwater came home a week later to a house cleaned so thoroughly she scarcely recognized it. Beanie even cleaned the recliner, and placed a soft coverlet that Sweet had never seen over the seat and back. Bubba John barely got her settled into the chair before Beanie brought a glass of sweet tea and a warm barley bag to drape across the back of Sweet's neck.

"Ah," Sweet sighed. "I could get used to this kind of attention."

Bubba John timed her arrival so she would have an hour or so to rest before the mob arrived home from school. It was two weeks before Halloween, and the kids were more excited than usual for the annual Trunk or Treat at the New Harmony Baptist Church. Being the seamstress she was, Beanie got a real kick out of sewing costumes for the little ones.

If Sweet was dismayed that these were the first thing the kids talked about when they got home from school, she did a good job of hiding it.

The girl's a genius, Sweet thought, and made a mental note to tell her - some other time when she wasn't feeling completely dispensable. For the moment, she just watched the chaos unfold, and reminded herself how lucky she was to have the help. Daisy, of course, was the most emotional, wanting nothing more than to climb into her mother's lap and stay there. But the doctor warned them not to let Sweet do anything too strenuous and risk undoing the healing that was finally evident.

Beanie put a pillow in the crook of Sweet's arm and placed Daisy gently into its center, where she stayed, occasionally stroking Sweet's jaw with one thumb, while the other four siblings wrestled for airtime.

"Mama, Travis bit me at school today."

"You gotta see the princess outfit Beanie made for Bitty, Mama. It's bedazzled and everything!"

"Mama, I'm gonna be a Ninja turtle. Bet you can't make a Ninja turtle outfit, can ya? Miss Beanie can. Want me to put it on for ya?"

"Mom, you gotta talk to B-Kay about letting me drive. She's been hogging the car the whole time."

"I got into the AP program, Mom. If I can go to Lake City twice a week, I'll have an AA degree before I even get out of high school."

"Hey, hey, hey," Bubba John said. "Let's give your mama a few minutes to breathe, how about it?"

"Y'all go put your stuff away and git your homework out. Supper ain't halfway done," Beanie said, somehow already accustomed to the commotion. "B-Kay, how about puttin' somethin' on the TV for the little ones. Pre-*fer*-ably somethin' quiet-like."

No one noticed the tears pouring down Sweet's face until Daisy piped up during one brief still moment, "Mama, why you cryin'?"

B-Kay ushered T-Ray and Bitty out of the room, while Beanie flipped the stovetop eyes to low, scooped up the little ones and took them "to the potty before they watch TV," she said on her way down the hall.

Bubba John rushed to Sweet's side and, kneeling by the recliner, took her hand, "What's the matter, hon? Are you hurting?"

Sweet threw an arm over her eyes and worked on controlling her sobs.

"Baby, what is it? What's wrong?" Bubba John was genuinely concerned.

"I don't know," Sweet snuffled. "I really don't."

Bubba John knelt there, stroking Sweet's palm with his own rough, work-weary hands.

"Baby, talk to me," he said. "What is it?"

"I think I'm just happy, really. I missed you all so much."

"But what?" Bubba John asked.

"I just...I don't know," Sweet said. "But, you're all fine, I guess. Everyone seems fine..."

"Aw, honey, that's just 'cause we're happy to see you."

"Really?"

132

"Of course, really. You just wait. You'll see. Everything's the same. Well, not exactly the same. It's kinda cleaner than usual, but we're adapting. Beanie runs a tight ship, that's for sure."

Sweet laughed then, hard enough to pull the pillow to her stomach to reduce the pain.

"That's good to know," Sweet said, pulling Bubba John to her for a kiss. "I missed you."

"Baby," Bubba John said with utter sincerity, "you just have no idea."

"But, look at the house! It's spotless. How does she do it?"

"Um, she doesn't do carpool and she doesn't run the shop," Bubba said. "Duh."

"Speaking of which, how's Dottie doing?"

Bubba John took a deep breath and prepared himself for what was quickly becoming habit, lying to his wife.

"She's doing great! Shop's hanging in there. Lots of camo going out, huntin' season and all."

That wasn't the lie. The shop was doing well. With a pay raise to match what she lost in tips, Dottie was throwing herself into sales like nobody's business. She was already gearing up for prom sales, which wouldn't start until January. She found a great deal on women's camo-wear and was making a killing on jackets for hunting season. She even ordered camouflage onesies, which sold out in a week.

Bubba John just couldn't bring himself to tell Sweet what he was paying Dottie. Hopefully, she wouldn't ask.

"How's Dottie holding up? I know she can't be happy losing the tips she always made during lunch hour."

"Dottie's fine," Bubba John said. "She knows this is just temporary and she's been closing up at five on the dot to work the supper shift."

"Makes for a long day, though," Sweet said.

"Dottie's *fine*, Sweet. I promise."

Bubba John wondered how long it would be before Sweet found out. He was on borrowed time and he knew it. Fortunately, the house was coming right along. Amazing what could be done in two weeks when the right amount of money was thrown at a project.

"Maybe I can get down there one day next week..."

"No!" Bubba said, more vehement than he intended to sound.

"Wow," Sweet said.

"Oh, sorry, but the doctor said not to let you overdo it and that's what I intend to do."

"You do realize your reaction only makes me more determined to go, right?"

"Yep," Bubba John grinned. "I do. Fortunately, you haven't been clear to drive yet, so I'm the only one who can get you there. Nothing doing right now, Sister."

Beanie returned with Daisy and Tater, who insisted on staying in the living room with their mother while Beanie finished up dinner. An hour later, they were all at the table together, minus Beanie, who took her meal out to the camper.

"Does she always do that?" Sweet wondered.

"Naw, I think she just wanted us to have some time alone. Besides, I think she and Suvi are going over to Walmart tonight. I heard her say something about it earlier."

"That's the cutest thing, those two together," Sweet said. "I never would have guessed."

"It's a little strange, if you ask me," Bubba said. "They don't seem suited somehow."

"How are people in town taking it?"

"Okay, I guess. Suvi thinks his business is falling off, but I can't really imagine anyone being hateful. They like to gossip, but I don't think they're mean-spirited people."

Sweet shrugged. "You never know. Can I have another one of those biscuits, B-Kay? Lord, Suvi would be a fool not to marry her is all I can say. That girl can flat cook."

"Mama," Tater piped up, his mouth full of collard greens. "Just wait 'til you taste her cinnamon rolls. You're gonna die. They ain't even out of a can or nothin'!"

"I'd be happy with canned after hospital food. It wasn't terrible, but that's the best I can say about it," Sweet said.

After supper, B-Kay took the little ones for baths while T-Ray cleaned up the kitchen. It was all so orderly and peaceful that Sweet felt, once again, a little melancholy.

"They're just on good behavior," Bubba John said. "Trust me on this."

26
Now That's More Like It

"Take it off!" Bitty wailed and tugged at the shoulder of the yellow and blue princess dress Tate had pulled on over his camouflage t-shirt.

"Stop, Bitty, I'm just tryin' it on," Tater swatted at his sister's hand, lifted the layers of tulle and spun several times on his heel.

"What's goin' on in there?" B-Kay yelled from the bathroom.

"No, no, no, no, noooo, Tater," Bitty pulled harder. "You're messin' it up!"

Tate spun again, but Bitty had stepped on the skirt and there was a long ripping sound as several layers of tulle pulled away from the waistband.

Bitty screeched and T-Ray came running.

"What in the heck is going on in here?" he asked, surveying the pile of netting Bitty was gathering in both arms. Tears streamed down her face and Tate looked terrified.

"I didn't mean to, brudder! I just tried it on..." Tate hung his head.

"Oh, for crying out loud, Tater, it's a dress!"

"So?" Tate looked confused. "I wasn't gonna wear it."

"You're wearing it now," T-Ray said. "What happened to it?"

Tater shrugged, "I dunno. Sissy did it."

"I did not," Bitty wailed. "He was spinnin' and spinnin' and he spunned it right off."

B-Kay appeared, her hair wet from the shower and a towel wrapped tight around her torso.

"What'sa matter Bitty-bug? Oh," she said, spotting the damage. "Oh, no, Tater! What did you do?"

"Can't you just watch them for one second?" T-Ray turned on his twin, his eyes narrowed and his face red with anger.

"I was taking a shower, T," B-Kay said.

"Well, I was fixing their damn *breakfast*, since there was no one else around to do it. No milk either."

"Tee," B-Kay admonished him. "Little pitchers have big ears. Watch your mouth."

"Oh, so now *you're* my mom?"

"Oh, for crying out loud. I don't know what has gotten into you this morning." B-Kay deftly pulled the costume over Tate's head and handed it to Bitty.

"Go take this to Beanie and show her what happened, baby. She'll fix it for you."

Bitty left the room sniffling and Tate followed dragging one shoe behind him by the laces.

"It might help if you paid just a tiny bit of attention. Notice anyone missing this morning? Dad's truck is gone and Beanie is not in the kitchen. That would be why you and I are left to deal with all *this!*" T-Ray swung both arms wide for emphasis.

"Shhh! Mom's right there." B-Kay pointed to the wall behind her.

"So what?"

"So, she's sleeping, you big jerk. And I'm trying to get dressed."

"So am I!" T-Ray pointed to the fact that he was still in boxers and a t-shirt.

B-Kay sighed and shook her head. "What do you want me to do, T? I can't do it by myself."

"I thought Beanie was supposed to be helping."

"Oh, come on. Are you clueless? She *is* helping. You wanna try it without her?"

T-Ray pushed past his sister to leave the room. "Never mind. You're no help, either."

B-Kay followed him down the hall and into the kitchen where Beanie had all three children sitting at the table eating cereal.

"Hey!" Beanie looked up from the stove, where she was stirring a big pot of grits. "Y'all hungry? I got cheese grits just about done."

B-Kay elbowed her brother. "Thought you said there was no milk."

136

"Oh, they wasn't any milk," Beanie said. "I had a little in the camper, so I went to get it. Your dad had some stuff to do in town, so he's gonna bring milk and bread later."

B-Kay gave her brother an *I-told-you-so* look, then turned toward Beanie. "I'd love some grits, Miss Beanie. I gotta get dressed first. We're gonna be late if we don't get outta here soon."

"Mommy!" came the chorus from the little ones when Sweet entered the room and sat down carefully at the table.

"What in the world are you doin' outta bed?" Beanie asked. "I was fixin' your breakfast to bring to ya in your room."

"Came to see what all the racket was about," Sweet eyed the twins, trying to figure out why they were both in the kitchen in states of half-dress. "Y'all need to go get some clothes on. What in the world is going on this morning?"

"T-Ray is being a jerk," B-Kay said. "That's what's going on."

"Am not! I was just -"

"Go get dressed for pity's sake!" Sweet ordered, and the twins complied.

"Tater broke my dress!" Bitty said, breaking into tears again at the memory.

"I didn't mean toooo..." Tater protested.

"Mommy, up!" Daisy threw both hands into the air, reaching toward Sweet.

"Oh, Lord," Beanie said. "I'm so sorry..."

"Don't be," Sweet said. "This is much more like it."

27
New Arrival

LouWanda Crump huffed as she wrenched open the door to the Mayhew Café and pushed past the crowd of young men standing expectantly in front of the cash register.

"Sit anywhere ya like," she threw over her shoulder before slumping into her usual seat at the round table. The men, divers staying at the hotel behind the café', shuffled to the far corner of the room and sat down.

"I swear, they oughta put up a sign." LouWanda said, miffed at having to expend the extra energy. "Sissy ain't got time to seat anybody anyway."

"And a very good morning to you, too, LouWanda," Dottie could barely contain her smirk.

"What's good about it?" LouWanda asked.

"What's *not* good is the better question," Dottie said. "You're fixin' to tell us anyway, so just go ahead and spit it out. What's got your panties in a wad?"

"That's disgusting, Dorothy. Don't be common."

"Well, what is it then?"

"I'll tell ya if you'll stop yappin' at me. I just passed by the old chiropractor's office on the corner and it looks like somebody's fixin' to set up shop, and Lord knows I don't need any competition. I'm barely makin' ends meet as it is."

Randy looked up from his paper. "The gray building by the stoplight?"

"Yeah, that's the one," LouWanda said. "I don't see any signs yet, but they's a cleaning lady down there now. Saw her pullin' a vacuum cleaner outta her Mercedes. I'd like to know how she can afford a car like that. Those people get on my nerves. Probably gettin' food stamps on the side."

"Black woman? Kind of tall?" Randy asked.

"Yeah, that's her," LouWanda said. "Dressed mighty fancy for cleanin' if you ask me."

"She's not a cleaning lady, LouWanda. She's the new owner of the building. It's gonna be a real estate office, I think."

"Oh, well, whatever," LouWanda said. "Looked like a cleaning lady to me. How come you know so much about her?"

"She filed for a business license and a permit to remodel. Her name's Gabriella Warren, and if that doesn't ring a bell, then you obviously don't follow the LPGA tour."

"The what?"

"LPGA, LouWanda," Dottie said. "I swear, sometimes you should just keep your mouth shut. Gabe Warren is a legend on the ladies pro golf circuit. I don't think she'd take too kindly to being called a cleaning lady. Jesus."

"Don't take the Lord's name, Dorothy. Besides, how was I s'posed to know that?"

"You're not supposed to *know*…just like you're not supposed to *assume*."

"Well, whatever…as long as she ain't takin' away my business, I reckon I can rest easy enough. Second colored owner downtown. Ain't we just movin' on up now?"

"LouWanda!" Randy and Dottie said simultaneously.

Dottie picked up her coffee mug and stood, scooting her chair back with her knees. "And you call *me* common? Really, Lou, that's just crossing the line."

"What? What'd I say?" LouWanda gawked incredulously at Randy.

Randy shook his head and raised his newspaper to hide his face. Dottie found a small table near the wall and sat looking out the window. Mac McConnell cleared his throat and looked around the room for Sissy, hoping to snag her for more coffee.

"Well, I swear, y'all act like you ain't never thought the same thing. Just 'cause I up and said it out loud don't make me any worse than y'all."

Randy leaned forward and flicked his head in the direction of Suvi Jones. "That's enough, LouWanda."

Mac McConnell stood and slapped Randy on the back. "Ready to go, ol' boy? I think we ought to stop by Ms. Warren's office a minute. You know, make her feel welcome and all."

Randy narrowed his eyes and searched Mac's face for signs of sarcasm.

"No, really, I mean it. We've needed a real estate office in this town for years. I'd hate for someone to get the wrong idea." Mac looked pointedly at LouWanda and headed for the door. Randy followed suit.

Across the room, Dottie Brentwood caught Suvi Jones' eye as he stood to leave.

Dottie's face conveyed her unspoken message – *I'm sorry*. Suvi shook his head and shrugged, but Dottie noticed his shoulders sagged just a bit more than she'd ever seen. He looked plain tired.

Meanwhile, LouWanda Crump fiddled with her coffee mug and wondered why everyone was angry all of a sudden. Her spirits rose a teensy bit when Eustace Falwell came in. He would change the subject to himself as soon as he sat down, and for once that would be a relief.

***

Suvi Jones left a ten-dollar bill under the lip of his plate, squared his shoulders at the familiar weight of depression, and strode out of the café with his chin just a shade higher than normal. It was a trick his mother taught him early in his life. *Think tall*, he told himself, though it was her voice he heard. He used to believe her constant reminder was designed to help him grow, but then he learned a little about genetics and realized he owed his tremendous stature to the father he never met. There was a book of photos that told most of the story: his mother, a cheerleader at the local high school, and his father, a basketball legend who led Mayhew High to its first state championship in the late sixties when the schools were finally integrated. The Vietnam War killed more than dreams of college careers. His parents married as soon as they could after high school, feeling the pressure to start their lives together when his father registered for the draft and pulled a ridiculously low number. Suvi was born a few days before his father died in the battle of An Lộc.

Think tall, he reminded himself again as he slid into his truck and turned the ignition. He looked up in time to see Dottie staring at him through the window of the café. He'd known Dottie for as long as he could remember. She was efficient and kind and one of the best waitresses he'd ever employed. And that was the key, he thought. *She's sorry because she works for me.* He turned off the engine and walked back into the diner. More than a few heads turned when he went straight to Dottie's table and sat down.

They didn't speak at first. Dottie's face grew pink and her hands shook. Suvi had no way of knowing that her nerves had nothing to do with fear, but were completely born of shame. She was ashamed of what LouWanda said, horrified that he had overheard.

Suvi relaxed in his chair, simultaneously aware of the tension in the room and Dottie's discomfort. His mother had warned him of this, too. *Be careful not to intimidate a white woman. It can cost you your life.* He'd never felt threatened in this town, but he was careful – just in case.

Suvi spoke first.

"How's it going at the dress shop?"

Dottie sighed and gave a brief, relieved snort of laughter.

"Couldn't be better unless I owned the shop myself," she said.

"I was just wondering 'cause, you know, you just never can tell when Cherry'll be callin' in again…"

Dottie laughed again. "Lord, that girl. I'll never know why you have so much patience with her, but right now I'm grateful. I got more than I can handle at the store."

Suvi nodded. "I just wanted to tell you that there are no hard feelings. Felt like it was important to say."

"I'm awful sorry, Suvi. I hope you know that we're not all like that, even though it seems that way sometimes…" The words tumbled from Dottie's mouth and, even as she said them she felt awkward and inadequate, so she stopped abruptly.

Suvi's lips drew in with his breath. "What does that mean – 'we're not all like that'?"

"Well, the town – us - *you* know…" Dottie stuttered.

"And what, I'm not a part of this town?" Suvi asked.

"You are a hero in this town, Suvi. You know that."

"Right, I'm *in* the town, but not of it. You said so yourself."

"I most certainly did not!"

Sissy came by and refilled Dottie's cup. "Y'all okay? It's gettin' a little tense over here."

Dottie gave a terse smile and nodded. When Sissy was gone, Suvi leaned forward and spoke a little lower.

"I'm not trying to hurt your feelings," Suvi said.

"I know you're not. It just seems like…no matter what I say, it's wrong. Like you just expect the worst every time."

Suvi sat back and shook his head in disgust. "You know, that statement right there just burns me up. Like it's my fault because I expect the worst. Well, you would, too. Trust me."

Before Dottie could respond, a man neither of them recognized, sitting two tables away, turned and caught her eye.

"Are you okay? Is he bothering you?"

Dottie's response was immediate. She forced herself to relax and appear in control.

"Oh, yeah, we're fine. Just talking, that's all," Dottie said.

Suvi raised his hands - palms forward. "See what I mean?"

Dottie said nothing, just stared down at the table. She picked up a tiny, wadded scrap of paper that once held a straw and worked it open with her fingers.

"I'm not even safe in my own town," Suvi said, more to himself than to Dottie, and so quietly it was almost a whisper.

"Oh, come on," Dottie dropped the straw wrapper and slapped both hands to the table. "That's ridiculous. He was just making sure I was okay."

"Right. From the big, black dude, I get it."

"Well, it's not like you can't take him if it came to that."

"Ha!"

Suvi's laugh was so loud and sharp the whole restaurant got quiet for a split second, and heads turned in their direction. He waited a moment, then spoke again, his voice dropped low.

"And what then, Dottie? You think I walk around this earth spoiling for a fight? Well, I don't." Suvi slid his chair backwards, turning it at an angle from the table. "But some people in the town sure do, and I'm tired of backing down."

He stood then and turned toward the door, nodding at the man who had spoken to him a moment ago and still sat staring in his direction.

Dottie sat and watched out the window as Suvi Jones folded himself into his truck, closed the door with firm control, backed out of the parking lot and drove away.

"Dammit," she whispered and dropped her head into her hands.

28
Beanie's Secret

The Atwater household settled into a nice routine in the first week of Sweet Lee's convalescence at home. Bubba was gone quite a bit, which gave Sweet time to bond with Beanie over countless loads of laundry. They fell into the habit of taking coffee together in the living room, just after the kids left for school. Beanie stopped in the laundry room on her way in every morning so, by the time breakfast was over and the dishes washed, there was a load to fold, which Beanie would bring to the living room while Sweet poured the coffee. This was the most strenuous task Sweet was allowed to do. Even the laundry was sorted so that Sweet had only to fold underwear and socks, which in the Atwater household was enough to keep her occupied until she tired.

On Monday morning, once the kids were packed off to school, Beanie settled Sweet into the recliner and gave her the TV remote.

"Now you just set here and watch whatever you want while I clean up the kitchen."

When she was finished with the dishes, she brought Sweet a glass of ice water and sat down on the couch with a whoosh, both from her skirt and her exhaled breath of exhaustion.

"I hate you're having to do all this Beanie. I don't know how we'll ever pay you what it's worth."

"You ain't got to pay me nothin'. Bubba John and I already worked that out. He got me out of a touchy situation and gave me a roof over my head. Besides, I'm happy to help out for a while. You ain't gonna be off your feet forever."

"I didn't realize there was any problem at The Château. I thought you and Will got along well."

"Oh, we did, but you know…I started seein' Suvi and it just got a little awkward is all."

"Ooohhh," said Sweet, as she mentally sorted the options for what that might mean.

Beanie shrugged and changed the subject. "How 'bout we get you into the shower while everybody's gone. You feel up to it?"

"Sounds wonderful, but I don't know what I'll do with this hair afterwards. I'm not supposed to raise my hands over my head for any length of time. I think blow-drying is out of the question."

"I can fix your hair for ya," Beanie said. "Won't take long at all."

And it didn't. Beanie knew when to step in and help without making Sweet feel uncomfortable or embarrassed. She was back in a clean nightgown and sitting in front of her dressing table before there was time to be tired.

Sweet refrained from comment until Beanie was finished drying and styling her hair.

"Is there anything you can't do?" Sweet asked. She stared at her reflection in the mirror, easing closer to admire the soft curls Beanie coaxed into her unruly locks.

"Well, yeah," Beanie said, "but I always loved doin' hair. Used to practice on my cousins when we was growin' up. That was 'fore I stopped speakin' to 'em, 'cause they was so hateful all the time."

"You have a gift," Sweet said. "A real gift. Have you ever thought about being a hairdresser?"

"Lots of times," Beanie nodded. "I even tuck one of them classes over at the Vo-Tech center after I got outta high school. But there's the proof I cain't do everything, right there. I ain't never been good at tests. I could do ever'thing they asked me to do in the shop, but I couldn't pass them tests for nothin'."

"Oh, Beanie, I'm so sorry," Sweet said, catching Beanie's eye in the reflection of her mirror.

"That's why I don't drive, either," Beanie admitted for the very first time in her life. "Will was gonna teach me, but I didn't have the heart to tell 'im it wouldn't do no good. I'd get down there and freeze up when it came time to answer all them questions."

"Beanie," Sweet said, turning to face Beanie directly, "have you ever been tested for learning disabilities?"

"For what?"

"Problems with learning, you know, like dyslexia or attention deficit or anything like that?"

"I don't recollect if I have or I haven't. Alls I can tell ya is, if it was a test somebody give me, I prolly failed it."

29
The Welcoming Committee

Gabriella Warren slammed the trunk of her 2011 Mercedes C300, a prize she won when she aced the seventeenth hole at Blue Bay. She didn't win the tournament but, for the first time, got noticed for something other than being a black southern woman on the LPGA tour. Truth told, she didn't think about it nearly as much as everyone else seemed to do. She first played golf on her high school team in a rural Florida town very similar to Mayhew Junction. She was a natural; the game itself suited her introverted personality as well as her love of being outdoors. Gabriella was recruited by three major universities, including Duke, but she chose Auburn for reasons only she knew. After college, Gabe toured with the LPGA for ten years, never winning any of the biggest titles, but earning enough money and recognition to transition into whatever career suited her fancy when it was time to retire.

Gabe chose real estate. After traveling extensively since her high school days, she was ready to settle down. She started out in Jacksonville, getting her real estate license, working for a few years, then taking the broker's exam, which she aced as well. She knew she wanted her own company, something she could grow without answering to anyone else. She looked at several small towns before settling on Mayhew Junction. It fit her criteria: small town, no local competition, and at least one family member nearby. In this case, it was her cousin who taught at the elementary school in Mayhew. Their mothers were sisters and, though they had never been particularly close, Gabe remember Delia with real fondness from family get-togethers over the years.

Their first meeting in Mayhew Junction had almost been their last. Delia, well-intended and misinformed, warned Gabe that the locals didn't look kindly on homosexuality and might blackball her business accordingly. Gabe almost got mad; she had never suffered fools gladly. But then it struck her as funny and she started to laugh.

"I'm not gay, Delia, despite what people think."

And they did think it. Gabe was well-aware, but did nothing to quell the rumors.

"Really? But they've always said…" Delia was genuinely confused.

"Who are *they*, Dee? Anyone who knows me, knows the truth. I'm just very, *very* picky."

"Why didn't you ever set the media straight about it? No pun intended…sorry." Delia gave a rueful smile and threw up her hands.

Gabe shrugged. "It made it a lot easier, trust me. Too hard to sustain a relationship on the road? Too hard to weed out the users? Too hard to avoid starting a family? Take your pick. I was happy. I liked my life. I wanted to keep it that way, that's all."

"Are you, then? Happy, I mean."

"I am," Gabe said, "And I'm excited about moving here."

"It's awfully quiet in Mayhew Junction," Delia warned.

"That's what I like most about it," Gabe replied. "I don't have a *lot* of money, but I'm comfortable. There are no quotas I need to meet, no pressure to increase company profits - I *am* the company. It's going to be great. Just watch."

"Okay, but do you mind if I dispel a few rumors in the meantime?"

Gabe sighed. "Does it matter that much to you?"

Delia thought about the question for a moment before replying.

"Only because they're wrong. It's a small town, Gabe. And gossip is the number one hobby. Well, hunting first, maybe. Then gossip," she grinned. "If they're going to talk about you, and they are, I'd like for them to at least have the facts."

"What people think about me is none of my business, Dee. I know who I am. You know, too. Isn't that enough?"

Delia did not respond.

"Look, it's no big deal. If you feel better about it, then knock yourself out. I honestly just don't care."

"I've made you mad," Delia said.

"Not at all. Not at *all.*"

"Are you sure?"

"Absolutely positive. Part of the reason I moved here is to have family nearby. You're all I've got. I don't want to make you uncomfortable, either, and clearly this issue does. So, no sweat. Say whatever you need to say."

"So we're good?" Delia asked.

"Yep, we're good. You know, it is what it is. No problem."

"Can I set you up on a date, then?"

"Absolutely not," Gabe said and grinned. "I have to draw the line somewhere and that one is uncrossable."

Dee laughed then, officially breaking the awkwardness of the entire conversation.

"Alright, then. How about if I just invite you to dinner one night?"

"That would be lovely, as long as you don't invite some strange man, too."

"The one I had in mind is not strange at all," Delia smiled.

"Don't do it, Dee. I mean it."

And she did. Gabriella Warren had no intentions of meeting, dating, or marrying anyone from Smalltown, USA. And that was how she set up her entire life – in avoidance of that which scared her half to death. No chance of finding anyone suitable in this Podunk town, and that suited *her* just fine.

Gabe stepped back into her new office and surveyed the room. It had been a chiropractor's office a year ago. The current décor did not suit her tastes, but it was clean and comfortable and would suffice for now. She exited the building and saw two huge pickup trucks parked on either side of her car. The one on the driver's side was so close, there was no way she could get her car door open enough to get in. Two men stood at the back bumper of the truck on the left. She couldn't help but feel intimidated, but she drew herself up to her full five feet, ten inches and took a deep breath.

"Morning, gentlemen. How can I help you?" Gabe asked, smiling broadly with everything but her eyes.

***

149

Randy Kerner pulled a toothpick from his mouth with his left hand and thrust the right one towards Gabriella Warren.

"Good mornin', Ms. Warren, nice to finally make your acquaintance. I'm Randall Kerner, County Commissioner, District Three. How you doin' today?"

Gabe gave the proffered hand a quick squeeze and stepped back immediately.

"Nice to meet you, too, Sir. Hope this isn't a political call, I'm not even registered to vote here yet."

"Oh, no, this is purely a social call. Just wanted to welcome you to Fletcher County. This here's Malcolm McConnell. He's the Town Clerk for Mayhew Junction."

Mac pulled himself up to his full five-feet-seven-and-one-half inches and gave a salute that looked more like a wave before sticking both hands in his pockets with a shrug.

"Good ta' meetcha. My wife follows you on the tour. Gets a kick outta you bein' – uh, you know – kind of a local and all."

Gabe squinted and gave Mac a sideways look. "I'm not from here."

"Oh, yeah, I know, but Delia teaches at the school with my wife, so we kinda count you as one of our own. Kinda like a claim to fame or somethin', ya know?"

Gabe nodded. "Kinda."

"Anyway," Randy said, "we just wanted to stop by and say 'hey' and let you know we are proud to have you settling here. Just proud as can be. And if there is anything we can do to help you in any way, you can stop by the town hall or the courthouse. I don't know what district you're living in, but it doesn't really matter. You can call me any time. Have you found a place to live yet, by the way?"

"No, not yet, but I'll get there. Staying at a hotel in Live Oak right now, but I'm going to go by The Château in the next few days and see if I can get a room there."

"Well, good. Will's a great guy. He'll be happy to have the business, too, I'm sure. Where you looking for property? I imagine you're going to want some acreage or something, huh? You thinking of putting in a golf course? County could use one, that's for sure. Closest one's in Suwannee County. The boys on our golf team have a forty-five minute drive each way."

"What about the girls?" Gabe asked.

"Don't have a girls' team," Mac said.

"Really?" Gabe smoothed an errant sprig of hair away from her face. "Why not?"

Mac scratched his head. "I don't rightly know, to be honest."

"Not many female golfers in the county," Randy said. "But I bet there will be now that you're here. You'd make a great coach for the team if you're interested."

Gabe laughed and kicked at a rock on the concrete pavement. "It'll be a while before I have time to even think about volunteering anywhere. I need to get this company off the ground, find a place to live… First things first, you know."

The pavement crackled behind them and all three turned to see Suvi Jones pull into the parking lot and exit his truck.

Ignoring the two men, Suvi extended a hand that, once she gripped it, engulfed Gabe's own strong and capable hand. Gabriella Warren had never been considered petite but, for the first time in as long as she could remember, she felt tiny, and a little intimidated.

"Vesuvius Jones. Folks call me Suvi."

"Gabe Warren."

"That probably goes without saying. You're a legend."

"Takes one to know one, I guess," Gabe said and smiled.

"I'm not even in your league," Suvi said, returning the smile, "but I wondered if you'd have time to talk to me a minute."

"I do have time. Is now okay?"

"Uh, sure, if I'm not interrupting," Suvi said.

"Not at all. We can go inside the office. It's not entirely set up yet, but it's clean."

"I heard." Suvi looked pointedly at the two men standing sheepishly behind Randy's truck.

Randy reddened immediately and nudged Mac. "Nice meetin' you, Ms. Warren. See ya tomorrow, Suvi."

Suvi reached around Gabe and pulled the office door open.

"What was that all about?" Gabe asked over her shoulder as she entered the building.

"A mistake in judgment, mostly," Suvi said. "I'll tell you later."

151

By the time Suvi Jones and Gabe Warren got around to discussing real estate, the two athletes had forged an easy friendship that included a tee time at Suwannee Valley Country Club for Saturday morning. Suvi was a little rusty, he was certain, but he had no intentions of turning down a golf game. Lord knows it was hard enough to find a golfer in Fletcher County, let alone one who invited him to play.

"So, tell me what you're looking for, exactly," Gabe said. "I've seen your house. It's gorgeous. Why do you want to move?"

"Well..." Suvi paused and leaned forward in his chair. "That's a difficult question to answer."

"Oh, Lord, here we go," Gabe laughed. "Spill it, sir. It'll do you good to say it out loud."

"I don't know that it's all *that* bad. I just want a change, that's all. The house is too big, for one thing."

"And the location isn't a concern?"

Suvi frowned, setting his lips in a grim line.

"Not on my part," he said. "I like my neighborhood fine. It's close to town. I can walk to work anytime I want."

"But you want to sell it now, so what are you looking for that's different?"

"I don't know, something smaller maybe?"

"You want some land to work? Something out in the country?"

"Shoot, no!" Suvi shook his head to emphasize the point. "I have enough work to do without trying to take on a bigger yard."

"What's the mortgage like on your house? You owe a lot?"

"Nope, my house is bought and paid for."

"Oh, good, I was afraid you'd be upside down in it."

"What's that supposed to mean?" Suvi was clearly annoyed.

"Okay, wait," Gabe raised her hands in mock surrender. "I need to back up. I have a tendency to come on strong, which is not going to help me get off on the right foot here. I wasn't trying to offend you."

"I don't know that I'm offended," Suvi said. "I'm just not sure what you're getting at."

Gabe sighed. "I don't know how to be anything but brutally honest. You can fire me before you even hire me, but I can't dance around anything just to make a buck."

"Dance around *what?*"

"You built that house on the edge of...what is it they call your neighborhood here?"

Suvi dropped his head and shook it side to side, blowing his breath out through pursed lips. When he looked back up, he said, "Obviously, you've already heard."

"The Quarters," Gabe said. "The *Quarters*, for God's sake. What does that even mean?"

"Everybody calls it the Quarters, even the residents. It's just always been that way."

"Now you know you don't believe that. They are referring to *slave* quarters and you know it. I almost didn't move here when I heard that."

"So why did you?"

"I'll just call us even and say 'that's a difficult question to answer,' but in the meantime, let's be real - your house is not going to be an easy sell. It's a mansion on the edge of the poorest neighborhood in this whole county."

"It's not a mansion," Suvi said.

"Compared to the houses around it, it is."

"So, what, I should just stay put?"

"I'm not saying that. I'm saying we need to be realistic about what you can expect to get out of the house. Comps will not do you any favors here. But, that's why I asked if you were upside down. If you own it outright, it may not matter that you won't get what the house is worth."

"So how much do you think it's worth?" Suvi asked.

"I need time to research it – pull some comps, if I can find any."

"How much time do you need?"

"Not much. You in a hurry?" Gabe rummaged through her desk drawer and pulled out a file folder labeled *New Client Forms*.

"Not at all. I just made up my mind to move the other day," Suvi admitted.

"Big decision. Why so sudden?" Gabe asked.

153

Suvi turned in his chair as if he were uncomfortable.

"It's kind of personal, actually," he said.

"Oh, okay, my bad…" Gabe began.

"No, no, I didn't mean that. It's a perfectly reasonable question. I can't really put it into words just yet. It just feels like something I want to do, you know?"

"Hey, whatever the reason, I'm happy for the business," Gabe said, smiling broadly. "We'll need to fill out some paperwork and then I'll get started looking."

"So how long is the paperwork going to take? I don't mean to rush you, but I need to get some wood burning in the pit for the lunch crowd."

"Good Lord, you still cook over a pit?"

"Oh, yeah, it's the only way to do barbecue right," Suvi said. "You should try it someday. I make the best barbecue in the county!" Suvi's grin gave him away.

"Let me guess," Gabe said. "You make the ONLY barbecue in the county."

"Bingo!" Suvi slapped his knee for emphasis.

After a brief discussion regarding the legal and financial details of listing a home with Suwannee Realty, Gabe walked Suvi to his truck and shook his massive hand.

"Can't even tell you how happy I am to meet you, Mr. Jones," Gabe said.

"Same here, Ms. Warren," Suvi said, "but I'm pretty sure we could dispense with the formalities at this point."

"We could," Gabe nodded. "Should I pick you up or do you want to meet at the club on Saturday?"

"Let's meet there. I have some shopping to do in Valdosta afterwards."

"Eight-ten tee time, right?"

"You got it," Suvi said and folded himself into to cab of his truck.

"See you Saturday, Mr. Jones."

Gabe turned and, waving one set of fingers over her shoulder, entered her office without looking back.

Gabe Warren

Sometimes I wake up in the mornings and the first thing I think is "Where am I?" That's a product of being on the tour so long. Sometimes you wake up in four different cities in one week. Since I've moved to Fletcher County, the first question tends to be "What in the hell am I doing here?"

Not that this is a bad place to live, it's certainly not. People are people wherever you go, and these people are no better or worse than others. I've been enough places to know that for a fact. But why here? What is the draw? Lot of people asking that. You take Randy Kerner and Mac McConnell – their first thought when they met me was "What can she do for us?" I'm a bit of a celebrity (though I hate the term), I'm bringing both money and commerce to the town, and I have a skill that makes me qualified to be a coach for one of their high school teams. If I was just another woman moving to town, they wouldn't look twice at me.

I, on the other hand, am just the opposite, which makes me an unlikely salesperson. I've been blessed by any standard and, though I worked hard to get what I have, I'm more likely to wonder what I can do for someone else. Don't get me wrong, I don't fancy myself a saint by any stretch, but I've seen towns like this before, where there is incredible potential and very little opportunity. And what it takes to change a town is outsiders moving in, and locals moving out. With my background, I can help on both counts.

Will I coach the girl's golf team? Maybe. But it won't just be made up of little white girls, and won't that cause a mighty little stir?

30
Trunk or Treat

Trunk or Treat was a huge community event on Halloween. It was held at New Harmony, but all the other local Baptist churches pitched in, plus two of the non-denominational churches in the county. Roped off with yellow caution tape, the churchyard became a fairground, with cars backed up to the resulting perimeter walkway. Each trunk sported hand-lettered signs and bags full of treats and various promotional goodies, mostly pencils or bracelets. With a county of only ten thousand people spread over endless acres of farmland, this was the only way the local children could get a decent haul of Halloween candy. A yearly contest of epic proportions, each church tried to outdo the other in quality and quantity - scrumptious cakes for the cakewalk, creative games, and spiritual entertainment in the form of youth praise and worship teams.

The first year Will and Marie moved to Mayhew Junction, they'd been amazed at the displays and the good-natured hospitality. They laughed themselves sick over the family of five who stayed at the event just long enough to eat all the free hot dogs they could hold, send the kids through the candy line twice, and win a cake for each family member before waddling back to their SUV loaded with loot and drunk on sugar.

The next year Marie convinced Will to set up a trunk of healthier treats featuring The Château logo. They dressed up like Laurel and Hardy and passed out homemade granola bars, popcorn balls, cheese straws and peanut butter brownies. The kids weren't terribly excited about their trunk, but the parents loved it, so Marie called it a success. After Marie died, Will didn't have the heart to tackle the event by himself, but he wouldn't miss going for the world. Last year, Beanie went with him; this year he was alone and feeling like the world's biggest creeper. What could he do but watch people? A few greeted him, but no one really knew what to say. He'd been warned three things when they arrived in town: don't run for public office, don't write about the town, and don't ever expect to be anything but a foreigner. He sure felt like one tonight.

He half expected to see Beanie and Suvi there and he braced himself for the possibility, but lo and behold, Beanie was there with Bubba John and the kids. Funny…Bubba John was the only one who looked out of place, given that everyone else was in costume. It was the only time Will ever saw Beanie blend in with a crowd.

Of course, tongues were wagging at the sight of them together. Will noticed the whispers and looks of shock and disapproval everywhere they went. Bubba John held Daisy on his shoulders, B-Kay kept a tight hold on Bitty's hand and T-Ray rode Tater on his back. It didn't take long for Beanie to notice the gasps and stares - she excused herself to go listen to the Primitive Baptist youth tackle shape notes with their own little twist. They weren't allowed to play any instruments, but they had obviously been listening to a variation of *a capella* music that was a bit less strident and it showed. Beanie knew all the old hymns and hummed along with them, tapping her foot in time to the rhythm.

"Great band, huh?" Will said, stepping into the space beside Beanie.

Beanie grinned when she saw him. "Will!" Of course, it sounded to him like she said, "Wee-yull!" but that, too, was music to his ears.

"Hey, Bean."

"They's a lot better than they was last year. Them kids've been workin', I'm tellin' ya."

"Where's Suvi?"

"Oh, he's at home, I guess. He didn't want to come. Says it's too early for anything quite so public."

The tempo changed with the next number and Beanie clapped along enthusiastically.

"This here was my diddy's favorite song," she said and clutched her hands beneath her chin.

Then she sang the words of the old hymn - her soprano voice sweet and pure and lovely, Will thought. He knew he shouldn't stare, but he could not look away.

"You're so pretty," Will said, then gasped when he realized he said it out loud.

"What'd you say?" Beanie clearly did not hear over her own voice.

"I said it's pretty," Will raised his voice a bit. "The music, I mean. It's pretty, isn't it?"

"I never get tired of hearin' it. My diddy knew ever' song in the Sacred Harp hymnal. Wore the cover slap off that little book, but he didn't even need it for the words. I 'member him sayin' he just felt nekkid without holdin' it out in front of hisself. He's prolly rollin' in his grave right now, though."

"How come?"

"Well, they got somethin' a little diff'ernt goin' on there. That ain't like they usually sing it in church."

"It's nice, though. I like it." *I like you,* Will thought, but this time held his tongue.

The song ended and the group took a break while the emcee for New Harmony pulled a few raffle tickets.

"Wanna go get a hot dog?" Will asked.

"Oh, prolly ought'n to do that. People may get the wrong idea."

"What people? Everyone here thinks you're with Bubba John. It's probably the *best* thing you could do."

"You got a point there. I was beginning to feel all scratchy inside walkin' around with Bubba and the kids. But I guess I was talkin' about Suvi anyways."

Will bit his tongue at that. He wanted to say, *if Suvi cares so much about who you're with, maybe Suvi should be here with you.* But he didn't.

"I'm hungry. How about you?"

"Starvin' half to death," Beanie said. "I hope they got some of them chocolate chip cookies left Cleo Roberts makes. They usually go pretty fast, but sometimes she saves me a few, 'cause I always bring her cranberry chutney at Christmas…"

Beanie chattered on like that through two hotdogs and four cookies apiece, and Will couldn't remember a better Halloween in his life. That is until Suvi showed up and ruined it all.

158

31
The Aftermath

At the café the next morning, Sissy approached the round table with a pot of coffee and two glasses of water. It was early yet, but half of the usuals were uncharacteristically absent.

"Anyone see Suvi?" Sissy asked. "He ain't missed a mornin' since his mama died. I'm kinda worried."

Conversation halted in all directions. Randy, Clyde and LouWanda stared at Sissy like she'd grown a third eye. LouWanda was the first to break the silence.

"You ain't heard?" LouWanda could scarcely contain her glee. It gave her immeasurable joy to be the first to break news as juicy as why Suvi Jones wasn't showing his face in public today.

"Heard what?"

"Mr. Jones done showed his butt last night at the Trunk or Treat. I ain't never seen Beanie Bradsher so fired up in all my life."

"My wife said Suvi had it comin' to him," Clyde Owensby chimed in. "But I don't know. I'm inclined to take Suvi's side of things. I don't like to talk outta turn, but seems to me Beanie's gotten a little full of herself now that she's won the lotto and all. First Bubba John, then Suvi, then Will Thaxton. I don't know who she's gonna turn her feminine wiles on next."

"I hope it's me," Eustace grinned and buttered his toast. "I been tryin' to go out with her since we was in high school."

"What in the world happened?" Sissy asked.

"Oh, she just never was much innerested, I guess..."

"No, Useless, at the Trunk or Treat, not in high school, for crying out loud."

"Well, I'm tryin' to tell y'all, but everybody keeps interrupting," LouWanda complained.

"Y'all shush," Sissy said. Not one to get involved in the gossip she heard every single day of her life, Sissy made the exception this time on the grounds that anything keeping Suvi Jones from his routine was something she needed to hear.

"Well," LouWanda leaned forward and cleared her throat, "Beanie Bradsher showed up at the Trunk or Treat big as you please with Sweet Atwater's family in tow. Lord help those poor children, they acted like they didn't think a thing in the world about their daddy takin' up with that woman."

"LouWanda, I don't think there's anything going on with Bubba John and Beanie. She's datin' Suvi Jones. He told me himself." Sissy didn't necessarily want to slow LouWanda down on her story, but it would help if she got the facts straight first.

"Well he told us, too, but that don't make it the truth. Seein' is believin', the way I look at it. Anyways, that was all well and good until Will Thaxton showed up and Beanie just up and took off with *him*. JoDeen Avery told me they was all but dancin' in front of the Primitive Baptist praise team, and that's just askin' for trouble. I like a good square dance myself, but I wouldn't do it in front of a *Baptist*, I'm just sayin'."

"So, where does Suvi come in?"

"Hold on, I'm a'gettin there. So, Will and Beanie ate supper together…you know they do free hot dogs and cake every year, though I don't know how they can afford it for so many people. Anyways, accordin' to JoDeen, Will and Beanie was gettin' along mighty well eatin' hot dogs and all, and they decide to go take a shot at the cakewalk, and that's when Suvi showed up and Beanie hit him square in the face with the cake she just won."

"Wait, wait, wait…" Sissy said. "I'm all for getting to the point, LouWanda, but it sounds to me like you left out some key information. Why did she hit him with a cake? What lead up to that?"

"I don't know exactly. I walked over to get something to eat and I was talkin' with JoDeen when the cake incident happened. But I sure saw Beanie Bradsher after the fact. She was fit to be tied, I'm tellin' ya."

"Well, I really don't like to gossip," Randy said. "But I was sittin' right across from the cakewalk with my wife and I saw the whole thing. The crowd thinned out in the Trunk or Treat line and Diane and I were laughing at Beanie trying to see the

160

little squares underneath her skirt. They put those numbers awful close together and she kept stopping to try to see, and Will kept runnin' into her. We thought it was awful funny. Everybody was laughing at 'em, even the kid in front of Beanie who kept gettin' tickled on the legs by her ruffles."

"Lord, that girl is a spectacle, that's for sure," LouWanda shook her head.

"I don't know, LouWanda. Beanie's just Beanie. She's always been that way. My wife and I think a lot of her, if you want to know the truth. She altered my niece's dress two days before her wedding and didn't charge her a dime. And you shoulda seen the way she had to wrestle with all them ruffles to get em to match up. My wife told Shayna not to go to the Bridal Mart over in Butler. Anyway, you got it right Suvi got a face full of cake. He sure did."

"But why, Randy?" asked Sissy. "What did he do? He musta done *something*?"

"Well, I'm not sure exactly. I can only go on what I saw, but Suvi looked a little irritated when he showed up. I noticed him walking across the courtyard of the church just as they called Beanie's number. Will poked her and tried to get her to look down to see she was standing on it, but she was looking at Suvi. She started hopping up and down like a little bird, but I can't really be sure if that was because of the cake or if she was just happy to see him. Next thing we know, Suvi's carrying Nell Wiggins' red velvet cake with Beanie skipping alongside him like a little girl. Left Will standin' there without a word. They got halfway across the courtyard when Beanie wheeled around in front of Suvi and started hollering something at him. I couldn't hear what she said, but she sure looked mad. Suvi all the sudden shoved the cake at her and, instead of takin' it from him, she put both hands underneath that thing and heaved it right up into his face. Then she started cryin' and ran back to find Will, but he was already gone. He left as soon as Suvi picked out Beanie's cake."

Sissy let out a long, low whistle. "If that don't beat all…"

32
Don't Mess with Mama

Monday morning Beanie met Bubba John coming out of the back door of the house.

"Hey, Bean," Bubba John said without slowing down.

"Hey, yourself!" Beanie had one hand on the screen door as Bubba climbed into the cab of his truck. Remembering something she needed from town, Beanie ran to the passenger side and opened the door. "Will you have time to run me into town sometime today? I need a few things from the grocery store and I want to stop by the pharmacy, too. We're about outta gauze for packin' Sweet's wound."

"I'll be back around noon, I think. I'm meeting the contractor out at the house this morning. They're having some issues with the foundation. I'm probably gonna need to go by the building department, so I could take you then. Or if you want to make a list, I'll pick it up when I come home. It'd be nice to eat lunch with Sweet if she's up to it."

"Well, they's some personal things I need to get, so if I could get a ride into town, that'd be better."

"No problem," Bubba John said. "I'll see you at lunch, then."

"I'll fix y'all something nice." Beanie waved over her shoulder and Bubba John pulled away.

Breakfast went off without a hitch and the kids made it out the door on time. Sweet made it to the kitchen just in time to kiss them all goodbye, before taking her coffee to the living room.

Beanie made two plates with toasted bagels and fresh cantaloupe slices and joined Sweet for their morning visit.

"Bubba John says he'll be home for lunch. What sounds good to you?"

"He told me he would try to make it, but the way things have been going lately, I wouldn't set any store in that."

"Ain't that the pure truth?" Beanie shook her head. "But, he said he'd run me into town after lunch, so I'm hopin' nothin' comes up. I'm all outta feminine products and I'm needin' 'em pretty bad right now."

The tears came so fast, Sweet didn't even feel them coming.

"Oh, no...Sweet, I'm sorry. I'm sorry. Oh, me and my big mouth." Beanie leapt up to grab a box of tissues from the coffee table.

Sweet gave what could only be described as a cross between a laugh and a sob. "Who'd have ever thought I'd feel this awful about never having another period? It just doesn't make sense, does it?"

"Of course it makes sense," Beanie pulled five tissues from the box in rapid succession and thrust them into Sweet's hands.

Sweet leaned her head back on the chair, buried her face in the wad of tissues and sobbed for a full minute. Beanie fluttered about her trying to think of what to say or do to make it better. She thought of nothing at all.

When it looked like Sweet's crying had settled, Beanie asked, "Did you...*want*...to have more babies?"

Sweet hiccupped softly and blew her nose.

"Maybe - I don't know. I always wanted to fill my table, and I'm one shy." Sweet laughed then. "That sounded ridiculous. An empty chair is no reason to have another child. What I meant to say is, I just wanted to have the option to have another one. I can't wrap my head around this being the end for me. It's funny, there was a time when I thought there would only be the twins. All those years of trying for the big family I always wanted, and every month I got the answer *not yet.* And now its absence means *not ever.*"

"I'm sorry, Sweet," Beanie said. "Sometimes I could just cut my tongue out."

"It's okay, really," Sweet said. "I'm just having a pity party. I need to remember to count my blessings. Lord knows there are many."

"Now that's the truth if I ever heard it," Beanie said. "I'm gonna leave you alone now so you can finish your breakfast. I'll come back in an hour or so to check on you. You need anything else 'fore I go?"

"Can't think of anything right now," Sweet said, and turned on the morning news program she started watching in the hospital.

As it turned out, Bubba John *was* late for lunch by about an hour. Beanie had made a pot of tomato soup, and had the good sense to wait until he arrived to make grilled cheese sandwiches. She took her lunch to the camper and told Bubba John to just honk when he was ready to go to town.

***

Beanie and Bubba John had only been gone about forty-five minutes when T-Ray burst through the back door and bee-lined for his mama's room. Sweet was napping when he knocked on the door and entered without waiting for an invitation.

"What in the world, son?" Sweet was startled by the entry and concerned by the look on her oldest son's face. "What's wrong?"

"I don't know, Mama, you tell me!" T-Ray dropped his backpack on the floor with a thud.

"I don't know what you're talking about. Has something happened?"

"Uh, *yeah*, something has happened. And you would know it if you weren't lying here in bed pretending nothing's wrong."

Sweet sat up in bed and moved her feet to the center to make room for T-Ray to sit down.

"I think you need to slow down a minute and tell me what you're upset about," Sweet said, patting the bed beside her legs.

"I don't wanna sit down, Mom. I want *you* to get *up!*"

Sweet sighed. "I want that, too, son. But right now, I want you to remember who you are talking to and tell me what the problem is. I can't read your mind."

"The problem is, Mom—the problem *is*—the whole school is talkin' about Dad bringing his girlfriend home right under your nose. So, we're coming home from school and there they are, goin' into the grocery store together, just laughin' and havin' a good ol' time."

164

"Oh, stop being so dramatic, T. Beanie needed some things from the store and your daddy gave her a ride to town, and that's all there is to it. It's not like I didn't know about it."

"Why'd she have to go with Dad? Why didn't she wait for me or B-Kay to take her? What was so all-fired important she had to go right then, huh? Well, I'll tell you something right now, Mom, if you had to listen to everything these stupid kids are saying, you'd be dramatic, too. It's disgusting, Mom, and I can't believe you're letting Dad get away with this shit."

"Whoa, whoa, whoa—stop it right there, son. Your daddy is the most honest man I know…"

"Are you kidding me? He's lying to you every single day, Mom."

"That's enough, T-Ray. I mean it. Don't you open your mouth again, and don't you dare leave this room before I say what I'm going to say," she said, as he picked up his backpack to leave.

"I don't know what it is you think I can do differently right now. I'm doing my best to get better. The only thing in the world that's important to me is my family, and I will not watch it be destroyed. Not by gossip, not by locker room nastiness, and certainly not by my own son. Sit down, T-Ray. Right now. Sit down."

T-Ray dropped his backpack again and took a seat across the room on the edge of a chair that held a stack of clean clothes.

"Your father has never, ever done a single thing to make me doubt his word. Maybe things don't add up right now. Maybe it does look a little weird having the two of them together in town. I'm sorry that's hard for you. I'm sorry kids are being mean. You're going to just have to ignore it until it settles down. Beanie won't be here forever, I can promise you that. But right now, she is here helping *me* and helping *you*, while I recuperate. And I will *not* have you being disrespectful to *any* adult, let alone the three in this house right now who all deserve better."

"Are you done?" T-Ray asked after a moment of silent reproach.

If Thomas Raymond Atwater ever knew he had crossed a line, he knew it at that moment. His mama, recuperating or not, flew out of her bed and crossed the room so fast he fell back in the chair and slid halfway to the floor trying to back up out of her way.

Sweet pointed her finger so close to his face she could feel her son's breath moving rapidly through his nose.

"Don't you *ever* speak to me that way again. Do you understand me?"

T-Ray tried to sit up and she laid one palm on his forehead and shoved him back down.

"Don't move. Don't you *dare* move."

At that moment, there was a soft knock on the door, and B-Kay stuck her head in the room.

"Mama?" she asked, taking in the scene before her. There was her brother, sprawled across a chair, and her mother, in a soft cotton nightgown, looming over him, her breath coming in short, sharp bursts. She turned to look at B-Kay and T-Ray took that opportunity to slide out from under her and make his escape.

Sweet said nothing, just returned to her bed and pulled the covers up to her neck.

33
Trouble is Brewing

"I'm sorry, what?" Sweet asked, not sure she heard her husband right.

"I have a meeting tomorrow about the house," Bubba John explained. "I'm sorry, I forgot about the appointment. Can't B-Kay take you?"

"All the way to Tallahassee?"

"She can drive. Besides, you'll be with her."

"What about school?"

"She can get out early. She hardly ever misses school. We'll write her a note."

"Why can't you just change your meeting time?"

Bubba John sighed.

"Well, I could, but it would be harder than you might think. I'm trying to work around other people's schedules, too."

"Right, and I'm one of the others. Except I should be a bit higher in the priority ranking, don'tcha think?" Sweet asked.

"Honey, *you* are my top priority and you know it." Bubba was annoyed and it showed.

"Actually…"

Not sure she was being reasonable, or if she was simply feeling a little emotional, Sweet stopped herself.

"That's not fair," Bubba said, answering Sweet's unspoken thought, which was just enough to push Sweet beyond reason.

"Not fair?" Sweet whipped her head up and gaped at her husband. "I'm not fair? The situation is not fair? What exactly is *not fair*?"

"Whoa, Sweet…"

"Don't you whoa me, Bubba John Atwater…I've already been whoa'd to damn death. You wanna know what's not fair? What's not fair is me sitting in this chair having to find someone else to take me to the doctor because my *husband* is unavailable. What's *not fair* is me losing all options for having another child.

They took my *womb* out and they didn't ask *me*; they asked *you,* and you didn't want any more kids anyway."

"Sweet, that's not true…"

"It *is* true! It is! And now I'm stuck here in this house being cared for by someone who the *whole town* thinks is sleeping with my husband – and what's worse is, I *like* her. That's what's not fair. And I can tell you this, Bubba, it's a good thing she can't drive, because if you let *her* take me to the doctor while you go see someone who's too important to change a meeting time, I'd lose my entire mind and not just the fragment of it I'm losing right now."

For the next minute or so the room was quiet, save for Sweet's ragged breathing and occasional sniffle. Bubba John said nothing, just stared at the floor. The silence was broken by the squeak of the back door. They both looked up then, expecting to see Beanie entering through the kitchen, but the room was empty, which meant she'd already been there and left.

Bubba stood then, looked toward the kitchen and back again.

"I'll take you to the doctor tomorrow," he said. "Right now, I'm going to go take a walk, because on the scale of fair and unfair, that was off the charts, Sweet."

Bubba John snagged his ball cap and his cell phone from the kitchen table before exiting through the back door.

Sweet was in bed when her husband returned fifteen minutes later. That night, for the first time in all the years they'd been married, Bubba John Atwater slept on the couch.

The next morning Sweet woke to find a note on the kitchen table.

Gone to Live Oak for meeting. Back in time to take you to Tally. Beanie said she'll do breakfast. Coffee in pot is ready to brew. Just hit go.

34
Time to Face the Music

At 6:30 that same morning, Suvi Jones walked into the Mayhew Café, morning paper in hand, as if he hadn't been missing in action for over a week now. He took his customary place, nodded at Sissy with a grimace that hinted at a smile, ruffled through the paper to find the sports page and snapped it open – all without glancing once at the round table. Had he looked, he'd have seen five regulars frozen in mid-conversation, eyes darting from one to the other with occasional sidelong looks toward Suvi himself.

LouWanda found her tongue first. Leaning forward, she used a stage whisper loud enough for aging ears to hear.

"Lord love a duck. Look what the cat drug in."

"It's been over a week," Randy Kerner said. "I thought he was never comin' back."

Sissy bumped the back of Mac McConnell's chair with her knee.

"Close your mouths and stop staring for cryin' out loud." Sissy refilled four cups, waited with coffeepot in the air while LouWanda drained the last drop from her cup, then refilled that with a bold pour that lasted less than two seconds and left the cup filled to the rim without spilling a drop.

"Well, can you blame us?" Clyde asked. "I thought he'd never show his face in town again."

"Prob'ly took him that long to get the cake off of it," Mac boomed, breaking into a wheezing laugh at his own joke.

The other four managed to contain themselves, but only barely.

"Knock it off," Sissy hissed between clinched teeth. "I ain't never throwed nobody outta here, but don't you bet I won't."

"S..s...sorry," Mac wheezed. "I c...cain't help it!"

"Well, go on outside 'til you can," Sissy said. "You're embarrassin' yourself."

Mac heaved his bulk out of the chair and stumbled out the front door. The others, chastened, but still slightly tickled, suddenly got busy looking at menus they hadn't used in ten years. Sissy, shaking her head in disgust, walked away muttering to herself.

When she got to Suvi's table, she sat an empty cup on the table and filled it carefully.

"I'm sorry about them," Sissy said.

"No need to be," Suvi said grimly. "I've learned to tune them out."

"You don't need a tuner. You need volume control, darn their hides. Whatcha havin' this morning?"

"Over easy with bacon," Suvi said. "I guess everyone knows, huh?"

"What they don't know, they make up."

"God's truth, isn't it?"

"Yep," Sissy said and went to put in the order.

Suvi had taken cover behind his paper when Will Thaxton walked in. The full house he'd had for the weekend all left the day before, so he decided to take the morning off.

Will was not accustomed to eating breakfast out at all, let alone enough to know where all the regulars sat at the Mayhew Café. So, he chose the quietest table he could find, which happened to be right across from Suvi Jones. Will sat facing the wall of newspaper without considering who might be behind it.

Sissy greeted him almost immediately.

"Hey, there. Long time no see. You having coffee this morning?"

"Please," said Will.

Will grabbed one of the menus propped between the napkin holder and condiments and winced when his fingers stuck to the plastic covering. He opened the menu using just his fingertips on the edges and laid it flat on the table, then made a mental note to wash his hands before his food arrived.

When Sissy came back with his coffee, Will ordered a Western omelet, egg whites only. That got Suvi's attention. He folded down a corner of his paper to see who ordered eggs without yolks and found himself face to face with Will Thaxton.

Had anyone been paying attention at that moment, they'd have seen two men in the throes of silent struggle.

Will spoke first.

"Morning, Suvi."

"Will." Suvi nodded once. "Egg whites, huh?"

"Watching my cholesterol."

"Hmph," Suvi said, and turned back to his paper.

Will slid back his chair and stood, casting a shadow over Suvi in the morning slant of sun. Suvi, without looking up, folded his paper and stood, expecting to face Will directly. He raised his head in time to see Will pass by on his way to the restroom. Now standing with nowhere to go, Suvi surveyed the room to see if anyone noticed. Sissy appeared from behind the buffet, Suvi's breakfast in hand.

"You leavin'?" Sissy asked.

"No. Huh-uh. I was…uh…stretching my legs," said Suvi. "You know…knee still bothers me some."

"Oh, okay." Sissy set two plates of food on the table and squinted at Suvi. "You all right?"

"Yeah…yeah, just hungry," Suvi said.

"Sorry it took so long. They're kinda backed up in there. You sure you're okay? You look mad."

"Nope. I'm good." He made a show of bending and flexing one very long leg before sitting back down in his chair. He was just settled in when Will returned from the restroom, drying his now clean hands on a white paper towel. Neither man acknowledged the other.

For the next five minutes Suvi focused on nothing but eggs, bacon, toast and pancakes. Will fiddled with his cellphone, sent a quick text to his daughter asking when she might have time for a vacation, and downloaded the app he deleted two days prior because he thought he might be addicted to playing card games, not to mention the fact that he really didn't like being reminded of his current situation.

Solitaire, indeed, he thought as he tapped the screen to deal a new set of cards.

And then, *damn these sound effects,* as the shuffling cards announced his pastime to the entire room.

Suvi chuckled.

"What's so funny?" Will asked, clearly not amused.

"Nothin'," Suvi said. "I play the same game. Drives me nuts."

"What's your best score?"

"Who knows? I keep deleting the app and starting over. If I don't, I'll stay on it for an hour, trying to get one second faster."

"Ha! Me, too," Will said, finally cracking a smile.

After an awkward moment of silence, Suvi stood and folded his paper under his arm.

"Have a good day, Will," Suvi said.

"You, too, Suve," said Will.

Suvi brushed past Will's table, handed a bill to Edwina at the register and nodded in Will's direction.

When Will finished his breakfast and asked for his check, Sissy told him someone had already taken care of the bill.

Will chuckled to himself on the way out the door.

"Well played, Mr. Jones. Well played."

35
If Loving Him is Wrong

Bubba John managed to get Sweet to Tallahassee for her one o'clock appointment, but with only minutes to spare. The ride over was anything but comfortable. Sweet was apparently not speaking to her husband at all. Bubba John noticed, but did not comment, preferring stony silence to a fight he could not win. It wouldn't be the first time Bubba John Atwater decided to wait it out, but it would be the longest time by far.

When the couple returned home, Sweet went straight to her room and later advised Beanie that she would be taking her supper in bed. At the dinner table, the kids were unusually quiet.

That is, until a fight broke out between Tater and Bitty about who got more french fries. Beanie, by now used to squabbles over how much juice and which superhero cups were used, quickly settled the matter by dropping more fries onto Bitty's plate. This allowed a brief reprieve while Bitty did a recount.

B-Kay finished off her burger quickly and unbuckled Daisy from her high chair.

"Time for a bath, Daisy-may," she said.

"Mommy do it," Daisy howled immediately.

"Mommy's sick, baby," B-Kay said. "Sissy do it."

"NO Sissy do it," Daisy wailed as B-Kay lifted her from the chair and headed down the hall.

"What's wrong with Mommy," Tater asked after the bathroom door shut.

"Mom's fine," Bubba John said. "The wound is healing like they expected. She's just not feeling good right now."

"She looks pissed if you ask me." T-Ray said, stuffing a spoonful of baked beans into his mouth.

"T-Ray!" Bubba John scratched his head and weighed his options. "Watch your mouth, Son."

"Well, she does. She's snapping at everybody. Even Daisy."

"Mom's a little upset with me right now, not you guys."

"Jeez, Dad, what'd *you* do?" T-Ray rolled his eyes.

Bubba John decided to ignore the obvious dig.

"Well, I don't think I prioritized things exactly right. Honestly, she's just a little touchy right now. I promise you, Mom will be all right when she feels better."

"Seventeen." Bitty announced. She gazed proudly at the row of fries arranged side by side from shortest to longest.

"Eat up, Bitty," Beanie said. "You're next in the tub."

"I'm full," Bitty said.

"Then why'd you make such a fuss over how many fries you had?"

"Only ten before. Now seventeen!" Bitty said triumphantly.

"Lord, help," Beanie said and smiled in spite of herself.

"I'll take her," T-Ray said. "You, too, Tate. Come on before the bathwater's cold."

"Thanks, T," Bubba John said. "I'll help Beanie with the dishes."

Beanie loaded the dishwasher while Bubba John cleared the table and put the leftover food away. They worked in silence for a while, neither having anything in particular to offer as a conversation starter. Besides, both were busy thinking of the person they'd rather have beside them in the kitchen.

Since the one day she talked to Sweet about smacking Suvi in the face with a cake, Beanie had not shed another tear over him. She figured when his ego was less bruised, he would call and things would go back to normal - or as normal as it ever had been. So, it came as a complete surprise to Beanie that, here she was, standing in some other woman's kitchen, thinking about a man who had never been hers to begin with, and missing him with a fierceness that made her stomach hurt. When she spoke, it was to herself and not Bubba John, whom she had forgotten was even in the room.

Beanie Bradsher slammed the door of the dishwasher shut and punched the start button.

"Oh, my God," she said, cupping her own face with both hands. "I *miss* him."

Bubba John, startled by the intensity of her admission, said the first thing that came to mind.

"Suvi?"

174

Beanie looked up at him, wide-eyed and incredulous.

"Noooo," she whispered as tears pooled over her bottom lashes. "Will!"

***

Beanie knocked on Sweet's bedroom door fifteen minutes later under the pretense of gathering her supper dishes, but what she really wanted was advice. How to ask for it, however, did not come naturally to Beanie Bradsher. She'd never had what you could call a best friend. She had cousins for playmates growing up, but they always found Beanie peculiar, and vacillated between bullying and ignoring her.

"Come in," Sweet said in a tone that sounded more like *go away*.

Beanie pushed the door open and poked her head in through the gap. The nightlight in the bathroom provided enough illumination to see Sweet sitting up in bed in an otherwise dark room.

"I just come to check on ya. You okay?"

"Yeah, a little tired is all," Sweet said. "Come on in."

Beanie entered the room and crossed in front of the bed to take Sweet's dishes from the bedside table.

"Kind'ly dark in here. You want me to turn on the lamp?"

"No, thanks. Dark suits my mood."

"I'm sorry," Beanie said. "Can I get you anything? You want dessert or somethin'? Sometimes pie helps."

"I don't think pie will do it this time, but thanks anyway," Sweet said. "Are the kids okay?"

"They's all fine. Last I looked B-Kay was a'readin' to the babies. They like it when she does that."

Sweet nodded and felt herself choking up. "I feel incredibly grateful and guilty at the same time."

"I know the feelin'." Beanie hung her head and stared at the floor.

Sweet turned on the lamp beside her bed and peered intently at Beanie's face.

"What are you saying?"

"I was kind'ly hopin' you'd ask. They's somethin' botherin' me and I don't know who else to talk to about it. I know it's wrong, given the situation and all, but I don't know what to do now..."

"I'm all ears," Sweet said.

"You sure? I don't wanna..."

"What is it, Beanie?"

"I think I'm in love with someone and it ain't Suvi," Beanie said.

Sweet pulled the bedcovers up to her chest.

"Go on..."

"Well, Bubba John and I was in the kitchen a little bit ago and I was thinkin' about how nice it was to have somebody in there helpin' me. So, then I realized I wasn't even thinkin' about Suvi, like I prolly ought to be, seein' as how I been kind'ly datin' him, though that's still up in the air 'cause he ain't even called since I humiliated him in front a'God and everybody. But anyway, then it hit me what I *was* a'thinkin', and I started feelin' guilty about it, and now I don't even know what to do with all this *feelin'* goin' on inside me, 'cause quite frankly it ain't never really happened exactly thisaway before." She paused to take a gulping breath. "And these feelings just came over me so sudden-like. You know what I mean?"

"Honestly? No, I'm not sure at all what you mean."

"Well, I am just the last person in the world that would ever want to hurt anybody."

"No..." Sweet stared hard at Beanie for a moment and tried desperately to weigh her words with care. "I can't imagine why you think it's all right to stand here and tell me what you are feeling, when you know there is not a damn thing I can do about it right now, especially in my condition."

Beanie's chin quivered and the dishes she held rattled in her hands as her whole body began to shake.

"I didn't mean to upset you, Sweet. Really I didn't."

"I think you need to leave now."

"Please don't be mad at me, Sweet. I shouldn't a'said anything..."

"Get out!" Sweet said, clinching the sheets of her bed with both hands.

176

Beanie fled down the hallway, through the dining room, past Bubba John preparing coffee for the next morning, and out the back door without stopping to deposit Sweet's dishes in the kitchen sink. Bubba John quietly finished his task, and settled onto the couch to sleep which, of course, did not happen.

36
The Lightbulb Goes On

Saturday morning was less chaotic in the Atwater household. T-Ray usually slept late, but B-Kay found it too hard to change her school routine and was often up before the little ones, who were perfectly happy to wander like little drunkards to the living room to watch cartoons. At some point, someone would thrust a bowl of dry cereal and a sippy cup of milk in front of each child and call it breakfast. This morning Daisy climbed up onto her sleeping father, nestled herself in the crease between his torso and the couch and promptly nodded off. Bitty and Tater managed to get the television set turned on and were sitting side-by-side in near catatonic states watching SpongeBob SquarePants when B-Kay entered the living room. Tater barely blinked, chubby fingers going slack when B-Kay pulled the remote out of his grip to lower the volume on the theme song's grating finale.

Seeing no need to interrupt or wake anyone, B-Kay shuffled to the kitchen to start a pot of coffee and look for something to eat. Beanie came in the back door just as B-Kay slid a bagel into the toaster oven.

"Mornin', B," Beanie said softly. "You the only one up yet?"

"Little ones are in the living room. Mom and T-Ray are still sleeping, though."

"You think I should make a big breakfast this morning? I got plenty of sausage and eggs."

"Ugh," said B-Kay. "That just sounds like a lot of work and a *lot* of cleanup. I think we're okay today. I don't know what Daddy is planning, but I can make Mama something to eat if she's hungry."

"She don't seem to be eatin' real good," said Beanie. "I think I upset her the other night."

"She stays upset these days."

"She's been recuperatin' a long time. I'd be outta sorts, too."

B-Kay shrugged. "All I know is, I'm ready to have my mom back. Dad, too, for that matter."

"Speak of the devil," Beanie said, nodding toward the doorway.

Bubba John appeared in the dining room holding a sniffling Daisy in one arm. A wet spot covered the front of his t-shirt and down one side of his sweatpants.

"Uh, we had a little accident here. Can somebody change her while I go take a shower?"

Without waiting for an answer, Bubba John deposited Daisy into B-Kay's arms.

"Oh, yuck," B-Kay twisted her sister's body away from her own in an attempt to stay dry. "Shoot, she hasn't wet the bed in weeks now. What in the world?"

At that, Daisy sniffles turned into full-bore tears.

"It's okay, baby, *somebody's* got you," B-Kay said, shooting a wry look over her shoulder as she left the room, which neither Beanie nor Bubba noticed.

"Is that coffee I smell?" Bubba asked.

"Yeah, B-Kay made it already. You want me to fix you a cup?" Beanie was already searching for mugs in the cabinet above the coffee pot.

"Do you mind? I don't think I ought to be in the kitchen with..." Bubba John trailed off, looked down at his soaked clothing.

"Gosh, no, it'll just take a minute. Lemme get the milk for Sweet's coffee and you can take that in to her, too."

"I'm not sure she's talking to me yet," Bubba John's face reddened at the thought.

"You and me, both," Beanie said.

"Really? What happened?" Bubba John took the two mugs of coffee Beanie held out.

"I don't rightly know what set her off, but she threw me out of her room the other night."

"She did what?"

"She told me to get out, and she meant it, too. I guess you didn't notice I been sendin' her food in with B-Kay the past couple of days." Beanie opened the refrigerator door and peered through a maze of condiments and juice boxes. "To tell the plain

179

truth, I'm a little worried about her. It ain't like her to go off on me like that. Where in the world is the milk?"

"Did she say anything in particular? I mean…like about the rumors and all?"

Beanie whirled to face Bubba John. "What?"

"Well, you know…the rumors with the lottery and everything, kind of got the town talking. I think Sweet's feeling a *little* insecure."

"About what?" she asked, punctuating the last word with a slam of the refrigerator door.

"About you and me."

"You and me *what*?" Beanie's voice rose an octave, which made it more like a squeal.

"I thought you knew…"

Beanie cupped her ears with both hands. "And Sweet thinks it's true, too?"

"Did you not hear us arguing the other night? I thought I heard you leave in the middle of it."

"Well, I stuck my head in, but I left real quick when I heard y'all yellin'."

Bubba put both cups of coffee down on the counter.

"Sweet got it in her head that there was something going on between you and me. I thought I'd gotten it settled before you moved in, but it's looking like I was mistaken."

Beanie sat down at the end of the table, too stunned to speak for a moment.

"How did this happen?" Beanie was speaking more to herself than to Bubba John. "How in the world did this happen?"

"Well, first it was the kids at B-Kay's school, but that was back when we got the lotto winnings and had to go to the lawyer together."

"B-Kay thinks so, too?"

"Not anymore."

"So wait… You knew they was gossip about me and you *before* you brought me out here to take care of Sweet?"

"Well, yeah," Bubba John's nervous hands found his pockets as his shoulders went up in an embarrassed shrug.

180

"Then why in the Sam Hill didn't you tell me about it? I bet I am the laughing stock of the whole town right about now. I thought Will was just bein' jealous when he accused me of sleepin' with ya. I had no idea Sweet thought it, too." Beanie doubled over in her chair. "This is just a mess – a mess, and it's your fault, Bubba John Atwater. You shouldn'ta never hired me in the first place. I'm goin' in to talk to Sweet right now. I ain't havin' her thinkin' bad of me."

Bubba John moved to stop her from storming out of the kitchen. "Bean, you can't tell her the whole truth. I gotta get this house built first." He looked desperate.

"I don't even understand why you're tryin' to surprise her with a house, for crying out loud. That's the dumbest thing I ever heard. It's *never* gonna work!"

Bubba John sat down in the closest chair he found. He looked at her for a moment as if puzzling over something complex.

"You really think so? It's a dumb idea?"

Beanie couldn't help but take pity on him, even as mad as she was.

"Well, maybe not totally dumb, but I don't know how you're gonna do it. It's crazy, really. And truth be told, if you don't do something about how your wife's a'feelin' right now, you ain't gonna have a wife left to surprise. I'm just sayin'..."

"What should I do?" He had never been more sincere.

"Well, first off, you gotta convince her we ain't...you know...what we ain't *doin'*. And I can prolly help on that, 'cause I am not the least bit interested in you and never have been. That's just crazy."

"Thanks, Bean," Bubba John said.

"Well, the feeling's mutual, and that don't hurt *my* feelings none. Oh, how did this happen?"

Beanie faced the sink, put her head in her hands and wept. Bubba John stood and moved toward her, laying one hand on her arm. "Don't cry, Beanie. You're right. If it'll make you feel better, I'll go tell Sweet the whole truth right now. I don't want you to be upset."

Beanie raised her head and sniffled. "You would do that for me?"

Bubba John nodded. "I didn't set out to make such a mess of things. I really didn't."

Beanie wiped her eyes with the drying towel. "It's okay. You was just actin' outta love, that's all. I'm okay. We'll wait 'til the house is done and then she'll know the truth, and that's all that matters."

Neither of them noticed T-Ray enter the kitchen and leave as quickly and quietly as he came.

When the dishes were done, Beanie took off her apron and went to clear up the misunderstanding with Sweet.

***

Moments later, Beanie squared her shoulders and knocked firmly on Sweet's bedroom door.

"Who is it?" Sweet's voice was weak and shaky.

Beanie opened the door and peeked her head inside.

"It's me," Beanie said. "Can I talk to you a minute?"

"I'm barely awake," Sweet said, though she'd been up for over an hour. "Can it wait?"

"Actually, no."

Beanie brought the rest of her body into the room and closed the door behind her. Finding no other place to sit, Sweet perched at the end of the bed and took a deep breath.

"Sweet, I ain't the least bit interested in your husband," Beanie said. "I don't know what exactly put you in mind that I was, but nothin' could be further from the truth, and I'm just sorry, sorry, *sorry* that you have been spendin' your recuperatin' time a' worried about such a thing."

Sweet sighed and covered her face with both hands.

"You don't believe me," Beanie said. "Sweet, I swear to you. I know you don't know me that well, but you do know Bubba John and, honest to God, he just ain't the type. And even if he was, I ain't at *all*. I'd sooner be boiled in oil than to fool around with somebody's *husband*..."

Beanie tried to choke back the tears that sprung up with the last word, but failed.

Sweet groped for a tissue on the bedside table and shoved it toward Beanie, who took it with a mumbled, "Thank you."

"Then why in the world did you come in here the other night saying you were having feelings about Bubba John?"

Beanie, by now in the midst of blowing her nose, snapped to attention.

"What in the world are you talking about?"

"The other night!" Sweet said, as if the repetition cleared everything up. "When you were talking about being in the kitchen with Bubba John and you realized you were having feelings for him. And the guilt and all that..."

"I was talkin' about Will Thaxton!" Beanie hiccupped and swiped at her nose with the tissue.

"But...you never once mentioned Will's name," Sweet protested. "I thought you were talking about Bubba."

"Why in the world would I do something so awful?"

"Well, I wondered the same thing," Sweet admitted.

"Exactly! I wouldn't. That's my whole point. I. Would. Not." Beanie punctuated each word slapping the footboard with her fingertips. "And I ain't havin' you thinkin' I would. I don't know what it's gonna take to convince you, but if I cain't, and if you still think I would sneak around behind your back with *your* husband, then I'll just up and leave today. I don't know where I'd go, though I'm sure Will would take me back in, but that'd be a whole nother can of worms, I'll just tell ya. Anyway, I can *find* somewhere to go if I have to, but honestly Sweet I wouldn't let that happen if I were you, because it smells really bad in here and I'm a'thinkin' it's because you need a bath. Whew...that's awful."

Sweet laughed then, but stopped abruptly. "Ow," she said, holding her belly low and tight. "Something's wrong. That really hurt."

"How long has it been smelling like that?" Beanie scrunched her nose up and winced. "I think we need to call the doctor, Sweet. That ain't right."

Beanie looked at Sweet long and hard. She hadn't noticed when she came in; she had avoided looking at her, out of embarrassment she supposed. Sweet's cheeks were flushed bright red. Beanie leaned forward and put her hand on Sweet's forehead.

"You're burnin' up. Can you stand?"

183

"I don't think so. I just feel…weak."

"You stay right there, then. I'm callin' the amb'lance."

Beanie left then, bolting out of the room at a run.

37
Lord Help

Bubba John and B-Kay were still sitting at the table when Beanie came flying down the hallway.

"Where's the phone?" they heard her say as she passed the dining room door.

"What's the matter?" Bubba John asked, but did not rise.

Beanie reappeared in seconds, telephone in hand.

"Here," she said, thrusting it toward Bubba John. "Dial nine-one-one. I'm shakin' too bad to see the numbers."

B-Kay stood, knocking the ladder-back chair to the floor. Without a word, she rushed down the hallway to her mother's room.

"What happened? What's wrong?" Bubba John said, punching the numbers without knowing why.

Beanie grabbed the phone from him and listened for the dispatcher to answer.

"Sweet's real sick," she said, covering the mouthpiece with one hand. "Oh, Lord, I think I done killed her."

Bubba John pushed past Beanie and headed for the bedroom.

"Nine-one-one, what's your emergency?" came the voice on the other end.

"I need an am'blance to Sweet Atwater's house, out here by Miller's Dairy."

"What's the address?"

"I have no idea. Bubba John, what's the address here?" Sweet looked around and realized he was no longer in the room.

"Never mind, I've got it now," said the operator. "What's the problem?"

"Well, Sweet's real sick. She's just outta the hospital, you know, and she was doin' fine, honest she was, and I'm s'posed to be takin' care of her, but she ain't been really talkin' to me for a few days, and I guess nobody's been doin' her repackin', and it smells real bad. Real bad."

"Whoa, whoa, whoa…calm down a second. I need to ask you some questions…"

"Is the am'blance comin'?"

"I'm dispatching it now, but I need to know what's going on. Is the patient awake and breathing?"

Beanie headed back down the hallway.

"Well, she was talkin' to me a minute ago, so yeah, she's breathin' okay. But she's burnin' up and she cain't hardly move for the pain."

"Where is she hurting?"

"Her gut, I reckon. It smells real bad."

"You said that. What smells bad?" the operator asked.

"Where they cut her for the surgery," Beanie snapped. "They was treatin' her for infection 'fore she came home, and Bubba's been takin' her over to Tallahassee for wound care. They've had a drain in, but they took it out a week or so ago. We was just packin' it with gauze."

Beanie entered Sweet's bedroom to find Bubba John kneeling beside Sweet's bed and B-Kay packing an overnight back with clean underwear and nightgowns. A washcloth lay across Sweet's forehead and her eyes were closed.

"What kind of surgery was it?"

"The female kind," Beanie said. "What's it called, Bubba?"

"What's what called?" he asked.

"Sweet's operation."

"She had a hysterectomy. Are they coming? I can load her up and take her over there myself if I need to," Bubba said, standing up.

Beanie waved him back down.

"Hysterectomy. That's what she had," Beanie said into the phone.

"Okay. Is the patient alert? Is she able to walk? I'm trying to determine if she really needs an ambulance or if you should take her to the hospital yourself. We only have one crew working tonight and they're coming back from Suwannee County right now."

"I thought you said they was on the way." Beanie's voice rose to near panic level.

186

"I said I was dispatching them, and I am, but it could be a good thirty minutes before they get there. I can send first responders if she's unconscious or having trouble breathing."

"Naw, she's awake," Beanie replied, then covered the mouthpiece and spoke to Bubba John. "They said least thirty minutes. What do you want to do?"

"Tell 'em never mind, I've got her." Bubba John didn't wait for a response; he wrapped the top sheet and comforter around his wife, lifted her from the bed and carried her to his truck. B-Kay followed with Sweet's overnight bag and tucked it into the back seat.

"I'm going with you, Daddy," B-Kay said.

"I need you to stay with the kids," Bubba John closed the passenger door and crossed behind the truck to get to the driver's side.

"Why? Miss Beanie's here..."

"Go back inside, B. I mean it."

B-Kay spun away from the truck, then turned back and wrenched the front door open.

"Mama?"

Sweet reached up and cupped her daughter's face with a feeble hand.

"Be strong for me, okay? Help Beanie..." Sweet said. Her hand flopped back into her lap and she moaned weakly.

Bubba John settled in beside his wife and reached to fasten her seatbelt.

"Daddy, please..." B-Kay begged.

"She's fine, B. Stay here."

"Mama?"

"Close the door, B-Kay. Close it."

B-Kay, wild-eyed and shaking, closed the truck door and turned to find Beanie with arms outstretched.

"Come on, baby, we'll make some coffee and wait for your daddy to call us, okay?"

Beanie led the frightened girl through the back door and into the kitchen as Bubba John's truck sped down the driveway toward the paved road.

"Sit down at the table and I'll make you something to eat." Beanie guided B-Kay to a chair and pushed her gently into it. B-

Kay had not uttered a word since her father left with his sharp rebuke. "You're shakin' like a leaf. Are you cold? I'm gonna get you some coffee. Do you drink coffee? How 'bout some tea? Now where does your mama keep the tea bags?" Beanie rummaged through the cabinets while B-Kay sat at rigid attention, neither moving nor speaking.

"Here they are," Beanie crowed, holding a box of Earl Gray in one hand and a handful of stray packets in the other. The child still did not move.

"Tea, B-Kay, can you drink some? B? Answer me now, you're scarin' me."

Beanie threw the tea bags on the table, pulled a chair from the side of the table and placed it in front of B-Kay. Then she sat in it and pulled the chair closer, so their knees were touching.

"B...look at me. Your mama is gonna be fine. Your daddy will have her to the hospital in no time and they'll get her fixed right up, you hear me?"

Two tears rolled down B-Kay's cheeks and plopped onto her t-shirt.

"Oh, honey, don't cry...don't. It's go'n be okay."

"How do you know?" B-Kay finally spoke.

"Well, I don't know *how* I know. I just believe she will be, that's all."

"I've been praying and praying and she just gets worse, Miss Beanie. Do you think God is mad at me or something?"

"No, I don't! And I don't think God works that way, honey. I just don't."

B-Kay leaned forward on her elbows and dropped her forehead into her palms with a soft groan. Beanie just sat without speaking and patted her softly on the back as her shoulders shook and tears landed on the floor between her feet.

Moments later, Bitty appeared in the doorway of the dining room.

"What's wrong, Sissy?"

Beanie rose quickly and ushered Bitty back to the living room.

"Come on, baby, let's find something else on TV. You tired of SpongeBob? What do you wanna watch now?"

"Why is Sissy crying?" Bitty's lip quivered.

"Sissy's fine, baby. Are you hungry? Did you finish your Cheerios?"

"Chee-ohs," Daisy piped up.

"I'm *hongry*. I want some shaushage." Tater staggered to his feet and headed for the kitchen.

"Lord help," Beanie said, meaning it. She picked Daisy up off the floor and swung her to one hip. "Okay, everybody to the table. Tater, go get your brother up and tell him I said to get in here now. Bitty, you collect all them bowls and cups and bring 'em with ya. We gotta have a family meetin' this morning."

Shortly thereafter, all five children were seated at the table, though Bitty's head was lolling so much Beanie thought she was going to fall back to sleep sitting up. B-Kay had gotten a grip on her tears, but still sniffled every few minutes.

"What's going on," T-Ray asked, annoyed that his one day to sleep in had been disturbed.

Beanie shushed him before sitting in Bubba John's seat at the end of the table.

"Okay, listen up. Your mama's had to go back to the hospital. Your daddy's takin' her over there himself, and we don't know exactly when they're comin' back."

The table erupted.

"Is she okay? What's wrong? What's the matter with Mama?" All at once.

Beanie held up both hands. "Shhhhh! Listen. Just listen. I don't know exactly what's wrong, but I do know this…your mama's in good hands at the hospital. We're just gonna sit here and have a little prayer together, and then we are going to get busy doing something to take our minds offa this thing until we hear from your daddy. Ever'body bow your head. Who wants to start?"

When no one piped up, Beanie led the way.

"Lord, we got a problem this mornin' and we'd sure like some help, if'n ya got some extry time. We all been worryin' about Sweet Lee – she sure needs a healin' hand today. These babies been doin' all they can while their mama lays sick in the bed, and now it just seems like she's a'gettin' sicker by the day. Lord help us, if you will. Help us with the worry and the fear, help us get right ever' which-a-way we can. And I ask a special

189

prayer for sister B-Kay here. You know what we talked about, Lord, 'cause you know ever'thing. She's a good girl, Lord, and I know she don't mean no harm. Help her feel better in her heart, like I do. I know it's gonna be all right, 'cause you got us in your hand and on your mind. Amen."

Beanie took a deep breath and smacked both palms lightly down on the table.

"Now, I'm gonna fix y'all some breakfast and then we're gonna tackle that laundry out there. It's piled up outta control. Ain't no reason y'all can't help with that. And then we're gonna clean the house, and ever' able body is helping."

"Daisy, too?" Bitty snapped to attention.

"Daisy, too," Beanie said.

"She's just a baby," B-Kay protested.

"She can learn to fold socks's good as the rest of ya."

"I don't know..." B-Kay shook her head.

"Well, we're gonna find out, aren't we?" Beanie said.

It was chaos in the Atwater kitchen for a few minutes, until everyone found something they could do to get food on the table.

***

Bubba John swung his truck through the Emergency Room entrance, took one look inside the sliding double doors, and pulled right on out again. He'd been to the ER on many a Saturday morning when Bitty or Tater had been up all night wheezing, or that awful time the twins both had croup and he and Sweet were just young, inexperienced parents. In a county with only ten-thousand people, there was never a pediatrician close by. When you couldn't leave other children home alone in the middle of the night, you went to the ER the next day. This was the closest hospital around for at least two counties, and it showed this morning. He could clearly see a waiting room filled with sleep-deprived parents and lethargic, nervous, and/or weeping children. He weighed his options within a matter of seconds. He could go in and hope they would airlift her to Tallahassee right away, but that would take every bit of an hour and more. He could drive her there in forty-five minutes.

190

"Baby, I'm taking you on to Tallahassee, okay?" Bubba John scanned the divided highway for oncoming traffic, then pulled out into the center turn lane. He glanced at his wife when she didn't respond.

"Sweet? Honey? Are you okay?" To which she responded with a low moan.

Bubba John punched the gas and felt the truck surge forward. *Too rough,* he thought and eased off a bit. Just a few miles down the road he could take the cutoff over to the interstate highway where he would make better time and not have to fly through the series of small towns along the way.

Sweet moaned again and tried to open her eyes. She reached out a weak hand and dropped it onto Bubba John's lap. Her fingertips dragged down the side of his thigh as her wrist continued its downward motion toward the seat.

"Baby, we're headed for Tallahassee, is that okay?"

No response. Bubba John was clearly not a man of many words, but at this moment he could think of a thousand things he wanted her to know.

"Sweet Lee Atwater, don't you leave me," he began. "I don't know why I don't tell you this, but I would be lost without you. Jesus, God, please don't take her from me. Sweet, stay with me, honey. You're gonna be fine, I promise, and when you get well, you're not going to believe what I have for you. It's a surprise...I know you don't like surprises, and I know you've thought the worst, but really, Sweet, you're gonna love the new house. It's gonna have everything you wanted. And you're not gonna have to worry about anything else, ever again." Bubba pounded the palm of his hand on the steering wheel. "Sweet, wake up. Talk to me, baby."

Sweet turned her head toward him, but did not open her eyes, nor utter a word.

"C'mon, c'mon, people, get out of my way." Bubba John braked behind a car in the left lane, riding directly beside a furniture truck in the right. There were no other cars visible in front of them, yet still the car would not budge. Bubba John flashed his bright lights off and on, then switched his caution lights on. No luck.

191

"Dammit, move!" Bubba John yelled. Using the heel of his hand, he pressed hard on the center of the steering wheel. The horn blared long and loud. Sweet mumbled something he could not understand. He saw the truck driver lean toward his side view mirror, checking to see what the noise was about, and they made eye contact long enough for the driver to realize something was wrong. He slowed immediately, allowing Bubba John to pull into the right lane ahead of him. Bubba John held up one hand, fingers splayed, by way of a thank you salute to the truck driver. He considered throwing an entirely different kind of salute at the offending car, but thought better of it and focused on the road ahead.

"Slow down." Sweet's weak voice was barely audible, but he understood her this time.

"I can't slow down, baby. I gotta get you to the hospital. Are you okay?

"I don't think so," she managed to mumble before closing her eyes. She did not wake again on the long ride to Tallahassee.

38
The Lay of the Land

The next morning was crisp and cool. The sky overhead was bright blue, though the horizon sported a shelf of dark clouds that might have discouraged a visiting golfer. Suvi, however, had checked the weather before he left home and the storm hovering over the coastal waters two counties over was moving more north than east and would most likely miss them. Wind would be a factor, both for golfing and comfort. Still, a light jacket was all he needed and he slipped that on and pulled his golf bag from the back of his truck.

Gabe's dark Mercedes coupe slid into the parking space opposite him just as he shouldered the bag.

"Morning!" Gabe called. "You beat me here."

"By two minutes at most," Suvi said. "Competitive much?"

Gabe's laugh was so loud and abrupt that it startled them both. She clapped a hand over her mouth. "Sorry!"

"Can I get your bag for you?"

"Never," Gabe said, still smiling. "The day I can't carry my own bag is the day I don't need to be golfing anymore." She popped the trunk of her car and slid her hefty leather golf bag out as if it weighed no more than a grocery sack.

"Impressive," Suvi said.

"Wait'll you see my swing."

"I've already seen it. I told you – I'm a fan."

"Yeah, yeah, that's what everybody says, but they actually don't watch us play."

"I watch," Suvi said, and he meant it.

Ten minutes later they were teeing up on the first hole. By the ninth, Suvi was three strokes behind Gabe, but the competitive camaraderie brought out a side of Suvi that he hadn't shown in years and barely even remembered in himself. Suvi Jones was laughing out loud.

***

After Saturday's golf game, Gabe spent a few hours riding through some of the neighborhoods in Fletcher County, though Gabe thought calling some of them neighborhoods was a bit generous. In Jacksonville, where she spent the past several years, there were countless planned communities with names like Summit Crossing and Augustine Oaks, all designed to create a pleasing aesthetic. They often included amenities like clubhouses, pools, and tennis courts, with houses of similar price range, painted various shades of one color scheme.

In Fletcher County, however, they had places like River Acres, marked with a homemade sign on a slab cut from a cypress tree. Dust from the dead-end dirt road leading both in and out of the "development" settled into the grooves left by the chain saw used to procure the wood. The background was painted white, and the letters had been routed by hand and painted red, which made it impossible to correct the sign-makers blunder: the sign read River Acers and no one dared protest.

A half mile down, the dirt road took a hard left and paralleled the river for a little less than a mile, coming to a stop in a small clearing surrounded by barbed wire fencing and "No Trespassing" signs. Along the river, dwellings of all shapes and sizes sat on the perfectly parceled half-acre lots, the only part of the neighborhood that could be described as "planned." On one, a vintage single-wide trailer, which may or may not have seen better days - on another a camper next to a double lot with a tidy gray and white cabin raised up on thick wooden pillars to keep it above the floodplain. Farther down the road another single-wide mobile home, encased in board and batten siding and riding high on concrete pylons sat next door to a two story brick house that had been grandfathered in with regard to new floodplain rules, and was subject to flooding every ten years or so.

An hour or so into Gabe's wanderings, she was beginning to feel discouraged. To begin with, she wasn't exactly sure what Suvi Jones was looking for; his description had been vague from the start. *Downsizing*, he called it. *How far down*, was the question. His house was huge, too big for one man, and a bachelor at that. But Suvi didn't look too old to start a family and he hadn't made a single remark that made her uncomfortable. Maybe he, like herself, was simply a loner. And yet he hesitated yesterday on a question she posed with every potential single client: Do you plan on marrying or starting a family anytime soon?

Important to know, of course. Should she be looking for a bachelor pad or a family home? It was a simple question, and Suvi had paused – squirmed in his chair, which was hard to miss, given his enormous stature. The guy was huge. Not fat, though. What was the word she was looking for? Imposing. Yes, that's it. *Suvi is an imposing man,* she thought. *But definitely not my type,* she added. *Where did that come from? Oh, stop.*

Gabe Warren shook the internal dialogue from her head and focused on the neighborhood next on the map she had printed from her internet search. It was small, somewhat planned – at least the roads were paved. Not on the river, so no floodplain to consider. Still no apparent zoning regulations in effect, since every other house was vastly different from the one before. Most yards seemed nicely kept, though only a few were landscaped. Nothing for sale so far, though. She turned the corner onto a short road that ended at a cul-de-sac, upon which sat a single house with a "For Sale by Owner" sign by the mailbox. Perfect. She stopped, knocked on the door and waited. After no answer, she rang the doorbell and heard it chime loudly inside. When there was still no answer, she grabbed a business card from her purse and stuck it into the doorjamb by the handle. *Every FSBO is a potential client,* her mentor had said repeatedly when she was in training. Gabe was nothing if not proactive. She got back in her car and headed toward town feeling somewhat accomplished with her scouting efforts.

Also on her list of Sunday chores was a stop by The Château to meet Will Thaxton and see about securing a more convenient living space. She had been staying in a hotel out near the interstate, but the distance was taking its toll. She was ready to settle into the town and start looking for a more permanent place to live. She could kill two birds with one stone looking for something for Suvi, as well as for herself. Several people had mentioned the local B & B, which was convenient to her office, being only a few blocks away. She liked the idea of walking to work every day.

She had called ahead to let Will know she was stopping by, but she was still surprised when he met her on the porch.

"You must be Ms. Warren," Will said, offering a firm, though slightly wet, handshake.

"Call me Gabe," she said, and patted her hand dry on the leg of her jeans.

"Sorry about the hand. I've been peeling potatoes for supper. Come on in, I'll show you around."

Gabe followed Will down the hallway and into the kitchen.

"Can I get you a cup of coffee?" Will asked.

"Got decaf?"

"Not in the pot, but I can make some. Won't take a second."

"I don't want you to go to any trouble," Gabe protested.

"No trouble at all. That pot has been sitting for an hour anyway. I could do with a cup of decaf myself." Will washed his hands at the sink and dried them on a hand towel dangling from his belt loop.

"So, do you provide supper, too?" Gabe asked. "I thought it was just breakfast."

Will laughed and shook his head.

"It's supposed to be, but I get a little carried away sometimes. I always tell my guests not to count on it, but the truth is, it's hard to cook for one."

"I hear you," Gabe said, nodding.

Will rinsed the coffee pot and put it back on the burner.

"Sit, sit," he said to Gabe. "As soon as I get this brewing, I'll take you on the big tour."

"I'm in no hurry at all." She sat at the long kitchen table and let her eyes wander around the spacious room. The cook stove was a massive mid-century affair with four ovens, one surely just for warming, she thought. The cabinets were painted white and the floor was covered in black and white tiles laid out in a diamond pattern. Everything was clean, if a little worn.

"So, I know you told me you were looking for a place to stay for at least a month or two," Will yanked Gabe out of her musings. "I hear you're opening a real estate office, is that right?"

"You got it. I'll eventually find something permanent, but I want to take my time and get the right thing," Gabe said. "Not to mention that I kind of need to see if this is even going to work here. I'm having a few doubts, to be honest."

"I know exactly what you mean." Will pushed the brew button on the coffee pot and joined Gabe at the table. "My wife and I fell in love with this place the moment we saw it, but we didn't want to sell our house in Minnesota right away. We thought we'd give it some time, you know, have a backup plan."

"So y'all are happy with it now?"

"Well, I am," Will said. "She's gone now."

"Yikes…and you stayed?"

"No, no…I said that wrong. She didn't leave me…well, she left me, but not like that. What I mean to say, and I'm saying it badly…" Will sighed. "She passed away."

"Oh, I'm so sorry," Gabe said.

"Thank you," Will said. "I keep thinking someday it will get easier to say, but apparently not. I still just trip over the words."

"How long has it been?"

"Gosh, at least five years or so." Will rose to get cream from the refrigerator, grabbed the sugar bowl from the cabinet and placed both by the gurgling pot.

"That's a long time to handle all this by yourself," Gabe said. "Just a little cream in mine, please. No sugar."

"That's how Beanie liked it, too," Will said.

"Beanie? Never heard that one before."

"Short for Beatrice," Will said.

"Beanie Thaxton," Gabe said. "That's a great name."

"What?" Will spun to look at Gabe. His eyes squinted in bewilderment. "Oh, no, no. Beanie wasn't my wife. Beanie just lived here a while. She's gone now, too."

"Oh," Gabe winced at her gaff. "How awful for you…"

"Ahhh, shoot. I'm an idiot." Will shook his head. "Gone. Moved out. Not dead."

"Coffee smells great!" Gabe was not good at deflection.

Will laughed out loud.

"That was smooth. Here you go." Will handed Gabe a hand-thrown pottery mug, one of the ones he used for important guests, which, if he were being honest, were rare.

"Thank you so much," Gabe said and took the steaming cup of coffee from his hands.

"So, let's go see the place, shall we? All of the larger rooms with separate baths are upstairs." Will chatted as he led the way out of the kitchen and up the staircase. "I have two rooms available for long-term rental. One of them is Beanie's old room. She used to live here and helped out in the kitchen, and with some light housekeeping and such."

"Ah," Gabe said.

"She moved out to help another family in need. No biggie," Will shrugged.

"I see." Gabe was not sure what to make of this information, but she got the feeling that Beanie was more important to Will than just kitchen help.

"Okay, so this room is a common area, though we try to keep it a quiet space. There is a computer, a fax machine and a phone with long distance included."

"My cell phone works in town, so I doubt I'll need any of that, but it's good to know," Gabe said.

Will opened the first door off the common area and held it open without looking in. "This is Beanie's room. It has a nice-sized bathroom *en suite*, I guess you call it these days, and a large closet."

Gabe had barely peeked her head inside the door when Will closed it so quickly she had to step back out of the way.

"I think the next one would be more to your liking," Will said.

He led the way to a second door and opened it, waving her inside with his free hand. Gabe entered the room and immediately felt at home. The room was decorated sparsely, but with great care, neither too frilly nor too masculine, but just the right touches of comfort and style. Through the open bathroom door, she could see a deep claw foot tub resting on black and white tile. Tongue and groove wainscoting was painted white, and the plastered walls above it were periwinkle blue. Gabe already had visions of restful evenings that would begin with a nice long soak, a glass of red wine, and a good book.

"I'll take it," she said. "When can I move in?"

"Whenever you like," Will said, "but don't you want to know how much it is?"

"I'm sure it's reasonable," Gabe said. "I'll move in this week."

And with that, Gabe Warren had an apartment a block from her office.

39
Daddy's Home

After a long, sleepless night at his wife's bedside, Bubba John Atwater returned home just before noon on Sunday to a spotless house and five bone-tired children who all lay, still in their pajamas, in various poses across the living room. Not one of them looked up when he entered until Beanie came out of the girls' room with an armload of dirty clothes from the night before and nearly collided with him. This startled her so badly she screamed and flung the clothes upward and outward, sending a pair of Daisy's panties into a spiral of pink that ended on Bubba's shoulder.

"Daddy!" came the chorus from the living room.

"Lord help!" Beanie panted. "You like to of scared me to death."

The little ones dragged and dropped blankets and fuzzy toys across the room as they rushed their father, pushing and shoving to wrap themselves around any unoccupied appendage. This left one arm unencumbered, which Bubba John used to pull B-Kay into a long and healing hug. He kissed the top of her head, and then her forehead when she leaned back and looked up at him.

"Mama's gonna be okay, baby."

With that, B-Kay buried her face in her daddy's neck and sobbed.

Meanwhile, Daisy wailed into Bubba John's kneecap, and Tater repeatedly punched his thigh saying *Daddy! Daddy! Daddy!* Bitty pulled at his hand for a minute, gave up and started counting the freckles on his forearm. Beanie broke the spell.

"Y'all get off your daddy now and sit down at the table," she said to the kids, then looked at Bubba John. "I got lunch fixed. You hungry?"

"Starved," he said, tucking B-Kay's head under his chin.

Moments later, after a loud snuffling breath in, B-Kay pulled away and gagged. "Shew! Why do you smell like pee?"

Beanie plucked the offending pair of panties off Bubba John's shoulder.

"Here, you guys help me get these clothes to the back porch. Come on now, pick up something," Beanie said.

After a full day of chores yesterday, even the little ones had gotten the hang of taking orders. All three of them snapped to attention and quickly gathered the rest of the fallen articles of clothing, which finally relieved Bubba John of his shackles.

"Gross," B-Kay complained, still sniffing back tears.

"Glad to see you, too," Bubba John said. "Mama said to tell you to stop worrying."

"How'd she know I was worried?" B-Kay wiped her nose on the tail of her t-shirt.

"She's your mama, that's how." Bubba John spun his daughter by the shoulder and gave her a little push toward the dining room. "Sit down and I'll tell you all what's going on."

After a general round-up of the straggling siblings, Bubba John explained the situation with their mother.

"Mama's real sick and they need to keep her there for a while. When they get the infection under control, they're going to move her to a rehab center where the nurses can take care of her better, and the doctors can keep an eye on what's going on. Mama said to tell you all how much she loves you and to be good for Miss Beanie while she's in the hospital."

Beanie was in the kitchen tucking hot dogs into buns lined up in a row. She turned and, looking as white as the paper plates lining the countertop, said, "I knew it was my fault she got so sick. I didn't take good enough care of her, did I?"

Bubba John looked up from the head of the table. "No, Beanie, that's not it at all. I promise. It's like they said, she just needed skilled nursing all along. They didn't want to send her home when they did, but Sweet insisted."

"But I wasn't skilled…"

"You're not a nurse, Beanie," Bubba John said. "And besides, you had enough to worry about with these guys. Please don't blame yourself. Honestly, if anyone is to blame, it's me. We've been asking you to do too much all along."

201

T-Ray, still groggy from lounging all morning, finally piped up. "Well, that changed yesterday, Dad. Miss Beanie taught us how to do laundry."

"Well, good, it's about time you and B pitched in a little more."

"Not just me and B-Kay, Dad," T-Ray said. "All of us, even Daisy!"

"Really! I may have to see that one to believe it."

Beanie brought the first three plates to the table. "T-Ray, could you get the rest of them plates for me, and Bitty, you can get the ketchup and mustard outta the 'frigerator."

"She's not playing, Dad," B-Kay smiled for the first time since he'd gotten home. "Daisy's folding the underwear. We tried socks, but she just couldn't get the hang of it. Turns out Bitty's got an eye for matching up size and color. Once we convinced her she could still line them up in order after they were twisted together, she did great."

T-Ray came back balancing three plates just like Beanie had done. "Yeah, and then she reorganized the refrigerator the same way. Now we can all find stuff, instead of asking Mom every time."

"Mama's gonna be so happy to hear that," Bubba John said as Bitty sidled up beside him with condiments in hand. "Great job, kiddo."

Daisy banged on the table with both hands. "I fold dee undies, Daddy!"

B-Kay reached out one hand to still both of Daisy's.

"You did good, baby girl," B-Kay said, then looked up at her father at the end of the table and grinned. "Though *folding* may not be the exact word."

"Lord, B-Kay, you sound more like your mama every day," Bubba John replied, shaking his head."

"I take that as a compliment," B-Kay said, and took a great big bite of her hotdog.

After lunch, Bubba John stretched out on the couch with Daisy and Tater, hoping to distract them into taking a nap. It worked for the youngest, but Tater waited for his father to start snoring, then rolled off of the edge of the couch and onto the floor to play with his race cars. T-Ray went outside to shoot at tin cans with his pellet rifle. B-Kay got herself and Bitty cleaned up and ready to take Beanie into town to run a few errands.

They met back in the kitchen and assessed the situation. Beanie pulled her grocery list from the magnet pad on the refrigerator.

"I'm sure I'm missin' somethin', but hopefully I'll think of it before I get outta the store." Beanie said. "Where's T-Ray?"

"He's outside somewhere."

"Well, we can't leave Tater here with your daddy sleepin'. How about if we take him, too, and y'all can play over at the park while I'm shoppin'?"

"Works for me," B-Kay said. "Come on, Tate, you're going with us."

"Noooo," Tater wailed from the living room. "I don't wanna go to the...where are we going?"

B-Kay stuck her head through the dining room door and looked at her little brother. "To the park."

Tater popped up from the floor. "Can I take my cars?"

"Yes," B-Kay said. "Come on now."

B-Kay headed for the door with a child in each hand. Beanie followed.

"When we get done, I wonder if you'd mind runnin' me by The Château for a minute. I want to talk to Will about helpin' me with my Avon a little bit. I ain't had time to drop any books off and some of my customers is askin' where they can get 'em. I'm hopin' he'll let me leave a few there in the hallway to pick up."

"Do you need me to start delivering some of your books?" B-Kay asked, remembering the times Beanie brought the catalogs into her mother's shop downtown.

"Well, that's a thought," Beanie said, "but I still want to stop by The Château, if'n you don't mind. They's somethin' I need to ask him about besides the Avon."

40
Unexpected Visitor

"Why don't you drop me off at Will's first," Beanie said as she and B-Kay approached downtown Mayhew Junction. "I'll walk on down to the Thriftway when I get done. That way you and the kids'll have plenty of time at the park."

"Ok," said B-Kay. "But how will I know when to come pick you up?"

"Good question." Beanie thought about that for a moment.

"You need a cell phone, Miss Beanie," B-Kay said.

"You're prolly right about that, but I just don't trust myself with one of them things. I got it! I'll just walk over to the park when I'm done. It ain't even two blocks away."

"With the grocery cart?"

"Yeah, it ain't no problem. Mr. Cunningham won't mind. I'll walk it back when we're done and you can pick me up."

"Sounds complicated to me." B-Kay glanced into the rearview mirror at the kids behind her. "Tater, don't eat your boogers."

Bitty laughed. "Boogers."

B-Kay pulled up in front of The Château and Beanie gathered her purse, a stack of Avon catalogs, and the folds of her crinoline skirt and exited the car.

"See you in an hour or so." Beanie waved and turned toward the front porch. She took a deep breath, climbed the porch stairs and paused at the door, wondering if she should knock or just go on in like most folks did. She hadn't yet decided when the front door opened and a woman Beanie had never seen exited with Will close on her heels.

All three exclaimed "Oh" in unison and took a single step back, though Will was a bit slower, and Gabe stepped on his toes.

"Sorry!" Three voices again, which made them all laugh.

"Beanie!" Will said, smiling from ear to ear, despite his throbbing toes.

204

"Hey, Will!" Beanie beamed over Gabe's shoulder.

"Have you met Gabe Warren yet, Bean? She just moved to town and is going to be staying here for a while. I just showed her the two upstairs rooms. She's taking the one next to yours..." Will stopped, embarrassed. "I mean, your old one."

"Well, welcome to Mayhew Junction!" Beanie's Avon training kicked into auto-drive, out of nerves, perhaps, or just years of forcing herself to greet people in a friendly manner despite being a natural introvert.

"So you're Beanie! Will was just talking about you." Gabe smiled and reached to shake Beanie's hand. "Great name, by the way."

Beanie, still processing what Gabe had just said, stared at her outstretched hand for an awkward second, then thrust a booklet into it. "I was just stopping by to drop off my new catalogs. Have you seen Avon's new jewelry line? They's some real pretty stuff in there, and we just got a-whole-nother range of foundations, just right for your own skin color. You got a gorgeous complexion, by the way. What do you use for moisturizin'?"

"Sunscreen," Gabe said.

Beanie wasn't sure if Gabe was joking, but she laughed just in case.

"No, really. I'm out in the sun most days. Sunscreen is the only moisturizer I've ever used. I'm not much for makeup, to be honest."

"Gabe's a pro-golfer, Bean," said Will. "LPGA."

"Oh," said Beanie. "Ooooohhh...I get it. Sorry, I thought you was just makin' fun of me or something."

Gabe laughed then. "No, I wouldn't do that. Not intentionally anyway." She turned to Will and shook his hand.

"Thanks for showing me around. I'll start moving first thing in the morning, if that's okay with you."

"Works for me. Let me know if I can help. There's a trailer out back you can borrow if you need it."

Beanie stepped back out of the way and let Gabe pass. "Nice to meetcha, Ms. Warren."

"Call me Gabe. Hope to see you again, and uh, thanks for the catalog. See you tomorrow, Will."

Will and Beanie watched until Gabe rounded the corner of the porch to the parking area, then they stood awkwardly staring at nothing at all until Will finally spoke.

"It's good to see you, Bean. How's it going?"

"It's going great!" Beanie lied. "Everything's great. The kids are fine. They's missin' their mama, but they're great kids…just great."

He could see her fighting back tears, so he just sat quietly and waited for her to go on.

"Sweet's back in the hospital, though. I don't think I'm doing so great a job taking care of her, 'cause her wound got infected, but Bubba John tuck her over to the hospital again and he says she's gonna be fine. I don't know, though…" She paused and swiped at her nose with the back of one hand.

"How's Suvi?" Will couldn't help himself.

"He's fine, I reckon," Beanie hung her head and stared at the Avon catalogs still clutched in her hand.

"You sure you're okay?" Will asked.

Beanie looked up at Will's sweet face, concern written all over it and something else. Something Beanie wasn't sure about, having not had much experience with people who cared about other people. But in that moment, Beanie saw something safe and open and welcoming, like he was glad she was there and she could tell him anything. And so she did.

"I'm not sure at all, Will," Beanie said, shaking her head back and forth so hard, her hat threatened to fall.

"What is it?" Will asked.

"It's just awful is what it is. Sweet's real sick and I think she might die and if she dies it's all my fault because I didn't pack her wound right, 'cause she thinks I'm sleepin' with Bubba John and she wadn't talkin' to me at all. And the kids is just sick with worry, but Bubba John don't even see it most times, he's so busy tryin' to fix up his daddy's old house for Sweet Lee, and why he wants it to be a surprise is beyond me. And Suvi ain't called once't since the cake incident, which is fine by me, if'n he's gonna be so jealous and suspicious. I ain't done nothin' wrong to nobody and ever'body's still thinkin' the worst."

Will took Beanie by the arm and led her inside, with her talking the whole way, and sat her down at the kitchen table.

206

"I just don't know how much longer I can stand it, though I don't really know why I'm complainin' cause the kids really *are* great, but I don't like bein' way out there and not bein' able to go by and see all my people downtown, and take 'em my Avon books and all. And I was wonderin' if it would be all right, not right now, but if Sweet gets better, I was wonderin' if it would be okay if I came back here to stay, because I miss my room and I miss bein' close to town and ridin' my bicycle ever'where, and I miss goin' to Walmart with you every Friday and helpin' you cook breakfast and wash dishes and, I miss laughin' at ever'thing and nothing at all, and I miss bein' appreciated, not just needed, and, and…I miss *you*, Will, I really do, and I wanna come home."

Will said nothing, just reached over and covered Beanie's hand with his own.

Sweet Lee Atwater

I hate what's happening to me. I've lost control of everything. And most of the people in my life will tell you I kind of prefer being in control whenever possible. I keep asking God to show me what it is He wants me to learn, so I can just learn it already and move the heck on.

When my mother and father split up, I was eight years old and had no idea anything was even wrong. Oh, they always fought like cats and dogs, but I had no frame of reference. I thought that was just how families were. So my first eight years were spent with parents who hated each other and adored me, and my next eight were spent in what I like to call a nuclear family; it just exploded all over the place. My daddy married a woman with two girls and a boy, and my mama married twice more, having one more kid with each husband. I stayed with my daddy on weekends and with my mama the rest of the time. And I floated around in the chaos of a disjointed, unstable home.

Even still, I knew I wanted a big family. I wanted to fill a table for eight and always, always sit down to eat together. I wanted my children to have a daddy who was irrepressibly there. That's what I thought I had. Bubba John and I have been a unit from the time we first kissed. I've never had reason to question where he was or what he was doing. He was almost always on his way home to me. He searches for me in the house, stops by the shop just to visit, hopes I haven't packed a lunch so we can eat together. He sits beside me on the couch, holds my hand in the kitchen, touches my face for no reason at all. He is always happy to have the kids with him, though not too many at once. He is not a man who looks at women passing by; he has always made me feel like I am the only one in the world he cares to rest his eyes upon.

And he's right...I am not the only one this has happened to, but I am the only one left alone for hours on end. I am the one left with an empty womb and a thousand doubts that are eating me up inside. Literally. I just want my family back. Even if it takes being the biggest fool in the world.

41
What's Going On Here?

Monday morning Gabriella Warren decided to stop by the Mayhew Café for a takeout order of a ham biscuit and cheese grits. She paid at the register and sat down to wait for her food at the table nearest the door, which had not yet filled with the round table crowd.

"You need a menu, Ma'am?" Sissy asked Gabe.

"No, thanks, I'm waiting for a to-go order," Gabe smiled.

"How about a cup of coffee while you wait?" Sissy asked. "On the house."

"That would be lovely," Gabe said, just as Randy Kerner walked through the door of the restaurant. "Mr. Kerner, how are you?"

"Ms. Warren," Randy nodded and took the seat on the opposite side of her table. "What brings you out so early?"

"Oh, this is not so early for me. I'm up at the crack of dawn pretty much every day."

"Well, welcome, welcome. Glad you're joining us. How'd it go with Suvi the other day? Is he selling his house or something?"

Here we go, Gabe thought. It was always tricky deciding what was okay to discuss with people she didn't know. She couldn't remember if Suvi mentioned his mission in front of Randy and Mac, and had no idea if he would want them to know about his business.

"No offense, Mr. Kerner, but I make it a point never to mix business with pleasure," Gabe offered a teasing tone so as not to appear rude. "I got a chance to play over on the Live Oak course yesterday. I understand that's where the high school team plays. I was pleasantly surprised."

"Oh, I hope you weren't expecting too much. They do a good job over there, but it's nothing like what you're used to," Randy nodded at Sissy as she brought two cups over and poured one for each of them. "Speak of the devil."

Gabe turned in time to see Suvi Jones enter with his Gainesville Sun newspaper tucked underneath one arm. She couldn't be certain, but he appeared surprised, and maybe not in a good way, to see her sitting there.

"Morning, Mr. Jones," Gabe said.

"Ms. Warren," Suvi said, then hesitated in a way that could only be described as awkward. He started to bypass the table completely, but thought better of it and leaned back to the left as if to move toward Gabe. He did this several times, his indecision glaringly apparent.

Randy, seeing the vacillation, pulled out the chair next to Gabe and said, "Well, don't just stand there, Suvi, sit down why don'tcha?"

"Well, I usually sit over..."

"Well, don't sit here on my account," Gabe snapped, by now offended. She didn't know what she had done to upset him, but she could see that Suvi clearly did not want to sit with her.

Suvi sat. Sissy took it in stride, or at least with only one double-take from across the room.

"Whatcha' havin', Suve," she asked from four steps out.

"Ham and cheese omelet," Suvi said.

"Well, that's new," Sissy said, clearing the fog from her brain with a swift shake of the head. "Comin' right up...you want it there or at your regular table?"

"Here?" Suvi said, thoroughly unsure of his answer.

"I'll bring it to you wherever you are," Sissy said without flinching, then turned to Gabe. "Your order's comin' out in a minute. You sure you don't want to eat it here?"

"No, I'm fine, thanks," Gabe said. The quicker that food arrived, the quicker she could get out the door.

There was a moment of awkward silence during which Randy and Gabe sipped their coffee, before the bell on the front door rang again and all heads turned to see LouWanda Crump struggling to get through the door on crutches. She was so focused on maneuvering past two couples at the cash register without assaulting anyone's feet that she didn't raise her head until she was nearly upon the round table.

"What in the world did you do, Lou?" Randy asked.

"I busted my big toe tryin' to get to the bathroom in the dark. And, for heaven's sake, Randall, don't call me Lou," she said, finally looking up to see Suvi and Gabe. "What in the…what are you doin' at this table?"

Gabe looked bewildered. Suvi cleared his throat and took a sip of coffee. Randy Kerner slid his chair back and stood. "Let me get that chair for you, LouWanda. I assume you have not met our new resident, Gabriella Warren."

Randy quickly skirted the back side of the table and pulled the chair out so LouWanda could sit.

"I'll take your crutches, too," Randy said, grabbing both in one hand as he helped LouWanda scoot her chair closer to the table. He leaned down then and put his mouth close to her ear. "Be nice!"

"I am nice," LouWanda snarled and swatted Randy away. "Whatcha settin' over here for, Suvi? Don't you usually set over there by yourself?"

"Whoa," said Gabe, under her breath.

"I believe that's what you'd call a rhetorical question." Suvi leaned toward Gabe and turned his head away from the table so only she could hear.

"Do tell," Gabe said, choking back a laugh.

"What's so danged funny?" LouWanda demanded. "All's I did was ask a simple question. Don't you usually set over there by yourself?"

With Gabe as both witness and support, Suvi took a more patronizing tone than usual. "I do, Miss LouWanda, but today I'm sitting here with Randy and Gabe. That's okay with you, isn't it?"

"Well, I don't know why it wouldn't be," LouWanda snapped. "I was just *askin'*, that's all. And who the heck is Gabe?"

"Gabe Warren! For crying out loud, LouWanda, I just introduced her," Randy said.

"You said *Ga-bri-el-la*," LouWanda enunciated. "Gabe's a man's name. How in the Sam Hill was I supposed to know?"

With customary timing, Sissy appeared with Gabe's order in a paper sack.

"Edwina says you already paid," Sissy said, setting the bag down in front of her. "You want another refill before you go?"

Gabe grinned up at Sissy. "No, thanks. I have apparently already overstayed my welcome, such as it was."

Suvi tried to disguise his snort of laughter as a cough, but failed miserably, and Randy shifted uncomfortably in his chair.

"All right, LouWanda, what'd you say now?" Sissy glared down at her with fists on her hips.

"I didn't *say* nothin'," LouWanda glared back. "I asked. And I been here a full five minutes and still ain't got no coffee."

"You've been here two at most, and you may not get any at all if you don't behave. Honestly, LouWanda, you're too danged much sometimes."

Sissy didn't have time to deal with nonsense this morning. Too many other customers. She spun on her heel and ducked back behind the counter to deliver the next order, and she did not bring coffee for LouWanda until she made another round for refills.

Gabe stood and patted Suvi on the back. "Come on, I'll walk you to your table."

Randy wiped one hand over his face, then cupped his chin and frowned. "Mind if I join you, Suvi?"

Suvi stood and offered one massive hand in Randy's direction. "Thanks, Randy, but I think I'd just like to read my paper a while."

Randy shook Suvi's hand. "No problem, Suvi, maybe next time."

Suvi threw his paper down on a nearby table and turned to Gabe. "Can I walk you out?"

"Nah, I think the waitress is coming with your breakfast. I'll catch you later."

"They're not all like that," Suvi said, his voice lowered to a near whisper.

"Yeah, right," Gabe replied. "Keep on telling yourself that, old son. Just keep on…"

And with that, she was out the door, passing Dottie Brentwood coming in.

Suvi caught her eye and nodded to her and was about to sit when Randy Kerner spoke up.

"Hey, Suve, you forgot your coffee."

Suvi spun on his heel and made his way back to the table and picked up his cup. He'd almost made his getaway when Randy spoke up.

"Hey, I was just wondering if you're planning on selling your house?"

Suvi braced himself. "I'm just thinking about it right now, Randy. No big deal."

Dottie took the seat on the other side of LouWanda. "You moving, Suve?"

"Thinking about it," Suvi repeated.

"Where to?" Dottie asked. "Not out of Mayhew Junction, I hope."

"Naw," Suvi said. "I'm not likely to ever leave here again. I just want something different."

"Where you looking exactly?" Randy asked.

"I don't know *exactly*, Randy. Maybe something on the river, or just something in a nicer neighborhood, but smaller. My house is just too big."

"Ya shouldn'ta built it that big to begin with," LouWanda chimed in. "That thing sticks out like a sore thumb where it is."

"Don't be rude, LouWanda," Dottie swatted her hand for emphasis. "Suvi's house is beautiful."

"Well, I know it is, Dorothy. That's why it sticks out so bad."

Suvi sighed. How much of this was a man supposed to take?

"My breakfast is getting cold," Suvi said and walked back to his table.

For the next ten minutes, Suvi Jones tried his best to ignore the whispers at the round table. *Where's he planning on moving to? Why don't he just stay where he is? Which neighborhood is he lookin' in? You reckon the Big Pig is going under? Your neighbor's moving, ain't he, Randy? How about that house next to you? Well, I would personally love to have Suvi next door, but I don't know how the rest of the neighbors will take it, to be honest.*

Dottie tried to hush Randy and LouWanda, but it only got louder when two other regulars got in on the discussion. *He's moving where? I don't think we've ever had nobody colored live out there. Maybe he's moving to Beanie's old place. Naw, Beanie's out there shackin' up with Bubba John, right under Sweet's nose...it's a cryin' shame how she's behavin'.*

"Can y'all just stop?" Dottie said finally. "Please, stop."

Four mouths suddenly went quiet and four heads turned toward Dottie Brentwood. *What?* They spoke in unison.

"First off," Dottie said between clenched teeth, "he can hear you and you know it. Secondly, it is no business of yours where he moves. And Beanie is *not* shacking up with Bubba John. She is *helping* them while Sweet is *ill*."

"Aw, he ain't listening," Mac McConnell spoke up. "He's reading his paper and paying us no mind at all."

Suvi looked up over the edge of his paper and glared at Mac. "Kind of hard to read with all that yapping going on over there. Can't y'all find something that *is* your business to talk about?"

As Suvi stood and approached the table, forty-some-odd-years of biting his tongue and hoping for the best from people who should know better threatened to get the best of him. He took a deep breath and willed his fists to stop clenching.

"Oh, shit," Dottie said under her breath. She knew Suvi well, and she had never seen him so angry. His jaw was clamped tight, and a vein pulsed in his neck.

"I'm only going to say this once, so I'd appreciate it if I had your full attention," Suvi spoke in measured tones to the entire table.

"Now, Suvi..." Randy began.

"Mac's right about one thing," Suvi cut him off. "I've been sitting over there for years, paying y'all no mind at all, or at least trying not to..."

"We didn't mean any harm, Suvi," said Mac. "Why you so riled up?"

"Well, see, that's the thing, Mac. Just because you don't *mean* harm, doesn't mean you're not causing it. So listen here...I'm looking for a house in this town, and if you have a problem with where I might live, I want you to say it. To my face. Right now."

Suvi waited for someone to speak. No one did.

"Randy," Suvi said. "Am I going to have trouble with anyone if I buy a house in your neighborhood?"

"Not from me, you're not, Suvi," Randy said. "Honest."

214

"But from your neighbors? Will I?" he asked. "And from the county commission. Will I have trouble getting a permit for anything? Will we suddenly have an HOA out there picking out colors for houses just in case I get a wild hair to paint something purple? That's what you think, isn't it?"

Randy squirmed in his chair. "I can't speak for my neighbors…"

"Yes, you can, Randy! Yes. You can." Suvi threw his hands up in the air. "You know exactly what they think about having a black man moving in next door. Same thing they think about having a black president. *Y'all go get your huntin' dogs, there's coons movin' into the White House.* You think we didn't hear those jokes y'all told? Well, we did, 'cause your kids didn't have the sense not to tell them at school, where *our* kids heard them. And we know exactly where they got those jokes."

A murmur rose through the café. Dottie stood.

"Suvi, let's go outside for a minute. I don't think this is the place, really…"

Suvi turned to his employee and softened slightly.

"So, where is the place, Dottie? Where is the place I'm allowed to say the truth? I eat here every day, same as all of you," he said, waving his arms out to both sides. "I didn't start this conversation. Y'all did. So where *is* the place?"

Sissy appeared with a full pot of coffee and started to pour as if nothing were happening.

"Suvi, you want some more coffee over there or are you gonna sit down here?"

Suvi looked at Sissy, then back at his table.

"Actually, I think I'm done."

Suvi drew a napkin from the box on the table behind him and wiped sweat from his forehead, then took his wallet out and walked to the cash register. Sissy met him there.

"You okay?" she asked.

"Yeah," he sighed. "I'm fine. Sorry about that."

"Nothin' to be sorry for," she said. "Nothin' at all. I'll see you tomorrow, okay?"

Suvi shook his head and pocketed his wallet.

"Okay, Suvi?" she asked again.

"Okay," he said, and left the café.

Sissy walked back to the round table, where the group was still sitting in stunned silence.

"I don't know exactly what happened here," Sissy said, "but in all my life I have never seen that man so angry."

"See, that's what I've been a'sayin'," LouWanda was nearly crowing. "Y'all keep fussin' at me, but I'm right. They's all walkin' around mad as hornets, and for what? Ain't nobody stoppin' them from nothin'. I'm sick of bein' in the grocery store and havin' 'em put their carts right in my way and darin' me to make 'em move. We ain't the ones causing the trouble..."

"Stop, LouWanda," Dottie said. "You're making it worse. I've never noticed any such a thing."

"I don't know...I think she has a point," Mac said. "I'm not saying they're bad. They're just different that's all. And I don't see what's so wrong with everybody just keepin' to their own. They segregate, too, and somehow it's fine if they say something about a black school or a black church, but we're bad if we say we want a white church. It's just not fair."

Dottie looked up at Sissy and shook her head. "I can't believe they just said that out loud."

Sissy stood looking down at the table for a moment, turned to walk away, then turned back.

"I want y'all to know something. That man," she said, pointing at the door Suvi just exited, "is the most decent man I ever met. If he's mad, he's got a reason, and I'm pretty sure the reason is right here in front of me. The problem with y'all is, you spend too much time at this table. From where you sit all you can see is each other, and the whole damn world looks ugly."

42

Trust and Believe

It was slightly more chaotic than usual in the Atwater house on this Monday morning. It had been determined that there was no school due to a scheduled teacher workday, which no one had noticed, except Bitty and her information was deemed unreliable at best. After a few phone calls, Bitty was vindicated and received both gratitude and apologies for doubting her in the first place. So, at the last minute, plans were drastically changed. Bubba John took T-Ray with him to work on the house and meet with Nonie Crawford. Not only had Bubba John been undeterred in his goal to surprise his wife, he was more determined than ever and wanted to be finished by the time she was released from the hospital. He and Nonie were going to sit down today, finish the outline for final changes, and call in the cavalry. The contractors would be able to knock out the work in no time.

Beanie would keep the little ones home with her. She decided to teach them how to make their own breakfast and lunch, and she also thought Bitty would be happy to reorganize the "Tupperware cabinet," as Beanie called the space beneath the pine hutch where Sweet kept all her plastic containers. Bitty would have everything sorted by size and shape faster than you could say *Bob's your uncle.*

That left B-Kay free to go visit her mama, which Bubba John intended to do before the change of plans.

B-Kay packed a suitcase with great care, and asked her father for a little cash to stop by Walmart and pick up a few things she thought Sweet would need, including fresh pajamas and underwear.

Bubba John handed her a hundred-dollar bill and a couple of twenties. "That enough?"

"Whoa," B-Kay said. "I don't think I've ever held this much money all at once."

"Well, the times, they are a'changin'," Bubba John said, flinging caution to the wind.

"Does Mom know you're spending all this money?" B-Kay tucked the bills into her purse. "I think she might freak out a little."

"She might, but you let me worry about that." Bubba John hollered for his oldest son, slapped his hat on and bolted for the door. "Come on, Tee, I don't have all day."

T-Ray stumbled down the hallway and through the kitchen. He had no intentions of staying home with Beanie today. Lord only knew what she'd be having them do next.

***

Sweet Atwater was sitting up in bed when her firstborn child entered the hospital room. Sweet's first thought was *she looks so young.* B-Kay's first thought was the opposite and it terrified her. She immediately burst into tears.

"Mama," B-Kay managed to choke out.

Sweet stretched both arms out toward her daughter and B-Kay fell into them, sobbing.

"Shhh, now," Sweet crooned. "Hush, baby, I'm okay. Aw, baby…"

Sweet held her stricken child until she quieted a bit, then she pushed her gently away, and tucked a strand of hair behind B-Kay's ear.

"Let me look at you, baby," Sweet said. "It's only been two days and it seems like a month."

B-Kay settled herself on the edge of Sweet's bed.

"You don't look good, Mama," B-Kay said. "Are you going to get well?"

Sweet laughed, then gasped. "Ow, ow, don't make me laugh, B. That hurts."

"Sorry…"

"No, no, I'm happy I have at least one child who will always tell me the truth," Sweet said. "I'm going to be fine, B, but it's going to take some time. Where's your daddy? Did he stop by the cafeteria first?"

"He didn't come with me. There was no school today, so he and Tee had some stuff to do. Beanie's keeping the babies."

"You came over here all by yourself? What in the world is he thinking?"

"Mama…it's fine. I wanted to. Besides, I have GPS on my phone. It's not like I'll get lost or anything."

"That's not the point," Sweet snapped. "What if the car breaks down?"

"Then I call Dad," B-Kay shrugged. "What's the big deal?"

"What's the big deal? Really?"

"Yes, really, Mom. Really. Look, I even stopped by Walmart on the way over. I got you some stuff Dad said you might need. New underwear, and pajamas – just like you like, all cotton, with no scratchy lace around the neck."

"What was so important that he couldn't come with you is what I want to know?" Sweet would not be distracted. "I'm sick of it, B-Kay. I am sick and tired of being sick and tired and your daddy not giving a rat's ass about it.

Sweet dropped her head back on the pillow, threw one forearm across her eyes and burst into tears.

"Mama, stop," B-Kay said. "That's just not true, it's not. If you had any idea how worried Daddy is…"

"Then where is he? I don't understand…"

"Mama, listen to me…seriously. Stop crying and look at me. I have to tell you something," B-Kay stood and faced her mother.

Sweet turned her sodden face toward her daughter. "What?"

"You have to promise me you won't tell Dad I told you…" B-Kay began.

"I'm not promising anything. What is it? Is it bad?"

"No, Mama, it's not bad at all. It's good…it's really good, but you have to promise me you won't tell."

Sweet sniffled and wiped her nose with a tissue.

"Okay, I won't tell," Sweet sounded more like a child than the mother of five children.

"First you have to stop crying," B-Kay said.

"Okay," Sweet said, drying her eyes with a clean tissue. "What is it?"

B-Kay took a deep breath. "I promised Daddy I wouldn't say anything, but I can't stand to see you this way, especially since it's half my fault in the first place."

"Why is it your fault?" Sweet pulled herself up in the bed, wincing at the pain in her belly.

"I'm the one who told you Daddy was having an affair with Beanie, but that's just not true at all."

Sweet groaned. "I know it's not. That's not what I'm mad about. It's just that all of the sudden he's too busy to do anything. It's not like him and, quite frankly, his timing stinks."

"You're the one who said I always tell the truth, and I do. All I'm going to say is this – Daddy is planning a surprise for you. It's something you've always wanted, and Daddy's working real hard to get it for you. That's why he's been gone a lot, but it's all about you, I promise."

"How do you know?" Sweet said, still not quite sure what to believe.

"I've known for a while, Mom. Beanie knows, too. Everybody is worried about you, but Daddy is so dead set on surprising you, he can't even see how hurt you are. He thinks everything will be fine once you see it. I think he's crazy, but that's nothing new." B-Kay grinned. "Mama, I promise you, you're going to love the surprise. You may kill him before you get it, but if you'll just be patient, I know you'll forgive him."

"You're not going to tell me what the surprise is?" Sweet was incredulous.

"Nnnnnope!" B-Kay said. "We have not worked this hard to spoil it now. But you gotta get better, Mama. We like Miss Beanie fine, but we're all tired of you being gone. So's Beanie."

"Oh, God, I was so mean to her…" Sweet covered her mouth with her hand.

"She understands, I think. But she thinks it's her fault you're still sick."

"Oh, no…I'm so sorry, B. Please tell her I'm sorry."

"Well, you can tell her when you get home. In the meantime, you will never guess what she has the little kids doing. The laundry! Can you believe it?"

By the time B-Kay left that afternoon, B-Kay felt like she had her old mama back, and Sweet felt like her daughter had grown into a woman overnight. And one thing Sweet was certain of, if her daughter told her everything was going to be okay, that was something she could believe. And she did.

What puzzled her the most, and she ruminated over it until they brought her supper, was why in the world did Bubba John think she wanted a ring so badly that he would sell his mama and daddy's house to get it? But far be it from her to spoil a surprise. If he was bound and determined to get her a ring, she was bound and determined to act happy about it.

Dottie Brentwood

Sometimes I don't even know why I stay in this town. I've been here all my life. It's all I know. Truth is, I know it far too well. It's equal parts good hearts and small minds. Sometimes all in the same person. There's some good ones who just don't know any better, and some bad ones who don't want to hear the truth, and sometimes it's really hard to tell them apart. Take LouWanda Crump, for instance. We've been friends since we were children, but lately it's been hard to take her. The older she gets, the less she keeps a rein on her mouth.

It's not that the things she says are anything new. People been saying stuff like that for years. They just learned to keep a lid on it in the name of political correctness. But lately, people have been emboldened to say things they know are wrong and to hell with who gets hurt.

I keep thinking of an Irish Proverb my mama had hanging on her kitchen wall. It read: May those who love us love us, and those who don't love us, may God turn their hearts. And if He doesn't turn their hearts, may He turn their ankles so we'll know them by their limping.

Now, I'm not particularly churchy myself. I believe in the Christian faith to which I was born and raised, and I pray to God on a fairly regular basis. In fact, I've been praying about this thing with Suvi a lot lately. But I get a little tired of going to churches set up like country clubs, where people use God as a tool for social-climbing and shutting people out. I mostly keep my faith between God and myself and it suits me just fine. Anyway, what I was saying about that proverb…seems to me that's kind of what God's doing with this political thing right now. Just giving people permission to say in public what they've been saying in their living rooms for years on end. He's turning their ankles so we'll know them by their limping. And isn't it better to know the truth about what your friends think, so you can choose them wisely?

See, the problem with this town is, we've always been like a big ol' boat rowing up-river. We aren't getting anywhere, but as long as we all sit tight and keep rowing, we think we're doing fine. At least we're not falling overboard. Well, we're not fine. We're not okay. And I don't care if we all stand up at the same time, we are going to turn this boat around or sink it and drown. Right now, I don't care if I get wet. I'm standing up.

222

43
We're Not Hiring

Dottie Brentwood opened Sweet Lee's Dress Emporium feeling like she'd aged about twenty years. She was tired, that was all. Tired of the big fat elephant that sat in every room of every establishment in this town. And, bless his heart, Suvi Jones just pointed him out, plain as day, and dared anyone to deny it. *We ought to be past this by now,* Dottie thought to herself as she flipped on every light in the store and opened the cash register.

She spent the rest of the day stocking new inventory and planning for the upcoming Woman's Club fashion show that the Emporium was hosting. Dottie couldn't wait to tell Sweet about all the things she had planned for the shop, but Bubba John had advised her to wait for some reason. She wasn't sure exactly why. She could only imagine that Sweet might be worried about how the shop was staying afloat in her absence. But afloat it was, and Dottie was thrilled. She felt like she'd found a new calling and, for once in her life, felt like she had a career and not just a job.

By shortly after lunchtime, Dottie had decorated the window with dresses and gowns for Christmas parties, and a new sign that advertised tuxedo rentals for next year's prom festivities. She hadn't stopped to eat, and her stomach was growling in protest when the front door opened and Kenya Green walked in asking to fill out an application.

"Oh, honey, I'm sorry," Dottie said. "I wouldn't have an application to fill out even if I did have a position open, which I don't. I'd love to have some help, but I'm not sure we can afford it just yet. What kind of work are you looking for?"

Kenya, a striking young woman with brown skin, clear amber eyes and thick dark curls all over her head, gave a small, resigned smile and shrugged her shoulders.

"Anything I can get, honestly," she said. "I'll wait tables, sweep floors, sell dresses…whatever it takes. I just need a job. Preferably one I can walk to from home."

"Aren't you still in school?" Dottie asked. "You're Addie Gee's granddaughter, right?"

Addie Green ran the Head Start program in town, where Dottie worked part time several years ago. Addie Gee, as all the children called her, ran a tight ship. She was determined that "her kids" were going to reach kindergarten on track, and she tolerated no slacking from her seriously underpaid staff. Dottie would have stayed, but the pay just wasn't enough to live on.

Dottie knew the whole story. She was still working at Head Start when Addie's daughter Chantelle died after an all-too-brief battle with cancer. She had raised Kenya by herself ever since.

"Yes, Ma'am, Addie's my gramma. I'm a senior this year, but I'm in AP classes and I get out before noon almost every day. I'll be close to having an associate's degree when I get out, but I need to save up some money so I can go to college next year."

That Addie Gee's granddaughter was going to college didn't surprise Dottie at all.

"Where you going?" she asked.

"I hope UF," Kenya said, "but FSU and FAMU aren't out of the running until I get all my letters back. Plus, it's gonna matter where I can afford to live. That's why I'm saving up."

"Do you have a car?"

"No, ma'am, and that's the other problem. There's plenty of jobs over in Live Oak, but I can't get there. I need to find something here."

"Well, honey, I would hire you if I could, but I don't own this shop and I just don't have the say-so. Have you checked next door at The Big Pig. I know Suvi's short a waitress right now. You'd get some good tips at lunch time if you can come in that early."

Kenya sighed. "I went there yesterday. He said he wasn't hiring right now."

Well, what in the world? Dottie thought.

"Hang on a second," she said, and picked up the phone. She dialed the number for The Big Pig and waited. Suvi picked it up on the third ring.

"Hey, Suvi, it's Dottie. I'm about to starve. Can you fix me up a hamburger and fries? I'll come get 'em in a minute."

"Sure thing. Want a coke to go with that?" Suvi asked.

"No, just the food. I got bottled water," Dottie said.

"Okay, give me ten minutes. I'm stacked up over here."

"No rush, but hey — while I got you — are you still looking for someone to cover the lunch shift?"

"Yeah, I could use someone for sure. Cherry's still hit or miss. I gotta let her go at some point. Why, are you ready to come back?"

"No, I was just checking." Dottie said. "I'll see you in a few."

When she hung up the phone, she turned to Kenya.

"I guess I was wrong. He says he doesn't need anyone right now," Dottie lied. "How about the new real estate office going in? I met Miss Gabe the other day and she seems real nice. Maybe she could use some help in the office."

"Is that the place on the corner by the traffic light?"

"Yeah, the old chiropractor's office," Dottie said.

"I went by there the other day, but no one was in. I thought maybe it wasn't open yet," Kenya said.

"Well, watch for a black Mercedes parked out front then. That's what she drives, so if the car is there, she should be, too. I'll be pulling for you, hon."

The two chatted for a few more minutes until a customer came in looking for a Christmas dress.

"Let me know how it goes at UF," Dottie said. "And thanks for stopping in."

"Thanks, Miss Dottie," Kenya replied, and slipped out the door of the shop.

***

Ten minutes later Dottie went straight to the Big Pig, entering the kitchen through the back door where she found Suvi and his cook discussing the heat of the fire in his smoker.

And speaking of *hot*, Dottie Brentwood had already worked herself into a lather.

"If you think you are going to get away with refusing to hire somebody because they're black, you have got another think coming," Dottie said, without even waiting to be acknowledged. "You know good and well this isn't about her age. We've had younger than her working here plenty of times."

"Aw, come on, Dottie..." Suvi avoided looking at her.

Dottie leaned toward him, hands on hips. "Please explain to me why you didn't hire Kenya Green."

Suvi sighed and shook his head. "I don't have time for this right now."

"Why, 'cause you got a restaurant full of people who don't have enough servers?"

"There is nothing I can say to make you understand, and nothing I can do to make these people any different than they are," Suvi said. "Somebody, at some point, will get a kinky black hair in their food, and my business will just go downhill from there. I'm telling you, it will. So, unless she wants to shave her head like mine..."

"So, you're going blame it on this *town?*"

"Why are you doing this?"

"To shake things up for a change...rock the damn boat."

"You wanna rock the boat, Dottie? You rock it yourself. I don't *have* that luxury." Suvi turned away and started loading plates of food onto a tray. "Y'all made these rules, not me."

"No, you didn't. You sure did not." Dottie's voice was heavy with sarcasm. "But I'll be damned if you didn't just fall right in line with 'em."

"That's enough," Suvi said.

But Dottie was not through.

"Do you really want that beautiful girl to live her life the same way? Feeling like there's always some kind of line she can't cross?"

"You think there's *not?*"

"Oh, I think people draw lines all right. All over the damn place. But that doesn't mean you can't cross them if you want what's on the other side."

"So what is it you think happens when one of us *po' black folk* cross that line, Dottie. You think we're just welcomed with open arms? You think it's *my* rejection that's gonna harm that child? She's been rejected worse than that in *grade school* by teachers who ought to know better."

Dottie spoke through the tightness in her throat. "You can't just give in to keep peace. Who's gonna change it, if not us?"

"Good question. Maybe you can figure that out sometime. Because let me just tell you, if your solution to this problem is to come over here and try to fix *me*, you are part of the problem."

"Do you really mean that?" Dottie said, her face quivering as she fought back tears.

"I wish I could say no," Suvi said. "But, yes, Dottie — I really mean it."

And with that, Suvi took the serving tray he'd been holding and exited the kitchen.

***

An hour after Kenya Green left her real estate office, Gabe Warren was down at The Big Pig ordering a slab of ribs and a side salad. Suvi seemed surprised to see her when he delivered the ribs himself.

"Hey! I didn't see you come in. What brings you out in the middle of the day?"

Gabe grinned. "Well, I was hungry for one thing, and I hadn't yet tried your famous ribs. I hope I'm not setting myself up for disappointment."

"Well, if I'd known it was you out here, I'd have taken extra care." He set the plate down in front of her. "Did Cherry tell you about the sauces?"

"Cherry?"

"The waitress. Cherry Allred, believe it or not."

"Ouch." Gabe winced and shook her head. "She took my order and disappeared, actually."

"Yeah, she stepped out for a smoke break. It's quiet this time of day and she had a helluva lunch shift. Anyway," Suvi said pointing to four bottles on the table, "those are our sauces. I make them myself. Clear is regular, red is hot, yellow is mustard sauce and white is sweet."

"Got it," Gabe said.

While Suvi headed back to the kitchen, Gabe replayed the conversation she had with Kenya Green, a charming young woman who she would love to hire if she could. Unfortunately, Gabe needed someone full-time who could grow with the company, and Kenya was leaving for college in less than a year. She was certain she remembered Kenya saying she had applied for a job at the barbecue place, the dress shop and the courthouse, and Suvi already said his was the only barbecue in town.

Gabe Warren grabbed the sweet and hot sauces and doused her ribs with both just as Suvi returned with a plate piled twice as high as hers.

"Whoa, buddy! That's way more than I can eat!"

"I thought I'd join you." Suvi slipped an empty plate from beneath the stack of ribs and placed it in the center of the table. "Boneyard," he announced, as if it weren't obvious.

"So, you're looking for another waitress, huh?" Gabe said before she could stop herself.

"Yeah, Cherry's not terribly reliable and I have two other part-timers who work when they feel like it. Hard to find good help these days."

Gabe took a bite of rib and hummed her appreciation. "You weren't kidding," she said, washing it down with a gulp of sweet tea. "These are something else."

"Secret recipe," Suvi said, and wiped a smear of sauce from his cheek.

"Kenya Green stopped by my office today looking for a job."

Suvi looked up from his plate and frowned. "Did Dottie call you?"

"Who's Dottie?"

"Never mind."

"Well, I thought she said she stopped by here but you weren't hiring. Seems to me like she'd be perfect for this job."

"Oh, she'd be great," Suvi said, "no doubt about it."

"But?"

"But the job would not be great for her. Dottie was just in here accusing me of not wanting to rock the boat and I hate to admit it, but that's probably closer to the truth than the excuse I gave her."

"What was that?"

"Doesn't matter," he said. "I could hire Kenya today and everything would *probably* go fine, but I can't take the risk. I know what would happen. Most people in this town wouldn't think twice about having her serve them, but they would *treat* her like a servant. They would tip her less, and talk down to her as if she didn't deserve better. But that's not even the worst of it." Suvi's hands tightened into fists beside his plate. "The first time some redneck son-of-a-bitch looks at her sideways, or calls her a name, or makes a joke at her expense, I will *take him out*. And then what? Then where will I be?"

Gabe said nothing. Just studied Suvi's face and nodded softly.

"I'll tell you where we'll be," he went on. "That boat I rocked will roll on by, and the only people in it will be white. And they will all say, 'Look at that big, angry black man. He's a danger to society. Better throw him in jail.' That's how it'll be. That's how close to the edge I live."

"Then why do you stay?"

"There's a certain comfort to living in a town you know, with people who know you. There is, and sometimes this boat is the safest place to be."

Gabe spoke through the tightness in her throat. "As much as I know this is true, Mr. Jones, it doesn't mean you shouldn't rock it a little. At some point you have to be willing to make white people as uncomfortable as you have been. Lord knows it won't kill 'em."

Suvi stared at Gabe for a moment.

"I'm tired, Gabe. Tired of weighing everything I say. Tired of trying not to look like a threat. Tired of being invited to the barbecue and not the birthday party. I'm tired of being tired."

"We're all tired, old son." Gabe reached into her purse and pulled out a yellow sticky note. "Here's Kenya's number. She wants to go to UF and she needs all the help she can get. If you won't hire her, maybe you can at least make some phone calls to your alma mater. I'm pretty sure you won't regret it."

Cherry Allred appeared then, reeking of cigarette smoke and alcohol. "You need me to get those, Suvi?" she asked pointing to the largely untouched plates of ribs and fries.

"No, thanks. I'll finish up here," Suvi said. "Why don't you go on home? I'll call someone to take the evening shift."

"I kinda need the money…"

"Go home, Cherry," Suvi said. "Just…go home."

44
Working on Mayhew Time

Bubba John Atwater was getting a good dose of his own medicine being on the receiving end of work done on Mayhew time. No one was in any particular hurry, and if you were promised a job complete in a week, you might just as well accept that it will take at least two. Everyone operated that way and the only people who dared complain were outsiders moving in, which is why that very thing was discouraged.

Bubba was having a heart-to-heart talk with the contractor's foreman when Nonie Crawford showed up at the house.

"Hey, I was hoping I would catch you out here," Nonie made her way through the construction debris wearing far more sensible shoes than one might expect with the suit she had on. In one hand she carried a clipboard and Sweet's idea book. In the other, she dangled three different sets of swatches all attached to metal rings. "I've got a box of tile samples in the back of my car. Do you mind grabbing that when you get done there?"

"I think we're about through now, but it isn't good news," Bubba said.

Nonie stopped in her tracks and turned to face the two men. "What's going on?"

"Materials missing, crew laying out, orders delayed, you name it, apparently." Bubba shook his head.

"I don't know what else to tell you, Mr. Atwater," the foreman said. "This ain't the only job we got goin'."

"I understand that, Carl, but y'all promised this job would be done on time when I hired you, and I don't mean just *kind of* promised. Y'all swore to me you could get it done."

"Hang on," Nonie interrupted. "What's the holdup, Carl? What are you missing?"

"Drywall, for one thing. And I ain't got any hangers right now if I did have the materials. Plus the flooring is delayed again. It ain't easy to get real hardwood on short notice."

"That's true, I'm sure, but it isn't impossible." Nonie dropped her swatches on the front steps. "Whew, that was killing my arm. Bubba John, can I talk to you for a minute? In private, I mean. Carl, don't you move."

Nonie turned and entered the house and Bubba John followed. Carl did as he was told and stayed put.

"You cannot let these guys run all over you now," Nonie said once they were out of earshot. "We are on a strict deadline and you told me yourself money is no object. If they can't get it done, I guarantee you my Jack knows half a dozen independent contractors who can be out here tomorrow. You go tell him that and see how fast they find drywall hangers. They've already got the permitted stuff done, Bubba. We can finish it ourselves if they won't move."

Bolstered by the pep talk, Bubba John returned to the front yard armed with newfound confidence. He did have plenty of money. And he had a trailer that would haul everything they needed from Live Oak.

"Nonie's right, Carl. I don't have time to wait around for y'all to get your act together. I'm gonna head over to Live Oak right now and get what we need to keep moving here. I don't know what you pay your drywall hangers now, but I bet I can find a crew that'll show up tomorrow morning for what I'll pay 'em to do a good job."

"How much is that?" Carl asked, expecting to get a good laugh.

He didn't laugh when Bubba John gave him the rate he was willing to pay.

"We'll get on it first thing, Mr. Atwater. You get us the drywall and I'll have a crew here. Hell, I'll hang drywall myself for that kinda money. What're you gonna do about the flooring?"

"You tell your boss I need to know when that shipment is due, and to cancel the order if it's any later than Friday. I'll drive over to Jacksonville myself if I need to. I don't have any time to waste, Carl. I'm not kidding. Tell him y'all are fired if you can't stick to your promise."

Bubba didn't wait for an answer. Instead, he opened the back of Nonie's Suburban, grabbed the box she requested and went back inside.

"That felt good," Bubba John said, putting the box down on the kitchen floor.

"I'll bet it did," Nonie nodded. "Money talks."

"I'm guessing it'll take a bit to learn the language, but my first lesson didn't go too bad, did it?"

For the next half hour Nonie and Bubba John made the final decisions on tile for the kitchen and bath, after which Bubba John went to see Jack about the drywall he needed. Nonie stayed for another hour taking measurements to make sure she ordered enough materials. The house was coming along nicely and she was pleased at the new layout which opened up rooms to give the old farmhouse a modern feel.

Later, when Nonie was home with her husband, Jack laughed about Bubba John striding into the store like he owned the place. "I don't know what you said to that boy, but he was on a mission when he got to the store. I think you may have created a monster."

"Sometimes it takes a monster to get things done around here," Nonie said. "I thought he was crazy to even attempt this, but you know what? I think we can do it. I'd give a lot to see Sweet Atwater's face when she gets her Christmas present. I sure would."

45
Not Going Back

For the next two weeks, it seemed that Mayhew Junction was a town in flux. Feelings were hurt and wounds were licked behind closed doors. Business at the café was slow for November, and Thanksgiving passed without fanfare. Bubba John and the kids all went to see Sweet at the rehabilitation center where she had been moved the day after B-Kay visited. They took her a full Thanksgiving meal, and proudly pointed out which child had helped prepare which food. T-Ray fixed a big pan of roasted root vegetables, most of which he peeled with a pocket knife, though no one admitted that to his mama. Bitty had helped crack pecans from the trees in their back yard for pie, and now knew exactly how many pecan halves fit into one cup. B-Kay did the turkey and dressing, and the two little ones helped make peanut butter cookies. Beanie mixed the cookie dough, then doled out a spoonful at a time to Tater and Daisy, which they rolled into balls with their hands, then flattened with a fork. While the cookies baked, they pulled the foil off the chocolate drops so they could place them in the center of each cookie while they were still warm. They made a mess of the entire affair and squabbled over who did the most cookies, but the task had kept them busy while the other dishes were prepared.

As thrilled as Sweet was to spend time with her family, the visit made her miss them all the more. She willed herself stoic, however, and basked in the attention as long as it lasted. She couldn't help wondering if they were all doing fine without her…they seemed so happy, like visiting your mama for Thanksgiving was the most normal thing in the world. And she chastised herself afterwards for even thinking like that when the departure was nothing short of traumatic for the little ones. B-Kay had to pull Daisy kicking and screaming from Sweet's arms. Tater had a meltdown of epic proportions, which was completely unlike him, and Bitty went stone silent and refused to come out from under the hospital bed. Later, Bubba John called to tell her that Daisy and Tate had slept all the way home and were fine by the time they got them out of the car. Bitty, however, had remained silent until T-Ray offered to play Chutes and Ladders with her, which brought her back to herself in no time.

Despite seasonal shoppers, downtown Mayhew was quieter than usual. Dottie Brentwood avoided the café for a while and kept to herself. She stayed busy with new inventory and increased sales. Bubba had been happy for Dottie to make changes at the shop, though he not-so-subtly suggested she not mention it to Sweet Lee just yet, if she did get a chance to talk to her, which was not often. Suvi did indeed hire Kenya next door, and she often popped into the shop to visit or look around a bit when it got slow. Kenya had a keen eye for fashion, suggesting outfits for display that Dottie would never have imagined. Business was booming and Dottie was fairly certain the store was turning a profit finally.

Two weeks before Christmas, Dottie asked Kenya how it was going next door.

"Great!" Kenya's eyes lit up. "Mr. Jones is quiet, but nice. I think he's happy with me. I heard him tell a customer he didn't know what he'd do without me."

"Oh, yay," Dottie said. "You hadn't said anything, so I wondered."

"The best part is, he called some of his friends at U.F. and put in a good word for me. I guess it worked, 'cause I got my acceptance letter yesterday!"

"Congratulations! So what's your major?"

"Honestly, I don't know yet. I'm not even sure what my options are, but I know I'll figure it out."

Dottie gave her a quick hug. "Smart girl! But here's a little unsolicited advice – don't come back here after you graduate."

"Oh, don't worry, Miss Dottie," Kenya said. "Once I leave this town, I am never looking back."

"Ha!" Dottie laughed. "What does your gramma say about that?"

"She's the one said it in the first place, I'm not kidding. She's always told me I had to get out of here when I could."

"That bad, huh?"

"Aw, I don't know – it's not a bad town. There's just nothing here for me. Never has been. When I get out of here, I'm gonna take voice lessons, and maybe do some theatre. All I've ever done is sing in church."

"I didn't know you wanted to be a singer," Dottie said. "Do you mind switching off the back lights for me? I need to close these windows before I leave. You working the supper crowd?"

Kenya walked to the back and pulled the breaker switch down. "Yep, he fired Cherry, so I'm getting plenty of hours now."

Dottie walked Kenya out and locked up behind them. She looked up just in time to see LouWanda Crump heading her way. They hadn't spoken since the last blow-up at the Café and Dottie had been laying low. The longer it went, the more awkward it became, but she was damned if she was going to deal with it now. She bid Kenya a quick farewell and rushed around the corner toward her car parked in back of the store.

Had she turned to look back, she'd have seen her old friend stop in the middle of the street and drop her chin to her chest in utter defeat. Dottie had never seen her cry, not once, and she didn't see it today, either. But, she would have. As it was, she had to hear about it later from Suvi Jones.

***

LouWanda stood in the center of Main Street until an approaching truck forced her to make a decision one way or the other. She chose to go forward. She walked straight over to the Big Pig and entered without stopping to wipe her feet, which was utterly unlike her.

She paused once inside, though, and grabbed a couple of napkins to dry her tears and blow her nose. Honestly, she never intended to call attention to herself, and that was the problem. Where other folks are hyper-aware of how they look and speak and who is listening, LouWanda Crump was just the opposite. She said whatever came to her mind and then, likely, never gave it another thought. She took care what she wore and how she looked, but she didn't dress for anyone but herself. This had

236

always worked for her before, but suddenly it seemed like the whole world had stopped talking to her, and more importantly, might possibly be, quite probably *were* talking *about* her, and she did not like that feeling at all. For the first time in her life, LouWanda Crump was ruminating about what she had said, and it was not sitting well, she could tell you that.

She wadded up her snotty napkins and headed to the ladies' room to throw them away and wash her hands. When she came back out, Suvi was going in—toward the men's room—down a hallway that barely fit two people if one of them wasn't the size of the mountain he was named after. LouWanda pressed herself back against the bathroom door and waited for him to pass. He nodded at her, but backed up into the dining room to allow her to come through. His upbringing simply wouldn't allow him to do otherwise. She smiled meekly and came on out.

"LouWanda," Suvi nodded his acknowledgement.

"Hey," LouWanda turned sideways to pass between his gigantic frame and the cash register counter. Doing so, she came face to face with her own reflection in the mirror behind Suvi and it did not make her happy. Her nose was red, her eyes swollen, and on her face was the awful-est scowl she'd ever seen on a person, least of all herself.

Well, she thought to herself, *is that what people see? I look like a haint.*

"Are you meeting someone here?" Suvi asked.

"No, no…I just…" LouWanda patted a section of her hair down on one side. "I don't rightly know what I'm doin' here, to tell the truth. I started over to say hey to Dorothy, but she apparently didn't want to say hey back. She took off like a scalded dog."

"I see." The fact that Suvi was not surprised was evident in the *way* he said, "I see."

"Do ya now?" LouWanda snorted.

"I do," Suvi nodded. "Nice to see you, LouWanda. Kenya should be right out, but you can sit anywhere you like. You know the routine."

"Well, I didn't act-chally come here to eat. I reckon I came to apologize, 'cause it don't look like I'm ever gonna live it down if I don't."

Suvi shook his head and winced. "So was that the apology?"

"Well, of course not. I'm not the fool you all apparently think I am," LouWanda snapped, then softened.

"All-righty then," Suvi said and turned to go down the narrow hallway. When he returned from the men's room, LouWanda was still standing in the doorway, looking at the floor.

"Excuse me," Suvi said and tried to squeeze by her, but LouWanda put up one hand, which jingled with the mismatched slew of bracelets she wore.

"Hang on a minute," LouWanda took a deep breath and looked up at Suvi's face, hand still in the air. "I am sorry if I offended you. I did not mean to run everybody off, nor make them all mad at me. You neither. So, I'm sorry, and I wish you'd forgive me and get it over with, 'cause I'm ready for things to be back the way they was before." Then she dropped both hands to her hips and waited.

Suvi closed his eyes and said a silent little prayer. *Help me, Lord.* When he squeezed one eye open, he saw that LouWanda was still in front of him. He sighed, shook his head back and forth, almost imperceptibly, and stared at the ground. When he looked back up again, he said, "Honestly, LouWanda, I can forgive you all day long, but I don't think I will ever wish for things to go back to the way they were. And if you were me, you'd understand."

He left her standing there, tears flowing unchecked down her marshmallow cheeks. She didn't know why she was crying, or why she couldn't move. She just stood there and cried until Kenya took her by the hand and walked her back across the street.

46
The Final Countdown

Bubba John and Nonie Crawford worked feverishly to complete the renovations on Sweet's "new" house. The hardwood floors were redone, two bathrooms sported all new fixtures and tile, and one bathroom was added on the second floor. Cabinets were installed in the kitchen and quartz countertops were due to arrive any day.

Nonie took it upon herself to outfit the younger kids' rooms, though B-Kay and T-Ray had a hand in designing their own. After all the years of the Atwater family barely scraping by, they were both trained to be frugal, which Nonie found thwarted her design ideas. She convinced Bubba John to let them in on the lottery secret as well. As it turned out, he was sorry he hadn't done it sooner, since there was not another word of doubt from either of them from then on.

Bubba was adamant that Sweet would get to decorate the master bedroom. Even he had sense enough to know when he had pushed his wife far enough. B-Kay saved the day, however, by suggesting that they replicate one room exactly as it was in the magazine pages Sweet clipped. There was one in particular that Sweet had scrawled across in Sharpie mark— *LOVE THIS!!* Nonie took B-Kay with her to shop for her mother, and they decorated the entire room together.

One week before Christmas, Bubba John's renovated family home was finished and ready for the entire family to move in. The two oldest Atwater kids were nearly bursting with nervous energy that threatened to spoil the whole surprise. They had to remember not to say anything in front of the youngest three, and *not* slip in front of their mother, who was due to come home any day now. Even Bubba John was nervous about sticking to his plan. As much as he wanted to take her straight out to the house, he decided it should be done as a proper Christmas present, under the tree on Christmas morning. And so he waited.

Three days before Christmas, the entire Atwater family, plus Beanie Bradsher, ate dinner at the long pine table Sweet insisted on buying when she and Bubba John were first married. Sweet was there, too, having settled in a few days before. The doctor had pronounced her "yard well," meaning she was healthy enough to be outdoors, maybe even go to the grocery store, as long as she didn't lift anything heavier than an egg carton. After dinner the kids impressed the heck out of their mother by all clearing the table without being told, then settled themselves in the living room for a little TV before bedtime. The twins squabbled a bit over who would get to use the computer first, but all in all, the transition was incredibly peaceful.

"I'm beginning to think you have brought me to the wrong house, Bubba John. Are these really our kids?"

"Beanie runs a tight ship. What can I say? It sure isn't my doing."

Sweet immediately felt a catch in her breath, then relaxed. She should be grateful, not angry, she reminded herself.

"I don't know how we'll ever thank you, Beanie. Really, you've gone above and beyond and I hope you know that I'm truly grateful. And, I just want you to know that I'm just sorry as I can be that I thought the worst. I wasn't my best self, and I hurt you. You didn't deserve that."

Beanie was not at all accustomed to heartfelt apologies, having never experienced one that she could recall.

"Oh, pooh, it was nothing. You was just sickly, that's all. I didn't pay it no mind."

"Well, it hasn't been nothing. It's been something special. I mean, just look at this house, and the decorations on the tree," Sweet said. "And I don't know what all you've been baking, but my house has never smelled so good. Even before I had boys."

In fact, the whole house looked homey and sweet and smelled of holiday baking. Sweet didn't know why Beanie wasn't big as a barn, except that she mostly baked, rather than tasted. She liked to give her customers edible gifts each year.

"I was hoping B-Kay could run me into town tomorrow. May take a while, 'cause I got to deliver all these packages, and Lord, them people can talk, I'm tellin' ya."

Sweet's eyes lit up. "Oh, yes, and I'll go with y'all. I'm dying to get down to the store and see how it's going. I can't imagine how Dottie has done this all by herself."

Bubba John was caught off guard. "I don't think so, Sweet. That's too much of a trip this soon."

Sweet squinted at Bubba across the table. "The doctor said I can do short trips into town."

"I know, but…" Bubba John began.

"This is short," Sweet cut him off with a wave of her hand. "I'm going."

Of all the bases Bubba thought to cover, this was one for which he was not prepared. What would she say when she saw the changes Dottie had made? The shop had never made enough money for Sweet to even take a real salary, much less provide for improvements.

"Dottie's been fixing it up as a surprise for you," he blurted without thinking. "I don't know if she's done yet or not."

"We'll see tomorrow," Sweet said. "I'm dying to get down there and I'm not waiting another day. I don't care if it's finished or not, I'll be tickled with whatever she's done."

Bubba John excused himself from the table, walked outside and called Dottie Brentwood, who was excited for Sweet to see what she had done. So what if Sweet got mad that he'd spent a little money. They were out of the red now, so the investment paid off. Bubba couldn't tell her that Sweet would know they didn't have that kind of money, nor could he tell her why they did. As far as he knew, only Beanie Bradsher knew they had won the lottery, and Bubba John wanted to keep it that way as long as possible.

Bubba came back in looking dejected and worried.

"What in the world is wrong with you, honey?" Sweet asked.

"Oh, nothing," Bubba said. "Just a problem on that job I've been working. No big deal."

Sweet wondered if his discomfort had anything to do with the ring she was sure he had bought. Maybe he hid it down at

241

the store, who knows. Anyway, she made a mental note not to look anywhere at anything that might give it away. B-Kay said she would like it, so she was certain she would. But a diamond ring? Nothing could be farther down on her list of wants.

"Whatcha thinkin' about?" Bubba John asked.

Sweet thought fast. "Just how lucky I am, that's all. I missed you so much."

At that, Beanie excused herself and promised to come back to clean the kitchen.

"I'll get the dishes," Bubba John said. "You get some rest."

"You sure? I don't mind…"

"Nope…go on. We'll see you in the morning."

Sweet put one hand on top of Bubba John's. "Looks like she trained you, too, Mister."

Bubba John laughed and scooted closer to his wife.

"I'm so glad you're home." Bubba John had never meant anything more in his life.

47
A Trip to Town

The next day, Beanie, B-Kay and Sweet headed for town with two dozen brightly wrapped boxes of candies and cookies Beanie had baked for her best customers. The first stop was The Château, of course, but Will was out and Beanie had to leave the package on the kitchen table with a note. On the way out, she noticed the Christmas tree in the formal living room. It was huge and lavishly decorated with Victorian ornaments and tons of ribbon. She wondered who had decorated it and couldn't for the life of her imagine it was Will.

Next stop, downtown, where they parked in front of the dress shop and left the car unlocked so Beanie could get more when she ran out. Sweet and B-Kay popped into the Emporium to say hello to Dottie, who had been forewarned and was thus not surprised. Sweet stood for a minute outside admiring the display Kenya had helped design. It was nothing Sweet might have ordered herself, but it looked fabulous. *Like a big city window,* Sweet thought. *Beautiful.*

But her reaction to the window was nothing compared to her stunned silence when she entered the store. It didn't even look like the same place. There were rustic crates along one wall with stacks of jeans in each cubby they formed. Old pallets were suspended from the towering ceilings and fitted with mason jar lights that added a warm glow to the room. Another free-standing hutch held an array of homemade soaps and candles and lotions, which changed the entire smell of the place. All of the merchandise looked new and different somehow – softer and less, what was the word? Camouflage-y. No. Masculine? Maybe. Whatever, the effect was striking, but she was confused. It didn't feel like hers anymore.

"Sweet!" Dottie wrapped her in a huge embrace. "I'm so happy to see you. How are you feeling? What do you think? Do you like it?"

Sweet laughed, but her smile didn't reach her eyes. "Sensory overload! One question at a time, please."

B-Kay whistled long and low. "Wow, Miss Dottie, you changed this place a lot."

"Yeah, business has really picked up, too. Maybe it's just the Christmas season, I don't know," Dottie said.

Sweet stood and took it all in.

"Are you okay?" Dottie asked. "You seem upset or something."

"No, not upset, I don't think," Sweet moved slowly between the racks of clothes. "More confused than anything. How did you do all this?"

"Well, Bubba helped some, and those crates and pallets I got basically free from different places. I wired those lights myself. Otherwise, it was just a matter of ordering what we wanted to sell."

"But how," Sweet asked. "With what money?"

"I…don't know, actually. But I know we're in the black. We've made a profit for the past six weeks." Dottie said. "I thought you'd be happy."

Sweet could hear the disappointment in Dottie's voice. "Oh, Dottie, I am happy. Really. I guess I'm just feeling like…a failure. Why couldn't I do this? I worked here every day for five years and I couldn't turn a profit. You've been here two months and—well—just look. No wonder Bubba John didn't want me to see it."

"Mama," B-Kay stepped in front of her mother and stood face-to-face. "Stop it. You're hurting Miss Dottie's feelings."

"Oh, gosh, no," Dottie moved from behind the register and touched B-Kay on the arm. "My feelings are not hurt at all, Hon. Your mama's just had a rough time."

"I'm sorry, Dottie," Sweet said, tears pooling in her eyes. "I don't know what's wrong with me. I should be praising you for what you've done, and I'm making it all about me. The shop looks wonderful. You've done an amazing job and I… I'm just… I'm sorry."

Sweet turned and fled the store, sobbing the entire way. Dottie started to follow and B-Kay stopped her. "Don't Miss

Dottie. She'll be okay. I promise. In a couple of days, she'll be fine."

B-Kay knew she was right, but this whole surprise thing was just breaking everybody's heart. She wished she'd never agreed to keep it a secret. Christmas could not get here fast enough.

***

After bolting from the store, Sweet sat in the car for ten minutes. B-Kay, unable to console her mother, joined Beanie in delivering gifts. When the girls returned to restock from the back of the van and hit the courthouse, Sweet dried her tears, blew her nose and grabbed a couple of boxes.

"Mom! Are you coming with us?" B-Kay held crossed fingers in the air.

"Yyyyyep," Sweet nodded. "Pity party's over. Time to do something for somebody else."

"You sure you're up to it?" Beanie remained terrified Sweet would relapse yet again.

"I feel great." Sweet silently willed herself to believe her own words, and repeated them for good measure. "Absolutely great."

By the time they were finished, all three were hungry and the lunch hour was long gone. They decided to stop by the café for a quick bite. Truth was, B-Kay wanted to go to the Big Pig, but Beanie couldn't bear the thought of running into Suvi, so she lied and said she wasn't in the mood for barbecue.

"Besides," Beanie continued, "the café is faster. I gotta get home and start supper."

Sweet took note of the word "home" and shuddered involuntarily.

"Where will you go when I'm back to myself," Sweet asked.

B-Kay had just pulled the van into the parking lot of the Mayhew Café, and Beanie sat with her hand on the door handle. She turned to face Sweet in the back seat.

"Will said I can come back to The Château, and I think that's prolly best. I'm plannin' on lookin' for a new house at some point, but you know — one thing at a time."

245

"Oh, good. You need your own house for sure—not that you aren't welcome at ours—but you know what I mean."

At that, Beanie and B-Kay scooted out of the car and slammed the doors shut. It was all they could do not to burst out in nervous laughter.

Sweet extricated herself from the seatbelt and followed the girls inside. Sissy greeted them warmly and handed them three menus.

"We don't need those," Sweet said. "We're all doing the buffet."

They were just starting to eat when Eustace Falwell came in, and boy, did he find a smorgasbord at the café today.

"Ladies!" His eyes lit up like roman candles. "I haven't seen y'all in a while. Who's this pretty lady? That can't be little B-Kay, can it?"

"Hey, Mr. Falwell," B-Kay managed a tight-lipped smile and dropped both hands in her lap.

"Oh, I'm not that old now, you can call me Eustace, cain't she, Sweet Lee?" He turned his attention to B-Kay's mother. "Wow, you look better'n I expected, what with all's been goin' on. I heard you were in the hospital, and it does show, if you don't mind me bein' a bit personal. I don't mean to offend you, but you do look a *little* peaked. You sure you're okay?"

"I'm much better, thank you for asking."

"Well, you've always been one of the prettiest gals in town, and that one don't fall far from the tree, if you know what I mean." Eustace jerked his head in B-Kay's direction and winked.

"You got somethin' in your eye, Useless?" Beanie nailed him without blinking.

He cackled at that, more amused than he should have been.

"You tickle me, Beanie." he said, still snickering behind his hand. "I prob'ly deserved that, though. I got in trouble for winkin' at a gal in church the other day. I don't know what comes over me, it's almost like it's involuntary or somethin'. You know like one of them tics my cousin's got?"

"You ain't got Tourette's, Eustace, you just cain't control yourself. It's two different things." Beanie picked up a fried chicken wing and took a whopping bite.

"Well if that ain't the truth!" he slapped his thigh and started toward the round table.

The girls breathed a sigh of relief, two seconds too soon. He wheeled back around, took his cap off, and scratched the top of his head before pulling the cap back down.

"I don't mean to be nosy, but I been hearin' all kinds of rumors about you gals and I sure don't wanna be spreadin' 'em myself, so it just seems kinda like I oughta go ahead and clear things up. I reckon one of 'em is pretty obvious – ain't no way you'd be settin' here with Bubba John's mistress. Dottie tried to tell 'em all it wadn't true, but you cain't stop some people from talkin', you know what I mean? Anyway, I was curious about you and your husband, I mean, you know, they's all kinda stories goin' around about him workin' on his folks's house, and why he was spendin' so much time with…"

B-Kay rose from her chair so fast the table slid straight into Sweet's chest. The plate B-Kay held flipped from her hands and ultimately landed on Eustace's feet, but not before spreading pasta salad and collard greens down his already grease-laden jeans.

"Oh, I am so sorry, Mr. Falwell. You better go to the bathroom and get cleaned up. I'll get this mess here," B-Kay said, pushing him toward the restrooms none-too-gently with one hand.

"B-Kay, what in the world?" Sweet gasped.

"It was an accident, Mom," B-Kay said. Her hands shook as she wiped up the food from the floor with napkins from the table.

Eustace stumbled into the bathroom, swiping at his pant legs with bare hands.

"That was no accident." Sweet straightened the table out just as Sissy arrived with a wet towel.

"Nice shot, B," Sissy said. "That's one way to get rid of 'im."

"Well, for crying out loud," B-Kay moaned. "He is so demeaning!"

"She just done us a great big ol' favor," Beanie offered. "Let's hurry up and eat 'fore he comes back."

"I think I've lost my appetite," Sweet said. "I'll pay the bill and step outside so I can call Bubba. Y'all come on out when you're done."

Once she left, B-Kay and Beanie sat in stunned silence for a moment before Beanie said, "That was close."

"I think we just need to go home and cook everything we can think of until Christmas arrives. I can't take any more of this. And, for the record, I'm gonna kill my daddy, just as soon as it's over." B-Kay said.

"I'll hold him for ya," Beanie replied.

48
Just Friends

The day before Christmas, Gabe and her cousin Delia stopped by the Big Pig to eat lunch. Delia was surprised to learn that Gabe and Suvi had already been introduced, which was the real reason she brought Gabe there in the first place.

"Well, I knew we needed to catch up, but I didn't know I was this far behind," Delia said after Suvi greeted them both by name and told Gabe to call him later about some property they discussed.

"Yeah, I thought I mentioned that last time we talked," Gabe lied.

"I'd have remembered that," Delia said. "I've been busting my brain trying to come up with a way to get you two together. He's perfect for you."

"Oh, stop. Suvi and I have a friendly business relationship and nothing more."

Kenya dropped off two waters and menus for them both. "I'll be back to take your order in a minute."

"Thanks, hon," Delia said and waited for her to walk away before launching back into the interrupted discussion. "Business? Really? The man is the most eligible bachelor in the county. What's wrong with you?"

"Delia, come on. Don't make me spell it out for you." Gabe made a point of looking at the menu, but Delia was staring at her across the table with her mouth hanging open. "Look, I'm just not interested, okay? And neither is he. That's all there is to it."

"I don't get it. If I wasn't married, I'd be all over that."

"Bah!" Gabe laughed and covered her face with the menu. "I can't be*lieve* you just said that out loud."

"Girl, you better believe it, 'cause I would."

"Well, I wouldn't, so stop it already. I like Suvi a lot. I think I would even go so far as to say we are friends, but there is simply nothing romantic going on at all. End of story. Can we change the subject now?"

"Sure," said Delia. "What are you doing on Christmas Eve? You headed south to see your parents?"

"Lord, no, they're on a cruise to the Bahamas."

"Oh, good, I was going to invite you over for our annual open house, but I just assumed you'd be going to Tampa for the holiday."

"I would love to come. Can I bring anything? Bottle of wine, maybe? 'Cause you know I don't cook."

"That'll work," Delia said.

Suvi interrupted then, pulling up a chair to visit for a minute.

"I was just telling Gabe about the open house tomorrow, Suvi. You coming this year?" Delia asked.

"Always do," Suvi said. Gabe rolled her eyes at Delia.

"Gabe's coming, too. Maybe y'all could ride together."

Suvi laughed. "I get the feeling she's trying to set us up," he said to Gabe.

"What gave it away?"

"Just trying to be helpful," Delia smiled. "Excuse me a moment. I've got to run to the ladies' room."

When Delia left, Suvi and Gabe both looked down at the table and shook their heads.

"She is too much," Gabe said.

"Always has been," Suvi agreed. "Who needs matchmaker dot com?"

"I don't think either one of us is looking for a match," Gabe said.

"No…no, I'm not anyway. No offense."

"None taken. I feel exactly the same way," Gabe said. "So, now that we got that out of the way, you wanna talk about going to see that house you liked?"

"No, I think I'm going to hold off for a while. I just got a job offer of sorts in Gainesville. I want to weigh my options before I make a decision."

"Really," Gabe said, surprised to say the least.

"Yeah, I called some buddies of mine at UF about Kenya and one thing led to another. There's a coaching position coming open in the spring. It's worth looking into." Suvi said.

"Interesting," Gabe said. "Mind if I ask you a question?"

"Not at all."

"What's there to consider?"

"What do you mean?"

"Well, I kind of heard talk around town that maybe you're dating someone. I mean, is that what might keep you from going? Because, the way I see it, anyone in your position would jump at the chance to coach at Florida. There has to be a reason you're—what did you call it—weighing options?"

Suvi leaned back in his chair. "I guess I shouldn't be surprised you knew, I mean, I wasn't keeping it from you or anything. There's just not much to say about it. The truth is, I'm not *dating* anyone right now."

"But?" Gabe asked.

"There is someone I care very much about, but I honestly don't see it working at all, much less in Gainesville. She'll never leave this town, I know that much.

"Somehow, I got the impression that *you* wouldn't leave it either."

Suvi sighed. "I might – under the right circumstances – but I'm not in any hurry. This is my home."

"So how much of that indecision has to do with the girl you're not dating?"

Suvi laughed and shook his head. "I honestly think that ship has sailed. She doesn't fit in my world, and I don't fit in hers."

"I hate that for you," Gabe said.

"I hate it, too."

Suvi stood then and patted the table twice.

"Good talkin' to you, Gabe. Here comes Dee. I already told Kenya lunch is on me. I recommend the chicken today. I just took it off the grill a few minutes ago."

"Sounds great, Suve. See you tomorrow?"

Suvi nodded. "You driving?"

"Yep," Gabe said. "Beat you there."

We'll see about that, he thought as he walked away, but he couldn't wipe the smile from his face for a long time afterwards.

49
Home Sweet Home

And arrive, Christmas did. There was a flurry of activity the day before Christmas Eve, when Beanie and B-Kay had to distract Sweet Lee to avoid her hearing phone calls and wondering too much about where her husband was.

On Christmas Eve, the Atwaters had their traditional Christmas dinner – pancakes for supper. They had started the tradition long ago, giving the kids the option of what to eat. After a few years of repetition, the menu stuck, even when the grandparents were still with them.

After dinner, each person got to choose one present from under the tree to open. Sweet knew exactly what she was looking for – something small. She wanted the surprise done, so all the whispering would finally stop.

Sweet and B-Kay made sure there were several presents for Beanie under the tree, but neither thought to ask if she wanted to invite anyone else, or if she had somewhere she wanted to go. Sweet thought of it when she saw Beanie sitting quietly off to the side.

"Beanie," she said. "Is there someone you want to invite over? Do you have cousins or aunts and uncles? Anyone?"

"Not really," Beanie said. "Will's the closest thing I have to family anymore and I ain't got a clue what he's doin' tonight. I got some cousins, but Lord you don't want those people around your children, I can tell ya that."

"Why don't you call and see what Will is doing? Maybe he'll want to come for coffee and dessert. B-Kay's gonna read the Christmas story before the kids go to bed."

"Oh, I don't know, it's kind'ly late now, ain't it?"

"Call him, Bean," Sweet said softly. "It can't hurt."

So she did, and the phone rang and rang and rang until the answering machine picked up.

Beanie left a short message. *Hey, Will? It's me, Beanie. Me and Sweet was wondering if you had anywhere to go tonight, and if you might wanna come out here for coffee. Just give me a call back. Okay. Bye.*

But Will never called, and Beanie did her best to smile through the evening, though deep inside her heart was broken in more places than one.

The children were clamoring to open gifts after supper, but tradition held that the reading came first. Sweet was surprised when Bubba John pulled T-Ray to him, whispered something in his ear and they left together saying they had to run to the store and would be right back. B-Kay took up the family Bible and turned to the place they had marked long ago with a Christmas card. The little ones settled in to listen as their sister read:

Luke 2:1-14

And it came to pass in those days, that there went out a decree from Caesar Augustus that all the world should be taxed. And all went to be taxed, every one into his own city. And Joseph also went up from Galilee, out of the city of Nazareth, into Judaea, unto the city of David, which is called Bethlehem, to be taxed with Mary his espoused wife, being great with child. And so it was, that, while they were there, the days were accomplished that she should be delivered. And she brought forth her firstborn son, and wrapped him in swaddling clothes, and laid him in a manger; because there was no room for them in the inn. And there were in the same country shepherds abiding in the field, keeping watch over their flock by night. And, lo, the angel of the Lord came upon them, and the glory of the Lord shone round about them and they were sore afraid. And the angel said unto them, Fear not: for, behold, I bring you good tidings of great joy, which shall be to all people. For unto you is born this day in the city of David a Savior, which is Christ the Lord. And this shall be a sign unto you; Ye shall find the babe wrapped in swaddling clothes, lying in a manger. And suddenly there was with the angel a multitude of the heavenly host praising God, and saying, Glory to God in the highest, and on earth peace, good will toward men.

Just as every other Christmas, the reading brought a sense of peace and wellbeing to Sweet Lee. When she sat back and considered her situation, she realized that abundance did not mean perfection, and discomfort did not mean disaster. Whatever would be, would be, and they would handle it together.

There was general chaos while the children tried to identify which package seemed the most promising. Bitty found a small square box with her mother's name on it and gave it to her. She looked around, but Bubba was still not back. *Really? This is your big surprise? Nice, Bub.*

Ten minutes later the living room was covered in wrapping paper and the little ones were playing with assorted new toys. B-Kay was programming her new Kindle Fire and Beanie was thrilled with the necklace Sweet had ordered online. And still no Bubba John.

It would serve him right if I opened this right now, without him even here, Sweet thought. She was just pulling the tape off when T-Ray and Bubba John came in through the kitchen.

"Glad you waited," Bubba John said, seeing the package basically intact.

"Almost didn't," Sweet said. "T, honey, pick you out a present to open."

"Go ahead, baby, open it." Bubba sat on the arm of her chair, and seemed a little breathless, which Sweet found endearing despite her annoyance.

When the package revealed a jeweler's box, Sweet laughed and said, "I knew it, Bubba. You shouldn't have done this, but it's very sweet that you did."

Bubba laughed. "Open the box, honey."

She pulled off the lid and lifted a small wad of cotton revealing…a key? Except it wasn't even really a key, just a half-moon of a handle with a long key-like prong.

"What in the world is this?"

"Here's the other half," Bubba said and handed her a key fob, which the key she held fit snugly into. "Let's go outside."

Bubba stood and helped Sweet to her feet. The older kids followed, but Beanie stayed in the living room with the younger ones while they played. Before they reached the door, Bubba

254

handed her a card. The front of the card had embossed wings, an emblem she recognized, and the note inside read, *So glad you're better. Enjoy your new car! Love, Angel. P.S. Dios es Buenos!*

Sweet tore the door open and went outside to find her beautiful gray minivan parked in the driveway.

"Oh, my gosh, Honey! Oh, wow, and I thought I was just gonna get a silly old ring!"

"What, you don't want a ring?" Bubba John laughed and kissed his wife.

"No, I don't," she said. "I thought you knew that."

He kissed her again. "Obviously...I did."

"For heaven's sake, honey, you have driven me crazy with this surprise thing, and it's a car? You could have just told me," Sweet fussed, but mostly in jest.

"Are you surprised?" Bubba John walked around the car and opened the driver's door with a flourish. "Your chariot awaits."

By then, the younger kids had caught wind of the grand surprise and all of them crowded around trying to get a good look.

"Wanna go for a spin?" Bubba John asked.

"But I can't drive yet," Sweet protested.

"You can ride. Come on."

And so, they all piled in and rode through town and around it finding all the Christmas lights they could before heading home. But when they got to their road, Bubba John did not turn. He went straight on by, turning right onto the highway that went toward the river.

"Where are you going?" Sweet asked.

"Just thought you'd want to see how the house is coming along. I've been working hard, trying to get it ready."

"Oh, I hope it sells so we can pay this car off," Sweet said. "I don't like owing money to anyone."

The kids were just beginning to whine when they pulled into the driveway at Mam and Pap's old place. Sweet gasped at the sight of the old farmhouse, now painted white and sporting new black shutters. The lights were all on and there were candles in the window, and a wreath on the front door, and—

what in the world? There was furniture inside, like the house was just waiting for its family to come home.

"You did all this?" Sweet turned to her husband, tears streaming down her face.

"Well, I had help, but yeah."

"How? It must have cost a small fortune."

"Worth every penny, don't you think?" Bubba John asked.

"It's beautiful, honey, but honestly — at this point — I just wish you hadn't even brought me out here to see it. How are we ever going to sell it? It's just…perfect."

Bubba John said nothing, just shut off the car and walked around it to open Sweet's door. T-Ray and B-Kay were busy shushing the little ones in the back, and they complied with little resistance.

Bubba John walked his wife to the front porch and dropped to one knee.

"What are you doing?" Sweet asked, her folded hands covering her mouth as if in prayer.

"Sweet baby," Bubba John began. "I have loved you from the first time I met you. I've never had much to give you, but you never wanted more than love, which is a good thing, because I have enough of *that* to last a long, long time. You, on the other hand, have given me everything. You have made what little we had seem like more than enough and then some, and you have always been happy. That's why, I'm pretty sure — no, I'm positive — you'll be happy with this, too." Bubba John reached into his pocket and pulled out another key. Holding it up to her, he said, "Sweet Lee Atwater, welcome home."

She could not answer, just stood and let the tears flow down her cheeks.

"Aren't you going to unlock it?" he asked.

"I can't. I'm shaking too much."

He unlocked the door, turned and swept his wife into his arms, then carried her over the threshold.

50
Goodnight, Will

Meanwhile, back at the Atwater house, Beanie Bradsher was cleaning up the mess from the Christmas tornado, and feeling more than a little lonely. When she finished the kitchen, she retrieved her lovely gift from the living room, took her hat off the rack and headed out the door.

The phone rang just as she stepped onto the back porch. She figured it was just family calling, and certainly not for her, so she stood on the porch in the chill winter air and listened to it ring. Finally, the machine picked up and she heard Will's voice on the recorder.

Hey, this is Will Thaxton. I was just returning Beanie's call, if you could just let her know and…um…Merry Christmas to you all.

The phone clicked off and all was silent again.

Beanie Bradsher was not a girl to wallow in her misery. This wasn't the first Christmas she'd spent alone, and likely wouldn't be her last. She thought of Suvi and how she had daydreamed many times about their Christmases together, all gathered at his house, nieces and nephews fighting over toys, aunts cooking in the kitchen and uncles gathered with Suvi in the living room talking about their glory days. And where did she see herself in that happy scene? She closed her eyes and realized she didn't see herself at all.

She saw herself at The Château making hot chocolate with Will, sitting quietly in front of the fire. She saw Will reading a book while she crocheted Christmas ornaments for the tree, Will gathering more wood for the fire while she set the table for breakfast the next morning.

But was she in love? That was the question. It was one thing to be comfortable with someone you like very much, and quite another to see yourself in their arms. Because, if she was honest, at the end of that scene, she still saw herself telling Will goodnight and going to her own room. And that would never be fair to him.

Beanie stood and looked up at the clear, cloudless sky.

"Goodnight, Will," Beanie said to the moon and the stars. "Merry Christmas."

Author's Note

Like *The Pecan Man* before this, I tend to write stories set in places I know well and love. I was raised and lived for most of my life in Leesburg, a small town in Central Florida. Just before the new millennium, my husband and I fell in love with a little town called Mayo in the Big Bend area of Florida. We built a house on the Suwannee River and raised our youngest daughter there. It is a lovely town and we are blessed to call it home.

There are places and settings in this new novel that many in our area will recognize. There is a building called the Chateau, which used to be the county courthouse, and has also been both apartments for rent and a bed and breakfast. Those, however, are the only details about the building that are real. Everything else about the building and its owners, past or present, are figments of my imagination. Likewise, the actual shops and restaurants along Main Street in Mayo are similar to those in the novel, but are not meant to be connected in any way to the story or to the fictitious characters I created.

Through the writing of this novel, the name of the town has gone through many changes. First Silo because there are many in our area. Then Suwannee Junction and a few others I don't remember now. Then Willow Springs, for the willow trees that mark the river entrance to Allen Mill, which is one of the spring tributaries that feeds the Suwannee and still bears the old beams that supported the mill that used to run there. I was going for a name that would be a nod to the Florida lifestyle, particularly *this* part of Florida, which has remained rural and natural and unspoiled throughout the building boom. The town name remained Willow Springs right up until we started focusing on the cover design and thus the name of the novel.

Its working title had been "Beanie Bradsher," but that was the series name. So, at some point, I landed on "What Matters in Willow Springs" as a title and finally felt good about it. But then, Patti and I decided we should have an alliteration in the title, mostly for marketing purposes. Of course Mayo would have worked, but I didn't want to use the actual town name. In Harper Lee's *To Kill a Mockingbird*, the town was called Maycomb, though locals recognized their hometown of Monroeville. I did the same in The Pecan Man, calling the town Mayville, but using similar landmarks from Leesburg. So, I pulled out a map and started looking for names that started with "M." I found a little town in Mississippi called Mayhew Junction. It suited my little town and all its quirky characters. It was perfect.

The character of Beanie Bradsher was inspired by a vague memory I have from childhood of a woman who wore colorful western clothes and rode a bicycle around town. I never knew her, but used the visual as inspiration to create a character I have come to love. About her name…Beanie comes from a nickname I call my beloved brother Bubba, who claims to go by Jim now, though I have never once called him that in my whole entire life. Bradsher is a family name on my mother's side. She and I once found the headstones of some of the Bradsher family on a trip to North Carolina. In a way, this helps memorialize that trip for me, as it was one of my favorites. I lost my precious "Mommer" this year, and there are days when I think I will never get over it. She was the source for many colorful stories in my life, and her voice can be heard in many of the characters who inhabit the stories I tell.

I'm taking the time to talk a little bit about this now, since some of the questions I'm asked most often at book clubs and readings involve how I come up with stories and characters. I have to admit that I've always been a people-watcher. And I'm drawn to those who are characters in real life. I don't write as much as I daydream, however, so when I see someone interesting and don't know anything about them, I just go on along and make stuff up. Always have. Must be why Mrs. Jean Miller, my beloved second-grade teacher at Skeen Elementary, called me a writer way back then. So glad I finally believed her.

I hope you enjoy my little imaginings as much as I enjoyed writing them down.

And now, please enjoy a preview of the second book in the Beanie Bradsher series.

1
What's Wrong with Bitty?

Sweet Lee Atwater pulled her mini-van into the parking lot of the Mayhew Elementary School, grabbed a Vera Bradley handbag from the back seat and sat for a moment to compose her thoughts. It was a bit more than two months since she had the surprise of her life, and she still hadn't gotten used to her newfound fortune. Literally a fortune. Sweet's unassuming and thoroughly reliable husband had gone behind her back for years, playing the lottery with money they could ill-afford to lose. Fortunately for them both, their numbers hit before she discovered his duplicity and they were now millionaires.

And what did that mean, actually? They still lived in the small town of Mayhew Junction, population roughly ten-thousand if you counted everyone in the entire county, who all shared Mayhew's zip code. Their kids still went to the same small schools, and they still didn't have the first fast food restaurant or even a Walmart for crying out loud. What they had was more money than they needed and fewer worries than before. Unfortunately, money would not help with the problem Sweet currently faced. Her middle child Bitty had always been a little different. She had habits that had been endearing when she was a toddler, but were apparently disruptive now that she was in a public school setting. She was a few minutes early for a meeting with Bitty's teacher and the guidance counselor. They were going to discuss what interventions might be necessary to make everyone's experience more – what was the word – tolerable? Sweet sighed. Bitty was a bright light in her life, always cheerful, smart as a whip, and incredibly kind-hearted. It was disheartening to watch that little light fade as her daughter grew more and more frustrated with the structure of the classroom.

No use sitting here fretting, she thought. *Time to face the music.* Sweet slid from her car, locked the doors and made her way to the entrance of the school office. Signing in at the front desk, she scarcely had time to give her name to the receptionist when the guidance counselor came around the corner, right arm outstretched and Pandora bracelet crackling heavily.

"Mrs. Atwater, so glad you could make it."

Sweet took the hand in her own and smiled. "Please, call me Sweet. Mrs. Atwater is so formal."

Libby Daniels laughed. "I know, and I agree," she said in a soft country lilt, "but we have standards here that make it a requirement. You're Mrs. Atwater and I'm Mrs. Daniels and we're both stuck with it."

Sweet decided right then and there she liked Libby Daniels very much. Though she had never met her personally, she knew the family Libby married into before moving to Fletcher County and they were good people.

"Come on back," Libby said. "Mrs. McMinn is waiting in the conference room."

Sweet did know Delia McMinn. They had gone to school together many moons ago, and Sweet had been happy that Bitty was assigned to her classroom for third grade. This was not a conference Sweet had looked forward to, but she allowed herself to relax a bit as they settled in to discuss what might be done to help Bitty cope with the classroom setting. She had a feeling she was going to need all the help she could get.

2
La Patisserie

"Will?" Beanie Bradsher called out from the kitchen of The Chateau, where she had lived since moving out of her flood-ravaged house on the Suwannee River, minus a stint out at the Atwater house while Sweet recovered from surgery. It had been one of the most dramatic Christmases Beanie ever experienced and she still wasn't sure she was quite recovered herself.

"You need me?" Will Thaxton appeared at the doorway with a bundle of firewood in his arms. "Thought I'd stock up in the living room. Looks like we have a cold front coming through, though it always makes me laugh saying that. You haven't seen a cold front until you've seen one in Minnesota. Now those are real cold fronts."

"Oh, shoot, I needed an extry hand here, but you ain't got one. Can you put that load down and come help me a minute?"

"Sure, I'll be right back," Will said and disappeared down the hallway.

Beanie could afford to get her own place, considering her lottery winnings were drawing interest, however meager, in her account at the bank. But she was comfortable here with the widower Thaxton, and he was happy to have her help, so she stayed. Besides, they were well on their way to opening a bakery, by accident mostly, but plans were taking shape and they were already filling orders for three months in advance. Will had once taken a cake decorating course with his late wife Marie and was surprisingly good at it. Beanie, on the other hand, had never had a day's formal training, but had made a name for herself with the baked goods she distributed to her Avon customers over the holidays.

Will was in the process of installing glass cabinets in the unused front room of the Chateau. Salvaged years ago from an old jewelry shop once housed in the small building on the same property, the cabinets were perfect to hold pastries and cookies and other baked goods. The Chateau, built in 1883, was originally the county courthouse, but had not been used as such since the current courthouse was built in 1907. It had been remodeled as a bed and breakfast over the years, and there were still several rooms left unused in the enormous wooden structure. Will had been looking for ways to increase his income, and there wasn't a bakery to be found in the entire county, so La Patisscrie it would be.

"At your service, Ma'mselle." Will had taken to using French terminology lately, which vaguely annoyed Beanie, though she couldn't quite put her finger on why. "Sorry it took so long. I washed up first."

"That's okay, I actually need help with this cooling rack here. It's all whoppy-jawed and I cain't have my moon-pies slidin' down into a heap."

"Beanie, we've talked about this. We are making macarons," Will said, rolling the "r" dramatically and giving the last vowel a nasal sound like he'd learned in high school. "They are not moon-pies. There's a difference."

"Look like moon-pies to me," Beanie said, rolling her eyes. "If they's macaroni, where's the cheese?"

Will laughed so hard he could barely hold the baking rack steady while she adjusted the height of the legs.

"Oh, stop," Beanie complained, smiling in spite of herself. "It ain't that funny."

But it was, which was why Will had found himself smitten with Beanie Bradsher months ago. She was only half-serious about the moon-pies. She knew the difference, but she wasn't one for pretense and, besides, she also knew how to milk a good joke.

They laughed a lot in this kitchen, and that carried as far as the living room, but no further. Their relationship was like the rack they were fixing, just a little off-kilter. Love on Will's side, great friendship on Beanie's, and it looked a lot to Will like *never the twain shall meet*. That did not stop him, however, from hoping.

Hickmans'

Made in the USA
Middletown, DE
21 April 2018